The
Ancient Tradition
of Angels

"Normandi Ellis is a masterful storyteller. She unfolds her understanding of the angelic realm not just from a profound scholarship but also from her personal perspective, and it is this rare blend that brings the subject to life for the reader. This is a wonderful and beautiful book carrying a message of hope at a forlorn time. Her words and stories uplift the spirit by showing that angelic messengers belong to all times and all traditions. This book feeds the mind with its scholarship, feeds the soul with an inspired vision of existence beyond the human sphere, and nourishes the heart with the certain knowing that angelic guidance is not limited to the past. No matter whether you come to this book from a faith tradition or from none, these words will open a window into possibility."

NAOMI OZANIEC, AUTHOR OF *BECOMING A GARMENT OF ISIS*

"A fascinating account of angels. This comprehensive study detailing angels throughout the ages and in different traditions is engaging and incredibly uplifting. It's a powerful book for today's world."

ROBBIE HOLZ, AUTHOR OF *ANGELS IN WAITING*

"Normandi Ellis's book *The Ancient Tradition of Angels* is a rare pearl and a welcome and inspired addition to human consciousness of who angels are, what their purpose is, and above all the unifying nature of angels, present in the contexts of all faiths and cultures (whether they are known by that name or another). Ellis's clarity allows for an ecumenical view of this divine assistance, ready to help all who are open to receive. The book begins with beautiful portraits from cultures around the planet, including depictions of the sacred, the divine, and the angelic. Highly recommended for angel newcomers as well as those who walk with angels already!"

KATHRYN HUDSON, AUTHOR OF
INVITING ANGELS INTO YOUR LIFE

"Weaving a tapestry between scholarship and personal experiences, *The Ancient Tradition of Angels* introduces the reader to the universal concept of divine messengers, from ancient Egypt to modern times. The common human experience of rescue by spiritual beings is captured in a treasury of vivid stories, along with beautiful full-color illustrations of icons by a selection of wonderful artists. Normandi Ellis's reflections about what all of these mysterious resemblances may mean is a journey through the universe of divine intervention."

TAMRA LUCID, AUTHOR OF
MAKING THE ORDINARY EXTRAORDINARY

"In her extraordinarily well-documented book *The Ancient Tradition of Angels,* Normandi Ellis once again shows us her skills as a wordsmith and scholar, capable of navigating the reader through the mysteries, historical foundations, and grace of angels. She opens doorways for the reader to consider this topic from every conceivable angle—mystical, esoteric, cultural, spiritual, chronicled, even within the field of physics. If angels serve the concept of God's powerful messengers, then with this book Ellis serves the purpose of authenticating those messengers."

SANDRA CORCORAN, AUTHOR OF *SHAMANIC AWAKENING*

"With a sense of wonder we are introduced to the worldwide history of angels in Normandi Ellis's tour de force of storytelling informed by serious scholarship and a lifetime of revelations. A gorgeously illustrated book that will fascinate devotees of all religions."

RONNIE PONTIAC, AUTHOR OF
AMERICAN METAPHYSICAL RELIGION

"I found Normandi's book to be exhaustively researched, incredibly beautiful, and inspiring. What's that—you say you don't believe in angels? Normandi would invite you to consider the words of poet Mary Oliver: 'Only if there are angels in your head will you ever, possibly, see one.'"

RAY GRASSE, AUTHOR OF *THE WAKING DREAM*
AND *WHEN THE STARS ALIGN*

The
Ancient Tradition
of Angels

THE POWER AND INFLUENCE
of
SACRED MESSENGERS

Normandi Ellis

Bear & Company
Rochester, Vermont

Bear & Company
One Park Street
Rochester, Vermont 05767
www.BearandCompanyBooks.com

Text stock is SFI certified

Bear & Company is a division of Inner Traditions International

This book derives from the author's dissertation, "A Crush of Angels: A History of Angels Across Faith Traditions," published in 2020 to the archive of the All Faiths Seminary International.

Cataloging-in-Publication Data for this title is available from the Library of Congress

ISBN 978-1-59143-439-9 (print)
ISBN 978-1-59143-440-5 (ebook)

Printed and bound in the United States by Lake Book Manufacturing, LLC
The text stock is SFI certified. The Sustainable Forestry Initiative® program promotes sustainable forest management.

10 9 8 7 6 5 4 3 2 1

Text design and layout by Virginia Scott Bowman
This book was typeset in Garamond Premier Pro with Gill Sans and Nocturne Serif used as display typefaces

The Vedic poem that appears in the chapter entitled "Eastern Traditions" comes from *The Myths and Gods of India* by Alain Daniélou, published by Inner Traditions, © 1991. Reprinted with permission.

To send correspondence to the author of this book, mail a first-class letter to the author c/o Inner Traditions • Bear & Company, One Park Street, Rochester, VT 05767, and we will forward the communication, or contact the author directly at **www.normandiellis.com**.

For my daughter, Alaina,
the dearest gift ever brought by an angel.

Nothing is more awe-inspiring than an Angel, nothing more seemingly unimpressive than a human being, and yet contained in a handful of dust is the signature for the entire universe of space-time. God is up to something. . . .

WILLIAM IRWIN THOMPSON,
THE TIME FALLING BODIES TAKE TO LIGHT

Contents

COLOR PLATE CREDITS

1. **Isis** – Cosima Lukashevitz

2. **The Tree of Life** – Kristina Sebenick Ellis

3. **Seraphim** – Bigstock

4. **Thrones** – Greg Zeman

5. **Jesus Ministered to by Angels** – James Tissot/Brooklyn Museum

6. **Archangel Michael** – Greg Zeman

7. **Archangel Gabriel** – Muhammad ibn Muhammad Shakir/Walters Art Museum

8. **Ascension of the Prophet Muhammad into Heaven** – Nur-al-Din/Walters Art Museum

9. **Jacob's Dream** – Jusepe de Ribera and L. Caracciolo/Indiana Association of Spiritualists

10. **Hindu Goddesses** – Nepalese, Walters Art Museum

11. **Mount Meru** – Trongsa Dzong, Trongsa, Bhutan

12. **Urvashi and Pururavas** – Raja Ravi Varma

13. **Cherubim Tetramorph** – Meteora, Thessaly, Greece

14. **Ahura Mazda** – Bigstock

15. **Egyptian Ba** – John Huntington Art and Polytechnic Trust/Cleveland Museum of Art

16. **Ethiopian Angel** – Willem Proos/Travel-Pictures-Gallery.com

17. **Taus Melek, the Yezidi Peacock Angel** – Gina Morales

18. **Yamantaka, Destroyer of the God of Death** – Tibetan, Metropolitan Museum of Art

19. **The Angels Munkar and Nakīr** – Muhammad ibn Muhammad Shakir/Walters Art Museum

20. **Michael/Samael** – Cosima Lukashevitz

21. **Night with her Train of Stars** – Edward Robert Hughes/Birmingham Museums Trust

22. **Raziel, Angel of Mystery** – Cosima Lukashevitz

23. **The Gift of Compassion** – Victoria Wilson-Jones

24. **Metatron** – Gabriel Schama

25. **NASA Star Angel Galaxy** – NASA, ESA, and the Hubble Heritage Team

Foreword

Jean Houston, Ph.D.

The book in your hands is both a marvel and a high mystery—luminous, inexplicable, and yet transparent to transcendence. Surely all of the angels are applauding.

I have known Normandi for many years, beginning in 1990 when I narrated an audio recording of her brilliant first book, *Awakening Osiris*. Its words were so profound, and the spirit behind those words so insistent, that it sent shivers down my spine. Leading a trip to Egypt in 1991 for a hundred students, she joined me in interpretating the depth dimensions and sacred psychology of ancient Egypt. She also worked with me on my book *The Passion of Isis and Osiris*, published in 1995.

Normandi's publishing record is formidable: fourteen books, and more to come. She is truly a masterful writer and scholar—witty, innovative, and always at the cutting edge of discovery. Her interest in metaphysics reveals a multidimensional mind and an elegant spirit.

Her work has not diminished over time, nor does she rest on her laurels. The angels called her and she answered. After nearly four decades of mining the gold of the Egyptian cosmology that she has so consistently evoked in great depth, she has given to this world and to our time a gathering of angels the likes of which we have not seen before. With wit, wisdom, and insight, she offers us a new understanding of our relationship to the spirit world. We are not just bags of ego;

we are participants in a divine architecture. And in elucidating this fact, she has given the divine dimensions more room and reality for their manifestation and cooperation, to remedy our planetary pathos.

I learn so much from Normandi, as do so many. Through this magnificent work, she invites the daemons of beauty, truth, and cocreation into the dark places in self and society that are so needful of the sacred gnosis that she brings. I believe this book will give new credence to a belief in and a partnership with the angels, bringing about a necessary spiritual renaissance. If Normandi's work causes us to believe in angels again, perhaps it will provoke the angels to believe again in us.

JEAN HOUSTON, PH.D., is a scholar, philosopher, and researcher in the human capacities movement, having long been regarded as one of the principal founders of the human potential movement. She is one of the foremost visionary thinkers and doers of our time, noted for her ability to combine a deep knowledge of history, culture, new science, spirituality, and human development into her teachings. She is the author of thirty books on sacred living and finding one's purpose, from *The Possible Human: A Course in Enhancing Your Physical, Mental, and Creative Abilities* to *The Quest of Rose: The Cosmic Keys of Our Future Becoming*. As advisor to UNICEF in human and cultural development, she has worked around the world helping to implement some of their extensive educational programs. Dr. Houston has also served in an advisory capacity to President and Mrs. Clinton. A powerful and dynamic speaker, she holds conferences and seminars with social leaders, educational institutions, and business organizations worldwide. Dr. Houston holds a Ph.D. in psychology from the Union Graduate School in New York and a Ph.D. in religion from the Graduate Theological Foundation in Sarasota, Florida. She has also been the recipient of honorary doctorates.

Foreword

Lynn Andrews

Normandi Ellis's new book, *The Ancient Tradition of Angels,* offers readers a fresh new approach to a potentially daunting subject, that of angelic presence in human affairs. A natural-born storyteller and attentive scholar, Normandi Elllis's narrative voice gives the work authority and makes it exceedingly accessible. In these pages the ancient and biblical stories, apocrypha, and contemporary observations she relates come alive. Much more than an academic treatise, this remarkable book seamlessly weaves Ellis's personal reflections and experience with scientific and scholarly research. It is a thorough and satisfying guide for the novice as well as those conversant with the holy world and the mystery of angels.

The text is inclusive; it gives equal substance to angels and other winged beings of Spirit in worldwide cultures throughout human time. Discussed are Judeo-Christian, Hindu, and Buddhist angels, Silk Road traditions, Zoroastrian and Yezidi angels, angels of death, and fallen and dark angels. Dark angels can be thought of as those errors in judgment in human concerns, or wrong thinking, which cause us distress—seductions that pull us in harmful directions. Quoting the author, "Thoughts are things. If you're looking for dark angels, you [will] find them. The book tries to answer typical questions [readers might posit]; but the only way to answer such [queries] is to talk about quantum physics because angels are made of light. And so are we."

Normandi Ellis contends that how we speak of angels and their purpose changes as our understanding of consciousness changes, as our awareness of our unique selves and the world around us, our perceptions, shift. Things in our lives that we never thought possible occur. Is consciousness then, in and of itself, forcing change in the way we perceive "reality"? Or is it possible that there is another mystery, that of consciousness ascending into the spirit realm, to be called "angel"?

Angels appear in every major and minor religion and spiritual practice as divine or spiritual messengers. When the spirit world confounds us, this book bridges the gap between that confusion and awareness—angel messengers come into our lives to imbue and inspire us with the mystery of divine creative intelligence.

Perhaps angels are antidotes to our overwhelming and illusory material world. Perhaps an angel is an experience to which our minds must give form. *The Ancient Tradition of Angels* does not attempt to solve the question of "What is an angel?" Rather, it offers a guide for delving into the *mystery* of angels, giving readers an opportunity to think about the true message of angels as part of us, as within us—inseparable. Perhaps this book is meant to be an instrument to be used to encourage nonbelievers and skeptics into saying "Yes . . . maybe."

Ellis—the author of numerous books, short stories, essays, poems, book reviews, and translations; lecturer; academic; seminar and metaphysical teacher; and workshop facilitator—writes with the expertise of the scholar, and the curiosity of the poet. Readers trust her narrative voice, for it connects us to the text rather than removing us from it. For those interested in and curious about ceremony, the book's addendum, "An Invocation to Archangels," is an extra gift.

Normandi Ellis writes, "We live inside a mystery" and, later, "The true message of the angels lies within us." These sentences alone are provocative enough to make this a must-read book for those who wish to more fully understand the complexities of the angelic state of mind.

THE LATE LYNN ANDREWS was the *New York Times* and internationally best-selling author of the Medicine Woman series, which chronicled her three decades of study and work with shamanic healers on four continents. In addition, Lynn wrote a total of twenty-one bestselling books and workbooks about her work. A shaman healer and mystic, she was recognized worldwide as a leader in the fields of spiritual healing and personal empowerment. She was also acknowledged as being a major link between the ancient world of shamanism and modern society and its thirst for profound personal healing and a deeper understanding of the pathway to enlightenment. Lynn hosted annual live gatherings for shamanic healing and empowerment in Hawaii and in Paradise Valley, Arizona, and led shamanic tours to Egypt, Peru, Alaska, Ireland, and other sacred sites around the globe.

Living Gratitude

This book begins way back, farther back than I can now recall. It began as a quest for understanding the phenomenon of angels, and resulted in my 2020 doctoral dissertation on the same subject. I received a doctor of divinity degree in comparative religions from All Faiths Seminary in New York. It is that dissertation upon which this book is based.

More than anyone else, I express my deepest gratitude to the angels for showing up, for answering prayers, and for allowing their messages to play upon the lips and through the hands of family, strangers, and friends. All of these individuals did the exact thing needed for me to find and create the next leap forward in my life. Often it would seem that just as I needed solace, a zap of illumination, or a boost of confidence, angelic messages would arrive—as expressed by the sudden appearance of a friend. "I don't know why, but I had the urge to check on you," they might say, or, "Hey, I just found this nugget of information, or had a revelation, and you came to mind."

Sometimes the angels showed themselves as glimpses of light caught out of the corner of my eye. Other times I perceived them as light breaking through dark clouds in the radiant form of angels, a feathery touch brushing my skin, or the sudden, firm embrace of a winged one at my back to strengthen me. Sometimes feathers dropped in front of my eyes on a windless and birdless day. I'm also a firm believer in the angel who appeared as solid as a human to say, "I think you dropped this," handing me a twenty-dollar bill with which to buy groceries and conveniently disappearing before I could say thank-you.

At Camp Chesterfield in Indiana, I live on sacred grounds amid the statues and energetic signatures of angels, devas, and masters, including the Christ. Here I have spent many hours of pleasant contemplation sitting by a fountain and its trumpeting angels. Here I have prayed for the healing of family and friends inside the Garden of Prayer amid guardian angels. Here I have also conversed with the busts of master teachers and prophets of the world's major religions—Vardhamana Mahavira, Gautama Buddha, Lao Tzu, Confucius, Osiris, Abraham, Mohammed, Zoroaster, Zeus, and the Christ—stationed along the Trail of Religion. Inside the metaphysical library at Chesterfield Seminary, while researching my dissertation, I found many a dusty, rare book whose wisdom can never be exhausted. This library also contains modern work that inspires me, and which sparks associations and further connection with the angelic beings. These contemporary writers are a grand gathering of religious folk, scientists, and "possibility thinkers," and I hope one day to create an annotated bibliography of their work. I want to thank those who so generously allowed me to quote them, or to cite their work in-depth. I applaud their visions, which have added to mine.

My original dissertation began to truly come together as a book for publication once I realized that hunting for angels carried the same energetic vibration as writing poetry or painting an inspired piece of art. These states of consciousness allow for serendipity, magic, and possibility thinking—or rather, possibility *allowing*.

No book stands alone, and this book has been built upon the work of countless authors, storytellers, and researchers before me, including those unknown inquirers of the world's sacred texts. I am indebted to the Tibetan and Egyptian scribes, and to the anonymous rabbis, Coptic priests, and monks who wrote and illuminated sacred texts in which the angels appeared. Brilliant minds have inspired me to look further into the nature of angels, including the in-depth studies of such modern authors as Rabbi Phillip Berg, Sophy Burnham, Rabbi David A. Cooper, Alain Daniélou, Gustav Davidson, Richard Foltz, Rabbi Louis Ginzberg, Manly Palmer Hall, Shaykh Kabbani, Rodger Kamenetz, Martin Lings,

Joseph Lumpkin, Valery Rees, Eszter Spät, and Rose Vanden Eynden.

I want to thank the poets, dreamers, and visual artists who inspired me. I'm thinking in particular of the poets Rainer Maria Rilke, William Blake, and Mary Oliver. I also want to thank, of course, the visual artists who granted me permission to include their works in my book. It is they who provided a necessary platform by which to celebrate the angels in all of our lives. Their visioning was vital and, to me, their original art allowed me to see that angels are "interpreted" creatures. They appear as states of mind. They conform to our intuition and to our thoughts. I offer my gratitude to the masons of temples and cathedrals in Ethiopia, in Scotland, in Asia, and around the world.

I am indebted to the vision and talents of close friends and artists Cosima Lukashevitz, Kristina Sebenick Ellis, Gina Morales, Victoria Wilson-Jones, and the photographic skills of Greg Zeman and Willem Proos, as well as others—James Tissot, Edward Hughes, Gabriel Schama, and Ravi Raja Varma.

I remember some years ago conversing with Cosima about the power of the hieroglyphs of Egypt, the word symbols and paintings. We agreed that many people thought of language and art as separate forms, but they actually are one stream of light consciousness. These angels, then, are concentrated light forms that we discover coalescing within the air, in active meditation, and on paper—or upon the canvas of our lives. (I can't even begin to count the number of inspiring cloud angel photographs that have been sent—unrequested—to me by friends over the last two years!)

I am blessed to have the beautiful images of the aforementioned artists appear in this book. Of course, I also want to thank the many art museums that generously allowed me to copy their images—the Birmingham Museums Trust, the Cleveland Museum of Art, and most especially the Walters Art Museum in Baltimore, Maryland.

Questing for angels amid the years of COVID-19 turned out to be a solitary task. Without the encouragement of supportive people like P. T. Wilson, Jon Mundy, and the committee members and faculty of All Faiths Seminary in New York, my research into the cosmos of the angels would have remained idle speculation. Encouragement from dear friends

Karen Klein, Gina Morales, Ray Grasse, and many others kept my life-long dream of attaining a doctoral degree in comparative religion afloat.

Sharon Kenton, my colleague and friend, spent speculative hours with me, sitting on my sofa and listening to my inklings, encouraging my ideas, and asking questions for my own clarification. Glenda Cadarette, my long-time mentor at Camp Chesterfield in Indiana, offered advice, encouragement, and conversation to carry me forward. My neighbor and friend Terry Hanks, my sister-in-law Sherry Ellis, and my brother Edward F. Ellis proof-read the manuscript when it was in its initial dissertation form. Later, old friend Jessie M Page offered suggestions and encouragement on the crafting of the narrative. My dear friend Peter Taylor assisted with reading the manuscript as he created a list for the index, thus also catching a few more errors.

What would I have done without the help of Pat Little, Mary Beth Hattaway, and Karen Klein who helped me through a health crisis? Auset Rohn, my dear priestess sister, came to my aid when my fingers were numb from surgery and my mind clouded in the days following it. She typed, converted images, compiled lists, double-checked me, kept me calm, and brought me food. The patience and compassion of my editors at Inner Traditions while I mended from four surgeries in five months kept me from giving up on the project. All these dear ones were the terrestrial angels who kept the celestial angels aloft.

I am indebted to my dear mentor Dr. Jean Houston and to my new friend and colleague Lynn Andrews for their rousing endorsements of my work. Finally, unequivocally, I am indebted to Dr. Anita Archer, my dissertation advisor, who continued to prod and encourage me to think outside the box long after she stopped advising me on the doctoral work per se. She asked the best questions, found hints to new directions, prayed with me over the book, and never allowed me to forget that it was something the angels intended for me to write. What an integral part of this work she has been, blessing me with her intelligent conversation and her beautiful, loving friendship!

I am grateful to all who inspired and encouraged me—and again, to the angels, to the angels, the magnificent visitation and illumination of the angels!

Answering the Call

Wonder tears open an otherwise closed cosmos.

THOMAS MOORE, *A RELIGION OF ONE'S OWN*

Do you believe in angels? People often ask me that.

The answer is: Yes, I do.

Do you work with angels?

Yes, I do.

Do you see angels?

Well, I perceive Spirit and angels are Spirit. Do I see them? Not always, but yes, at times.

See, in this case, becomes a bland, misshapen word. What happens are moments of wonder that come upon us unexpectedly, as the angels did for me. Whether angels appear to us as winged, as light, or as human—or not at all—depends upon the viewer's state of mind, our garment of belief, and the circumstances in which we find ourselves. We cannot imprison our minds nor the understanding of a god-filled universe with padlocks demanding keys of absolute proof. As the poet Mary Oliver said, "Only if there are angels in your head will you ever, possibly, see one" (Mary Oliver, "The World I Live In").

Let me give you an example. For most people the perception of color varies according to the individual and to the circumstances. My blind masseur astounds me with his clairsentient perception, sensing color with his hands. He feels the aura, which few sighted people can even see with physical eyes much less touch with their fingertips. Friends who have experienced traumatic situations assure me of the appearance and intervention of beings of light, visible angels, who brought comfort to them and relieved their fears.

MY OWN EXPERIENCE OF ANGELS

As for myself, I certainly have experienced angelic interventions. For one thing, I feel presences, and I have witnessed miracles, fleeting images of light, and unbelievable healing. Although I did not physically see an angel on the night my daughter was conceived, certainly I heard one. It revealed itself as the most beautiful, hauntingly expressive music I had ever heard. My husband heard it, too. That sound followed us for several blocks as we walked beside Boulder Creek (in Colorado). What a beautiful way to conceive one's child!

At a separate time in my life, when I was not in a good state of mind, feeling mentally and emotionally exhausted, I did feel the foul energetic presence of something I can only call demonic. It stayed around a while, flinging objects off the mantle, physically restraining me in bed, and even frightening my friends and my dog. Finally, recognizing that this energy reflected an ill will within me, I had to exorcise it with powerful intention, angelic invocation, forgiveness, and love.

I want to offer my stories as evidence that we do participate in the good or ill that surrounds us. It doesn't always "just happen" to us. The Spiritualist creed professes that we make our own happiness or unhappiness as we obey or disobey spiritual laws.

I grew up in the Episcopal Church, enfolded in the spiritual energies of my maternal family of Roman Catholic aunts, uncles, and cousins who prayed to Mother Mary, to saints and to angels, as well as to God and Christ. I relished their beliefs in the availability of legions of spiritual beings. My lifelong mysticism began when at the age of five I heard a wavery woman's voice singing outside and in a beautiful moment that snowy, blowy winter morning, I knew that it was "God's Wife" calling at our front door. I told my mother that "God's Wife" was calling to us. I could hear Her voice in the whistling eaves; it was cold out there and we had to let Her in. She wanted a cup of coffee. My mother did not seem to hesitate. She made coffee for herself and for God's Wife, and then we sat at the kitchen table and chatted. Mother asked questions and I repeated what God's Wife answered. That may have seemed sacrilegious to my Catholic relatives, but to my father's side of the family it was a quasi-normal event. A few of them were already Spiritualists engaged in seances of one type or another and talking to dead relatives, spirits, and angels all the time.

I grew up on gossip, anecdote, and oral storytelling. Wild tales about neighbors, relatives, and friends abounded. Those sightings from the "other side"—a mysterious, unseen world, complete with near-impossible but very true details—blazed themselves into my memory. Stories of one relative in particular became a lifelong touchstone. My great-aunt Arzelia practiced as a Spiritualist medium, therefore mysterious visitors from other dimensions have always piqued my interest.

Most adults might think of my conversation with God's Wife as the byproduct of an overactive childish imagination, yet it is the imagination that creative individuals develop and draw upon as they age. Those of us whose mothers read books to us as children, or whose fathers painted, encouraged *us* to paint, and engaged in conversations with angelic beings (as mine did) are exercising our so-called "angel lobes." As a child, William Blake saw angels in the windows. As an adult he sketched and compiled his poetic visions into his visionary book *Heaven and Hell*. Such children at a young age use creative imagination to develop their capacities to later access higher dimensional beings. This endeavor is deeper than expressing an overactive imagination. Mystical children, I believe, continue to develop into deeply mystical adults.

Yet the fear that such children will develop into deeply disturbed individuals tends to cloud our interpretations of early mystical experiences. The spirit world often confounds us. Humans are experiential beings, and most adults have had their sense of wonder crushed. Taught to trust only what we can grasp with our senses or intellect, we often will second-guess what comes knocking at the door of our sixth sense. The celestial message succumbs to dismissive labels, such as *imagination, dream,* or *coincidence.* Perhaps worse, these mystical experiences are deemed to be *hallucinations.* Creatures from another dimension, alternate worlds, or separate planes of existence disturb our intellectual need to create solid, verifiable meaning from random events. The angels and the fallen ones become part of the ineffable mystery of the mind of God.

My mother did not discourage my conversation with God's Wife. As I grew older, I recognized that the God's Wife I knew as a child was Isis, the Egyptian goddess. This angelic being impressed me as being beautiful, almost human, winged, and filled with the energy of air, clouds, wind, and wooded places. Quite unlike the God hiding inside His lonely cathedral off Main Street, She could appear instantly whenever I needed Her. More available at times than a human mother, I thought of Her as My Other Mother. Later, as a grown woman, I found her image in Coptic churches. Here she wore the cloak of Jesus's mother, Mary, surrounded by her attendants, whom the Copts identified as angels. They seemed to resemble the winged *ba* souls of the ancient Egyptians; that is, human heads with wings. In other words, cherubim accompanied Mary, and ba souls accompanied Isis.

Did I actually see God's Wife as Isis robed in white and blue standing at our front door when I was a child? Again, not with physical eyes, but yes, I am absolutely certain it was She. I had never heard of Isis then, nor had I seen pictures of Her, but I was impressed that I stood in Her presence. I *knew* Her. To my inner vision She appeared exactly as described by the ancients. She definitely approached me as a messenger. Was she a deity or an angel? you might ask. Does it matter? I might ask in reply. Angels appear in all cultures and religions. One group identifies such a being as deity, another as deva, another as angel. But are they real or imagined? Ah, now that is one of the questions we will be drawn to examine more closely toward the end of this book!

THE FUNCTION OF ANGELS

Aside from childhood lessons delivered from pulpits and parents, most of us learn about heaven's messengers through scripture and mythology. Is one version of the origin and purpose of angels truer than another simply because it happens to be older? Not really. What amazes me is how alike these angelic sightings tend to be across religions and throughout time and space.

The belief in divine messengers is a tenet of every major religion. The wingspan of angels and spiritual beings, as messengers of God—the Ultimate Reality covers nearly all Western and Eastern faith traditions. In my opinion, all spiritual beings belong to the category of angels, whether they have wings or not. As long as they exist in a stratum of greater spiritual command, a hierarchy, if you will, I call them "angels."

The word *angel* derives from the Greek or Italian word for messenger, *angelos*. The Hebrew word *mal'akh* identifies that messenger as one from Jehovah and it is associated with words such as *melek* or *malachi*, which equally mean "God's messengers." In addition, they may do other work as well, but their appearance seems to be God's way of telling us that life is more than we can imagine. We spend our days inside a mystery. Angels fly into our lives to remind us that an awesome divine intelligence created and sustains the universe for its own cryptic reasons. Summoned by God at the beginning of time, they infuse us with the mystery of the divine creative intelligence itself.

Divine messengers appear in Western traditions, which include the Jewish, Christian, and Islamic faiths, and in Eastern traditions, which include Hinduism, Buddhism, and Shintoism. Similar angels appear in religious traditions found along the Silk Road, specifically Zoroastrianism and Yezidism. In every religion where angels appear as beings of light, their counterparts fly in as dark beings—angels of death and fallen ones. Some are demons, and some are Nephilim, the so-called children of fallen angels.

What are we to make of this complex landscape populated with such a variegated assortment of angelic beings? In seeking to answer this question we might try to determine what God may have had in mind during his cosmic creative process. In so doing, in this book we enter into a discussion of how angels—as messengers of God—and their fallen brethren—the dissenters of God—interact with human beings, to whom God gave choice and free will.

Most religions posit that angels, quite unlike humans, have neither choice, free will, nor souls. I suppose that without free will there would be no need for a soul to progress. There would be no need to work through one's karma. Neither would there be the wisdom of experience. Angels have no karma. They are perfect and never die.* On the other hand, humans are a mess of free will, and our souls try like heck to outgrow our mortal errors. And while I am of the opinion that humans do not evolve into angels, the mystical poet Ralph Waldo Emerson claimed that "every man contemplates an angel in his future self."[1] Perhaps he did suggest that humans do turn into angels, but I interpret this to mean that humans long to become a more angelic, light being in the future.

So what exactly *is* an angel's function? If my dreams are accurate, angels help us to evolve and work out our karma—karma being that resultant pattern we experience based on the choices we made in previous lifetimes. My understanding of such occurred in one of my dreams when I found myself in a starry kitchen stirring an enormous kettle of soup, working with five congenial angels. We placed in the soup cauldron certain colored, gelatinous plates of geometric shapes—squares, triangles, rectangles, and trapezoids.

I recognized these geometric shapes as astrological patterns floating around in a cosmic soup. When I realized the plates could slide over each other, lock into place, and light up, I became excited. In that moment I understood that the configurations the angels and I had created had formed natal birth charts. Each pattern connected to a life lesson that a particular soul needed to learn. I felt so honored to be working with the angels to craft opportunities that would unfold in the life story of specific individuals. I had no idea whose

*Not all religions believe this.

life I was creating—past, present, or future. It was simply an honor to work with the angels. Finally, I saw an unusual pattern that really excited me, and I shouted to the angels, "Golly, look at that! That's perfect!" And the angels clapped their hands, smiled, and said, "Okay, then. Jump in!"

What a powerful dream I dreamed of how, before my birth, I stood in the starlight with angels to craft my life! Perhaps everyone does.

Again, angels make themselves known in human affairs at the service of evolution and the soul's progression. They see events in the past and the future because they exist within and without all dimensions, which all come back to the Mind of the All, the All being the universal life force of God.

THE NATURE OF ANGELS

Angels can take whatever form they wish. When the occasion warrants, they may appear as human. Groups of people will see, dream, or have visionary experiences in a certain way because of the group's social or religious conditioning, which anthropologists call "cultural patterning." This might explain why the "People of the Book"* all envision angels in a similar manner, and why devata appear differently to those in the Eastern tradition. The celestial visions adapt themselves to the understanding of the seer.[2]

The more I learned about angels, the more intrigued I became. Who *were* these beings that I had become so fascinated by? Some say God created angels as a separate species. While this may or may not be true, humans and angels share a common origin in the way that early on most creatures—frogs, birds, cats, and humans—resemble each other in shape, at least embryonically. Genetic design determines the outcome. And theology and physics seem to agree that angels and humans are both comprised of light. Humans are perhaps more or less light in frozen form.

*Those adherents of the scriptural texts of the Abrahamic, monotheistic faiths.

It also must be said that both mammals and angels establish themselves in a type of organized structure. Specifically, each religious tradition offers a hierarchy of seven (or nine) heavens, hells, or planes of existence. Within those planes dwell innumerable angelic or divine beings. Beyond the hierarchies of angelic hosts and above the demigods, we find Deity. Its Cosmic Being-ness appears so ineffable that humans deem it the "Ultimate Truth" or the "Ultimate Reality."

Although angels appear to have an intelligent design behind their diverse appearances, forms, purposes, and so on, not all angels are the same and they don't all have the same agendas. Hindu devas (divine beings) evolve through many human lives and states of consciousness in order to attain their divine status.

Another example: Mormons believe that the angel Moroni dictated the Book of Mormon to their patriarch, Joseph Smith. Mormons identify Moroni as the last great leader of the Nephites, who eventually ascended beyond his human life.[3] Perhaps the evolution of humans into angels requires a mental development rather than a physical one.

Maybe it becomes more important to think in the way that angels think. Perhaps the more we understand that all of Creation—angels and humans alike—has sprung from the mind of God, the more humans and angels will be drawn close together. This connection is underscored by the richness of the literature that exists about angels. In my opinion, angels exist beyond metaphor, but we have difficulty expressing exactly *how* they exist. They are not necessarily more in favor now than they have ever been. In fact, angels have never fallen *out* of favor. Reports of angelic appearances span many, many thousands of years. How we speak of angels and their purposes, however, changes as our understanding of consciousness changes.

Why do reports of angels abound? Perhaps we long for what lies beyond the veil in the same way that salmon swim toward a home they've never actually known. One might say it's in our DNA.

Humans crave a sense of purpose and order. Whether we define ourselves as religious, spiritual, or a-spiritual, one of the most frequently asked questions about the plan of one's life on this planet is, "Why am

I here?" Life purpose is a question that religions try to answer. Religion tends to codify its answers into prescriptive rules and cautionary narratives, but no religious faith began as a list of tenets. Most were preceded by an angelic intervention, or through mystical appearances to individuals. An angel appeared, delivered a message, and that changed everything.

Religions begin when humans try to interpret what that message means and for whom. Religions gather strength and force of will by gathering followers and adherents. The faith machine then requires adherents to keep the momentum of the institution. That, in my opinion, is where the angels vacate the building. Without the monument of a stolid religious tenet, the appearance of angels remains a solitary, mystical experience.

ANGELS AND RELIGION

In this book I intend to tell a number of stories, some of which are personal. A few I've gleaned from reported modern sightings, but most derive from myth, ancient literature, biblical literature, and the apocrypha, those tales that fell out of the official canon. Modern Theosophists, Sufi masters, Eastern gurus, kabbalists, and Christian mystics and psychics add their stories and revelations to those I will recount.

The medieval inquiries of the Christian saints Thomas Aquinas and John of Damascus, together with those of Eleazar ben Judah of Worms, laid the groundwork for modern angelology: the study of angels. Aquinas and John of Damascus spent decades contemplating angels. And for centuries, clerics dubbed Rabbi Eleazar ben Judah of Worms "a madman" obsessed with analyzing and conjuring angels. Each theologian wondered: "What are angels? Do they possess a form? Why do they come bidden or unbidden? Have they always good intentions? Are they sent by God's command only? Or can humans invoke angels; and, if so, for what purposes?" Then follows the question about whether one has a personal angel. The author of Matthew 18:10 seems to say that everyone has a protective angel watching over them. Could this really be true? What *is* true is that whether or not we believe in angels, they believe in us. In my opinion, most people will experience an angel one day—whether personal or by whatever means or names.

Have *I* ever seen an angel? Maybe.

If you asked the biblical Abraham the same question, he might have given you the same answer: "Maybe." Maybe those three messengers sent by God who stopped to rest beside Abraham's tent and enjoy Sarah's delicious cooking with him were angels, even though they looked and ate like men (Genesis 18). Perhaps angels may take human form long enough to alter an event, foretell a joyful occasion, or provide dire warnings of terrible things to come.

In any event, at my age I don't have thirty years or more to continue to study the angels. My finite mind can only go so far in its understanding. I am not attempting to persuade detractors of my position and thereby prove one particular religion. My own faith and upbringing, however, will color the way I use particular words or concepts in this book.* I admit to cultural biases. My intention is to unfurl the kaleidoscope of angels across many religious traditions to reveal the unified essence of angels and to underscore their eternal mystery. Angels continue to exist despite the ever-changing theological perspectives upheld by various clerics. No one sees the same thing, but most clerics agree that the study of angels offers an engrossing, magical understanding of the cosmos.

In my own case, even before I wanted to learn the mysteries of Egypt, I wanted to know the secrets of God. I wanted to know that which seemed whispered behind the blue curtain of sky and who exactly conversed with whom amid the wind in the trees. I wanted to see the big angels. Apparently, I am not the only one.

---

*My bias is Spiritualist Episco-pagan. You can't join this religion. It's just how I roll. The Bibles I choose to cite derive from diverse traditions. Sometimes I like the poetry of the King James Version, although not always its patriarchal qualities. Sometimes I prefer the etymology of Greek, Hebrew, or Aramaic texts. Thinking like an ancient Egyptian is also part of my psychospiritual practice; therefore, you will find many thoughts derived from that.

This Infinite Intelligence that sourced all life and all of the angels is called "Jehovah" or "Yahweh" by some. Others call it "Allah," "Wakan Tanka," or "Krishna." Whatever this divine force and ultimate reality may be, and whether it may be envisioned as impersonal or personal, as natural law, or as Truth, *it* creates and sustains the universe.

Let me further define God as consciousness. The Russian grande dame of Theosophy, Helena Petrovna Blavatsky, defined God as a consciousness having its center everywhere and its circumference nowhere.[4] A former Anglican priest turned Theosophist, Charles Leadbeater went on to emphasize that either you see God in everything, or you never see God and his angels at all. Neither one is wrong; one is just more burdensome than the other. Most theologians will tell you, as the Franciscan friar Richard Rohr puts it: "If God is not the center, you are burdened with being the center yourself. What an impossible and self-defeating task."[5]

Angels are impossible to explain to one with no experience of them. Yet all the time we believe in things we can't always see. Physics, for example. We believe there is light we can see and light we cannot see. Most people believe scientists who say that light is both a wave and a particle. We may not be sure how this is true, but scientists now tell us that it depends upon whether or not that light is observed. At any rate, we can prove that light vibration adapts to thought, or consciousness.

Likewise, angels seem at times to be formless and at other times to be a luminous substance. Does their form depend upon whether or not we humans are consciously seeking them? Do these "God thoughts," which is what Meister Eckhart called them, appear as our own thoughts?[6] If angels are ideas, or mentalities, as Eckhart suggests, can they, being a mental construction, also take form? Thoughts, metaphysicians tell us, do become things and, in that regard, ideas are not vagaries, but precursors to manifested experiences. First, perhaps, there is emptiness, and then God fills the empty form with its mental form. Then something happens—a thought flies forth.

What else might thought require in order to become form? Perhaps a will to be known, such as God's will, or even a desire to have a truth become manifest. Either way, the request to become takes shape in the heart and mind. "I will to do thy Will," so to speak. Buddhists attribute the appearance of angels to the divine mind conceiving objects and forms. Before the name and identity, however, there is samsara, the source of the identifiable world in the beginning. That is: emptiness, stillness, an egg of potentiality.

Potentiality is and it is not. (To be or not to be. Is that even a choice?) Once thought stirs, the choice defines the perception of form. How variable that must make the angels! In attempting to define the word *spirit,* Dr. Peter Kreeft, professor of religious studies at Boston College, suggested that angels consist of two things: "the power of thinking—conscious, deliberate, rational understanding," and "the power of willing and choosing and deliberately loving."[7] In that case there is never a time, no matter how lonely, isolated, or afraid one feels, that any of us travels through life without the possibility of an angel's accompaniment.

GUIDANCE FROM UNSEEN ANGELS

Often in my neurotic youth I couldn't figure out the next step in my life. Always I felt called to follow a spiritual path. In fact, I recall my first husband saying, "You act like you are on a mission from God." I thought, *Of course. So are you. You just don't recognize it.* Sometimes, sitting on my porch, I prayed for a big white panel van with an arrow on it to pass by the house. That van would give me clear direction in a message painted in letters two feet high: "Normandi, Go This Way." But the van never arrived. That perhaps would have interfered with a divine alternate plan in which I had to make a choice. Fate or karma is part of the human experience. Any angel commandeering that white van would not be allowed to interfere.

Perhaps unseen angels have guided most circumstances of my life as it's unfolded. Angels might overshadow the right human and send him or her along at the right moment to engage in a conversation that will result in a life-altering course. For example, one conversation with an acquaintance resulted in my purchase of Wallis Budge's hieroglyphic text *The Egyptian Book of the Dead: Papyrus of Ani*. That event initiated me into a lifelong journey of spiritual and metaphysical thought.

Then there was the time, on a snowy Sunday, that the angels maneuvered a MapQuest malfunction that sent my friend Gina and me driving, hopelessly lost, for thirty minutes in the wrong direction, until we righted ourselves. We soon realized that had we not exited that same interstate thirty minutes previously, we would have been involved in a fatal auto accident.

Once I believe I encountered an angel inhabiting a human form. During my first trip to Egypt, I traveled alone, and earlier in the day, I'd found in the Luxor street market a gorgeous black basalt statue of Isis. Pressed for time, I promised myself I would come back for her.

Returning to the street market that dark, cold, and foggy January night, I found myself lost. It grew late. The sound of kiosks and shops shuttering their doors and windows filled the air. A particularly thick blanket of fog kept rolling through the streets. I could barely see two feet in front of me. I remembered having seen the statue on a high shelf in one of the shops. Could I find her again? I hurried from store to store, alley to alley, trying to rediscover the spot I had visited in the daylight. After an exhaustive search, I zigzagged through the labyrinthine streets—and then, lo and behold! There she was!

The shopkeeper who was rolling up the striped awning and shuttering his doors grudgingly stayed open only long enough for me to buy that statue. He wrapped it in newspaper, and I carried my bundle back through the maze of alleys and darkening, silent streets. In the deep emptiness of closing time with all the shop lights clicking off in a town that had but a single stoplight and few streetlights, I could not tell where I was; but I could very distinctly hear footsteps behind me.

I grew nervous and crossed to the other side of the road. The steps followed me. I picked up my pace, crossed the street again, and turned quickly around a corner. So did those footsteps behind me! I hurried, scanning doorways, right and left, picking up the pace. So did the feet that followed! I panicked and ran as fast as I could run, clutching a sixteen-inch stone statue, and the footfall behind me drew closer. Totally lost now, and quite afraid, I whispered "Goddess, help me!"

From out of the fog appeared a black horse pulling a black-topped carriage driven by an Egyptian boy. He slowed his horse just long enough to point to the left and say "Lady! Your hotel is one block this way."

Thank you!

I ran to the street corner, turned left, and there was my hotel! I practically burst through the glass front door and into the lighted lobby. The shadowy figure who had been following me strode on.

Later that night, tucked into my bed in the hotel, my mind returned to that encounter, and I kept returning to the image of the boy who had saved me. How did he know where my hotel was? I hadn't told anyone or even ridden in any carriage to or from the hotel. In retrospect, I have decided that he was an angel—a divine messenger in a human form.

Perhaps he descended from a higher realm to save my younger self so that I could grow old, write my books, live a life imbued with mystery, and now, on this particular future day, recount that miracle of the past when an angel appeared and possibly saved my life. Or perhaps an angel overshadowed this good native son of Egypt, using a human vessel to deliver a message to a frightened traveler. Okay, it wasn't a white panel truck, but a black horse-drawn carriage. Still, that lifelong prayer to Spirit to point the way for me becomes more enigmatic now.

Who or what did I encounter that night? People not only believe in angels, they also rely on them. In uncertain times they are an antidote to an overwhelmingly illusory material world. Angels appeal to our childlike desire to know what is going on behind that closed door— behind the curtain in Oz, so to speak. Angels draw us that much closer to the mystery of God.

And what happens if we ignore angelic messages? Certain apocryphal texts assure us that angels know the future. Humans have choice; angels do not. Having no say in the matter, the angels tried to talk God out of including humans in the composition of the universe. Being creatures of prophecy they could foresee the flawed decisions that humans would make and the disastrous outcomes, but their warnings fell on deaf ears. The story of fallen angels demonstrates the disastrous result of angelic free will.

In our preliminary look at angels, there are many heavenly neighborhoods and more avenues to wander through than there are back alleys and shops in the bazaars of Luxor. Beautiful, haunting, puzzling, mysterious . . . Many authors have tackled this subject. Why the widespread fascination with the hellish and heavenly attributes of angels? Contemporary Jewish writer Rabbi Philip Berg may have summed it up best: "The subject of angels is not one to be regarded as a curious notion that simply captures our imagination. It must be considered as a serious matter. Our lives may very well be affected by this knowledge."[8]

So, what *is* an angel? Perhaps an angel is an experience to which our minds must give form. The mind (knowledge) can awaken, just as the Buddha's mind snapped into awakened consciousness with an ineffable experience (mystic wisdom). To hold onto that awakened state, to define it, to live within that consciousness, the experience most often needs a shape. Thus the mind will provide us with shape or a symbol—a touchstone for the experience to which the mind can return. The mystic may express the feeling with the cry: "Oh, that's what it was—an *angel!*"

Once I received a vision of the angelic residence in heaven. Early one summer morning I saw on the eastern horizon the "City of Gold." An equally stunned and reliable witness sitting beside me corroborated its appearance. At the time this vision appeared, I didn't know about that celestial mountain in the sky, Mount Meru, and the Tibetan vision of the realm of Shambala. I didn't know about the ascended masters of the Theosophists who, in etheric bodies of light, attend vigils in the Wesak Valley for planetary and spiritual transformation.[9] Perhaps I should have known, but that might have ruined the impact of the complete, decade-long revelation that came to me about the place of angels, the creation of the world, and the City of Gold.

On this particular day in August 1987, according to the Mayan calendars, a certain planetary alignment was to come into being. New age hype swirled about the Harmonic Convergence that had been prophesied by Dr. Jose Arguelles, the new age author and artist. On that same day, throngs of people gathered in spiritually potent locations to see the wheels and gyres of the universe slip into place. With no desire for a group experience, my friend Jessie and I decided to celebrate her birthday—the alignment of her solar return—in a private sunrise meditation. In the dark, we climbed Mount Sanitas, which juts out of the landscape near my house in Boulder, Colorado.

As Jess and I waited in silence, gazing east across the plains north of Denver, we witnessed in the clear sky a golden light formation. Just before sunrise, without a cloud in the sky, Jess and I observed the building up of a towering city of gold. Perhaps it was the Shambala of the Tibetans, or Mount Meru, the residence of Hindu devas. On a golden mountain fully made of brilliant light, thousands of temples appeared built upon its plateaus. Stunned, I watched in silence, trying to take in the vision that offered a portal into an alternate universe. Then I elbowed Jessie, saying nothing. "I see it, too," she whispered. We marveled at the sight, flooded with a sense of peace. When the sun rose, blindingly, the vision disappeared.

Upon such an occasion, the rational mind kicks in, attempting to think away or interpret the message. The mind whirs as it tries to categorize and diminish the experience. Stunned by what we have seen, we keep trying to fit it into a container too small to contain it.

Scientists say that our entire essence changes after such an experience. How so? Every religion celebrates the central sun as the source of light, life, and the symbol of an awareness of God. Exposure to this light, or to the enlightenment of meditation, increases the presence of biophotons in the brain, which increases our capacity for consciousness. Angels emanate an intense, powerful light. The more of their light we experience, the higher our consciousness becomes. And seeing an angel (or a whole city of angels) pierces the witness with awe. *Awe,* sometimes *dread,* are the words used in sacred texts to describe seeing a phenomenon that doesn't fit within our worldview. It stops us in our tracks. Let's face it, the familiar road is not the one that leads us into a new life. The experience of awe, scientists suggest, can assist our bodies in producing more light, more consciousness, more enlightenment.

What deeper understanding, what "new life" did the cosmos instill in me that day beyond the witnessing of the City of Gold in a transmission of light? In short, my life changed. At a fevered pace I began to complete the sunrise meditations, which led to the eventual translation of the hieroglyphs of the Egyptian Book of the Dead. Phanes Press published my book of translations, *Awakening Osiris,* in 1988, and since then I have followed a path of spiritual inquiry and writing.

I firmly believe that in August 1987 an angelic vision pulled back the curtains of my psyche to let in more light, thereby elevating my consciousness. To me this proved that I was, as are we all, part of a grand cosmic scheme. Knowing that we are part of a larger plan and accepting our place in that plan affords us a sense of peace and wellbeing—if we are but open enough to sow the seeds of our own divine awakening.

1
Western Traditions

*The original fire out of which the angels burn and live,
that is God himself.*

HILDEGARD OF BINGEN, *LIBER VITAE MERITORUM,*
AS QUOTED IN *PHYSICS OF ANGELS*
BY FOX AND SHELDRAKE

JUDEO-CHRISTIAN ANGELS

On the first day in the infinite nothingness before Creation, something happens.

The ancient Egyptians would have said that at the core exists an ineffable Being. He longs for companionship, for an Other, for a way to know himself. Rabbis and Christian clerics tell us that a divine mouth moves over the water, intoning the Word: "Let there be light." The Muslim sheikhs say that the one god simply said, "Be." Scientists tell us that at the moment of the big bang, universes flung themselves into existence. Beingness and consciousness begin with the light. All the heavens, the particles that exist in time and space, spin out from the vibrations of that light.

On the second day before he makes the Earth, God makes the heavens, and many angels appear as flames of fire in the seven heavens through which they move and sing their praises. On the third day when

18

the Earth forms, the angels soar and float as wind, or sometimes move among its people and creatures clad in flesh as if they were beings like them (Psalms 104:1–4). The closer to Earth they move, the denser they become—and yet they can flutter off, up into the highest heavens to dance like flames before the Throne of God.

On the sixth day, God makes all his creatures and humankind. Apparently, like the angels and the entire contents of the universe, they, too, are crafted of light. "And God said, 'We shall make men in our image, according to our form, and they shall rule among the fish of the Sea, and among the birds of Heaven, and among cattle, and among all animals of the Earth, and among all creepers that creep on the Earth'" (Genesis 1:26 The Peshitta Holy Bible Translated).

Here is the crux of it: through the divine mind of God everything is made of light; that humans, angels, universes, and all creatures partake in the light that may be particular to their species, but all are a part of the collective conscious mind of God in conversation with itself. So refined is the intelligence of the One Great Light, Meister Eckhart says, that "if a tiny fragment or a little spark were to fall from him, it would fill this whole world with rapture and bliss."[1]

An Angel: Some Definitions

Simply defining an angel proves to be a daunting task. Melek (Muslim), or mal'akh (Jewish), or simply akh (ancient Egyptian), these winged creatures symbolize the spiritual forms of light and intelligence. Both *melek* and *mal'akh* translate as "divine messenger," but a messenger of what? Sent by whom? For what purpose? Their duties and proclivities define them. Their names are many; still more exist whose names are unknown. They appear everywhere, maybe right beside you now, or nowhere in particular. They come and go as thoughts do.

In the Middle Ages, somewhere around 1192 CE, marauders attacked Rabbi Eleazar ben Judah of Worms, a Hasidic Jew and German mystic. Some believe Crusaders broke into his house looking for money. They left the rabbi maimed, but murdered his wife, Dulcea, and his daughters Hannah and Bellette. The sins of men did not deter the rabbi. A metaphysician who worked with angels, Eleazar ben Judah authored an ethical code known as the Rokeach, which married the rabbinical teachings of the Talmud with the mystical traditions of the Kabbalah.

A pious man and a devoted Talmudic scholar who practiced metaphysics, the rabbi worked tirelessly as a translator, an astronomer, a poet, and a gifted liturgist. As we mentioned in the introduction, his critics labeled him a "madman." He believed that by manipulating his breath he could produce angels and demons with whom he conversed. His critics berated him as a kabbalist swayed by hallucinations. "He saw legions of angels and demons and exerted himself to spread cabalistic systems which went far beyond the conceptions of the authors of the Cabala."[2]

Critics scorned his use of gematria (the numerological codes that he applied to prayerful petitions), however, he believed his white magic amplified the angelic forces that he invoked to create miracles. His book *Sefer ha-Ḥokmah,* a mystical treatise on the various names of God and angels, documents his formulae. Whether such invocations are sanctified, recommended, or even possible, the use of gematria indicates just how far down the rabbi(t) hole one can go in the study of angelology. In the book known as Rokeach, Eleazar ben Judah detailed a concept known as *kavod,* or divine glory. The kavod (angels) appear as an emanation of God, he said, and remains the only way for us to know the infinitely transcendent and unknowable author of the universe.[3]

"Ageless and changeless angels originate from an eternal, changeless God at the beginning of time. They transcend every religion, philosophy, and creed," the Dominican monk and philosopher Thomas Aquinas wrote in the thirteenth century. They have no religion because they preexist every religion. Love is their religion.[4]

We identify angels according to their jobs, qualities, appearances, and names. The study of angels began long before Eleazer ben Judah began his compendium of angelology. The modern *Dictionary of Angels* by Gustav Davidson lists thousands. Only five appear by name in the Bible; the Kabbalah offers seventy-two. John of Patmos, attributed author of the book of Revelation, described their number as "ten thousand times ten thousand, and thousands of thousands."[5]

It proves impossible to name that many angels. An infinite number appear because they emerge as swift and as light-filled as thought. The expanded size of our universe—one hundred thousand light years from end to end—means that even if angels moved at the speed of light and thought, it would take one hundred thousand years to cross from one side of the galaxy to the other. And this does not account for the appearance of angels in other universes and dimensions. Certainly many angels appear in many orders, and in other universes many take their places in their hierarchies. Thomas Aquinas suggested in *Summa Theologica*, "The more perfect a thing is in nature, the more ought it to be multiplied."[6] In 1619 the English clergyman William Sclater asked the question: "How many angels can dance on the head of a pin?" We can look to Thomas Aquinas for our answer. He would say that because angels have no physical bodies, the answer would be: "an infinite amount."[7]

To the ancients, angels swarmed into existence at the break of dawn above the watery deep, offering humankind a variety of inspirational, awe-filled, and terrifying appearances. Whether in the field at night or sitting outside an empty tomb, the appearance of an angel often filled the viewer with dread. We even meet them in dreams as when Jacob, asleep in the desert with his head on a rock, sees angels ascend and descend on a ladder stretching from Earth to heaven (Genesis 28:12–17).

Similar ladders to heaven appear in the ancient Egyptian Pyramid Text of Unas in which one sees the akh spirits flying up and down a ladder that opens into a window in the sky. In this vision Unas learns he belongs to heaven and earth. To Jacob, the angel prophesies that he and his children will inherit the earth upon which he lies. To Unas, the divine being acclaims his birth as a spiritual being created of earth and of sky. But when he sees the shining spirit beings, Unas feels both overwhelmed with wonder and afraid of the "magic" these ancient Egyptian angels possess.[8]

Angels appear to the chosen and pagan alike. To each, their messages instill awe and fear. When an angel said that a holy child and savior was born, the shepherds who heard that voice felt "sore afraid." Who, indeed, are these messengers, and why does nearly every religion include angels in their theology? Why do terrifying messengers initiate so many religious traditions with philosophies that often seem to be at odds with each other? Yet, simultaneously, each tradition argues its veracity based on the words of divine messengers.

In the thirteenth century Thomas Aquinas began answering these age-old questions about angels, only to bump up against their ineffable mystery. In his book *Summa Theologica* (1265–1274 CE), he enumerates the questions, pontificates, and speculates on all matters of theology. His musings became a voluminous sequence of tracts that epitomized a lifetime of monkish enquiry. A mere portion of it (167 pages) poses 72 questions and answers about the function and nature of angels.

Among his questions were: Do the angels exercise functions of life in the bodies they assume? Can an angel be in several places at once? Does an angel pass through intermediate space or is their movement instantaneous? Does an angel's act of understanding reflect his substance? Is an angel's power of intelligence his essence? Do higher angels understand more as a universal species than do the lower angels? Does an angel know himself? Does an angel know God by His own natural principles? And so on. Some of the questions may seem unusual, leading to conundrums. On the other hand, inquiry into invisible things has a way of getting convoluted. For Aquinas these questions offer an answer to the "what" and "from where" regarding Judeo-Christian angels. The work then branches off into speculation on the interrelationships of the angelic, divine, and human worlds. Angelic messengers span time and space. They cross religions, and have become one of the unifying themes of theology worldwide.

Theologians, scholars, and scientists ask similar questions today to the ones posed above. In order to understand the powers of angels and their influences on us, we return to our first question, which tries first to determine *what* they are. Aquinas asks intriguing questions such as these: How do we define an angel? Are they etheric or mental, that is, incorporeal, or are they composed of matter and form? Have they human-like bodies? Or do they differ in species? Are their forms eternal and incorruptible? Do they pass away? Are angels limited to our understanding of time and space? These ponderings encompass Questions 50–53 in the *Summa Theologica*.

The question "What is an angel?" can hardly be separated from the question "What is the nature of God?" According to Genesis, God created every angel individually and simultaneously during the first six days. Theologist Marc D. Angel suggests that the Hebrew word *yom* was translated to mean "a day," but really served as a metaphor for "process." Of the six processes of God's creation, the concept of time was one.[9] When the angels witness God's creation of the Earth, Job 38 declares "the morning stars sang together, and all the angels shouted for joy" (New International Verson). Thus one might surmise that jubilant, witnessing angels emerged during the first process or on the first day.

The Zohar, a book of kabbalist wisdom, says that when God said, "Let there be light," angels emerged.[10] God saw the angelic light as good. I'm inclined to say that if God *is* a verb, as Rabbi David Cooper suggests in his book title of the same name, then the angels are God's action figures. In his book, *Angels: An Endangered Species,* visual artist and author Malcolm Godwin suggests that "The primary significance of angels lies not in who or what they are, but rather in what they do. Their inherent nature cannot be separated from their relationship with the prime mover, the God or Ultimate Source."[11]

Being of the same substance as God, His angelic messengers must also speak the same language as God, whether that is as thought, speech, or angelic light code. The angels understand His commands because they are formed of his very substance. Its form passes away, yet its substance remains eternal. In Genesis 1:25 we read that God made man in his own image, which shows man with an eternal, spiritual essence. Again, in Genesis 3, God apparently addresses the angels, saying that He has made humankind "like one of us" (NIV). While our mortal bodies die (a result of willful decisions made in Eden), we nonetheless share the eternal essence of God and the angels. We simply occupy different forms in a physical realm than they do.

Jewish legend says the angels disagreed about the creation of man. "The Angel of Love (Chamuel) favored the creation of man, because he would be affectionate and loving; but the Angel of Truth (Uriel) opposed it, because he would be full of lies. And while the Angel of Justice (Raguil) favored it because he would practice justice, the Angel of Peace (Phanuel) opposed it, because he would be quarrelsome. To invalidate his protest, God cast the Angel of Truth down from heaven to earth, and when the others cried out against such contemptuous treatment of their companion, He said, 'Truth will spring back out of the earth.'"[12]*

Still, when the bands of angels under the highest angel, Michael, protested, God "stretched forth His little finger, and all were consumed by fire," except for Michael. Gabriel's angels protested, asking God, "What is man, that Thou art mindful of him?" Poof! The same thing happened! Then Raphael counseled his angels to say nothing, and he said: "Lord of the world, it is well that Thou hast thought of creating man. Do Thou create him according to Thy will? And as for us, we will be his attendants and his ministers, and reveal unto him all our secrets." In this way, Raphael the healer leads all healers in heaven and on Earth, offering knowledge of celestial and planetary medicine.[13]

In the mid-thirteenth century Aquinas suggested that God's thoughts formed both the angels and mankind.[14] But what is form to God varies in density and intention. As thought forms, angels are etheric beings unbound by time and space.

Aquinas's philosophy relies upon the work of John of Damascus (ca. 675 CE), a Greek Franciscan monk who authored *An Exposition of the Orthodox Faith*. That book became as pivotal to the Eastern schools of religion as Aquinas's book *Summa Theologica* was to the Western. A difference between angels and humans is that we mortals perceive ourselves as having form, yet most people believe that angels are primarily etheric and insubstantial, if not entirely a mental construction. John of Damascus described the angels as God having "brought them into being out of nothing and created them after his

---

*Identifications of the unnamed angels in the legend are mine.

own image, an incorporeal race, a sort of spirit or immaterial fire . . . "
He continues to describe the angels as "an intelligent essence" who
are light, keen, sharp, and filled with ardor, and who hunger to serve
God.[15] Thomas Aquinas believed that God made angels of the incorporeal substance of itself, without bodies of any kind. Because angels
are incorporeal, he reasoned, they do not die, and thus eon after eon
appear to first one person then another, without ever changing in
essence from their original appearance.

Spirit beings and angels dominate the landscape of nearly every
religious tradition. While it seems that humans seldom cross through
the veil to interact with God and return, we do more often encounter
angels on the Earth plane who are the emissaries of a hidden Infinite
Intelligence. Because these messengers derive from a godly mind, they
respond at the speed of thought, and so they resemble divine thought.

It may be simpler to accept the fact that angels are God's messengers and an army of light, and to leave it at that; but that is not what
defines angelology. Kabbalists like the rabbis Z'ev ben Shimon Halevi
and Eleazer ben Judah of Worms spent decades meditating on the
meaning of verses and the actions of angels. Their exploration of this
realm of angelology takes on its own weighty mythos. They surmise
that the density of consciousness determines an array of manifested to
unmanifested angelic forms. Their philosophies run in tandem, trying
to elucidate the many planes of existence, the many mansions of heaven.
The locks of their many doors require innumerable keys, and an inexo-
rable amount of chanting the thousands of sacred names whose gematria unfolds the angelic and spirit worlds.

In Halevi's *A Kabbalistic Universe* the reader discovers seven heavens. Layers of angels reside in various locales inside those heavens and
discharge particular duties. Angels were not the first creations of God,
Halevi says. Created by the Elohim on the fifth day, they appeared
when "the waters brought forth winged creatures to fly above the earth
in the open firmament of heaven." Halevi sees these winged ones as the
angels, and the "swimmers" as lesser angels inhabiting the lower material world.[16]

The Hierarchy of Angels

Nearly all religions envision hierarchies of angels, most often nine particular planes that are like the rungs of a ladder moving from ethereal existence with expansive duties to more densely felt angels with simpler messages to deliver. As in Jacob's dream, all these interpenetrating angelic lights weave together the scaffold of a Jacob's Ladder. That ladder is one way to depict the hierarchical structure of the angels and their duties, but it is also an image of the kabbalistic Tree of Life—a tree with three pillars or branches that is a mirror for the divine hierarchy. It is a replicate ladder of Spirit within the human being—heaven in earth, so to speak.

Dionysius the Areopagite (1st century) recounted a similar story of Jacob's vision in his mystery school teachings about the glorious beings of light. He later codified this information into the hierarchy that included the nine classifications of angels. The guardian angels stand in the heavenly realm closest to mankind, and the seraphim stand before the celestial throne.[17] Each class of angels differs from the other, but all emanate from the divine source. Because they bear a common ancestry, they are all part of God. Their names identify their attributes. Seraphim are the "Glowing Ones" because they kindle and make hot the mental plane. The "Streams of Wisdom" that are the cherubim emerge from the eternal, angelic contemplation of the beauteous godhead, and the subsequent outpouring of their wisdom to those in planes below them.[18]

Not all mystics see the heavens as hierarchical. The twelfth-century sibyl and Christian mystic Hildegard of Bingen notably said, "God is a wheel," by which she meant angelic hosts existed on various spokes of the wheel, supporting and stabilizing the whole.[19] Both analogies work for our discussions of physics and angels later on.

Inside the middle pillar of this tree, the God Yahweh placed Adam (the first man).* The creature Adam, made in the image of God, pos-

---

*The words *Yahweh* and *Elohim* are interchangeable in Genesis, but *Elohim* is a plural form of this divinity. The word also indicated pagan progenitors and came to refer to the high angels of Yahweh's court, who approached nearly demigod status. There may be a connection between the words *Elohim* and *El-Hem*, meaning "of Egypt," or the divinities of the ancient land of Khem.

sessed choice. "All other spirits having no volition of their own, had no choice: they simply carried out the directions given to them according to the will of the Elohim."[20] This idea begets later conflict among the angels regarding their roles in heaven. Various angelic beings enter earthly manifestation by becoming part of the lightning flash that sears through the veil between worlds in a fiery, spirited unfoldment. As it descends the three pillars of the Tree of Life, the light-force energy passes through a trinity of states of being. In this it moves quickly from supernal thought, then tears through the veil of illusion into the etheric and astral planes of existences until its brilliant light touches into the physical plane, Earth. Seed thought becomes form.

Each of these angels emanate from the supreme creative intelligence of God. Included among the hosts of angels that live with Yahweh are:

Metatron, also called the Angel of the Presence, seated next to Yahweh; then follows

Raziel, a recording angel called the Angel of Revelation;

Zaphkiel, the Angel of Contemplation;

Zadkiel, the Angel of Mercy and Compassion;

Samael, the Angel of Death, called "Poison of God";

Michael, the Chief of Hosts;

Haniel, the Angel of Grace;

Raphael, the Angel of Healing;

Gabriel, the Angel of Spiritual Knowledge; and

Sandalphon, the Guardian Spirit of the World and the World Tree.*

Life emanates at the top of the tree from the divine creative intelligence contained in the godhead. Here resides Metatron—the supreme archangel who reigns over all the angelic hosts. Metatron and God sit

---

*Note that three of the four archangels—Raphael, Gabriel, and Michael—appear on the Tree of Life. Sandalphon may represent the fourth archangel who simultaneously oversees the physical plane and yet remains close to Yahweh. He epitomizes the dictum "As above, so below."

nearly side by side, says the Kabbalah—Metatron being the highest created archangel. Because he commands the other angelic beings, mystical scholars refer to him as the "Lesser Yahweh." A few Talmudic authors suggest that his name should not be invoked arbitrarily. Like "G-d," or "YHWH," the secret vowels protect the powerful energy of his true name. Metatron appears in the image of God as a coauthor of the universe, and as second in command. His name may derive from the Greek words *meta* and *throne*, being "one who serves behind the throne." Others say the name derives from *metator*, which means "guide," and that this angel manifested to the Israelites as the cloud of fire that guided them and Moses through the wilderness.[21]

Metatron has been described as "surrounded by storm, thunder, whirlwinds, and lightning. He has seventy-two wings and countless fiery eyes. His eyelashes are lightning, his bones are made of embers, his sinews and flesh of flame."[22] It does not say who saw this vision of the highest of angels. While Metatron is united to Enoch in Jewish lore, he actually does not appear until the mid-third century. His name appears on Babylonian incantation bowls of the fifth to eighth centuries, giving him such epithets as "Great Prince of the Entire Universe," and "the protector, who is the one that causes shaking upon all those of the upper world." Yet other incantation bowls identify him as "Yah," the abbreviated name of God in ancient Hebrew, and elsewhere as Azazel, a fallen archangel.[23] That Metatron and Enoch merge as one entity, according to esoteric literature, has been debated by the Jewish community. Yet the powerful reputation of this archangel remains.

Sandalphon collects the prayers, and Metatron handles God's responses. Overseeing the material plane does not offer Sandalphon the same power as Metatron, but still, the other angels and all beings bow their heads in awe of him. If he were visible, his body would stretch end to end across the universe. His name means "coworker," which underscores how the two angels—one in heaven and the other on Earth—work together.

These two angels hold an intimate connection with humanity because both Metatron and Sandalphon assumed human forms on

Earth. Metatron, son of Jared, was the prophet Enoch "who walked with God" (Genesis 5:22 English Standard Version). Sandalphon was the prophet Elijah, who did not seek to be a messenger of God, but God chose him. In the years following their earthly incarnations, God lifted to heaven each prophet in order that he might become an angel presence. "There are hundreds of stories describing Elijah's appearances on earth in various guises," says Rabbi Cooper, including his key appearance at every Passover Seder table.[24] Constantly battling the dark forces, Elijah, the "Robin Hood" of prophets, took from the rich and gave to the poor, working for social and economic justice. His presence often appears as the beggar at the side of the road or the simpleton with unusual wisdom. Known as one to raise the dead, Elijah becomes Sandalphon, the angel of life who fights the angel of death.[25]

Depending on circumstance, angels assume whatever shape helps them to deliver God's messages and teachings, or in performing any other God-given duty. The cherubim guard, wait, and watch outside the Garden of Eden and can turn themselves into flaming swords. "When they descend to earth, to do the bidding of God here below, either they are changed into wind, or they assume the guise of men."[26] Some kabbalists ascribe these angelic flaming swords to the lightning flash of energy that moves down the three pillars on the Tree of Life. The lightning flash moves through each world above, bringing Spirit into manifestation.

Do angels ever possess a tangible form? Apparently so. Many religious patriarchs and matriarchs recount visions in which they claim to have either seen, heard, or felt an angel's presence. It would seem that angels can glide along on a scale of materiality from embodied, to subtle, to felt but unseen. Angels working at the highest levels may be incorporeal, yet at other times their forms are composed of matter that varies in density. Our material perceptions are, of course, three dimensions. Obviously, existence in the fourth and fifth dimensions are not readily apparent to those of us with three-dimensional, rational minds. In essence then, it is nearly impossible to tell whether angels are mostly invisible or only sometimes invisible. Like water or fog, the solidity of their visibility varies.

As corporeal beings, our understanding is primarily sensory. Our own spiritual nature seems veiled in flesh. Once we deepen our spiritual understanding—whether through sitting zazen, undertaking shamanic initiation, or studying Kabbalah—we find that worlds beyond our everyday ken will appear. We can see these worlds in a different light, worlds filled with mysteries. "Included in those mysteries are realms beyond our ordinary reality, filled with supernatural energies," says Rabbi David Cooper. "They are not 'real' in the ordinary sense that we can measure them to meet scientific criteria, but they are real on some other level. They speak to us, guide us, protect us, caution us; they are voices and visions that appear clearly in the mind's eye."[27]

Quoting John of Damascus, Aquinas said that angels are "incorporeal substances [that] rank between God and corporeal creatures."[28] It helps to imagine angels existing along a continuum of polarities of essence. This is not dissimilar to the way we look for infrared and ultraviolet light on either end of the spectrum and further beyond at the unseen edges of the electromagnetic waveforms: microwaves and X-rays, radio waves, and gamma rays. It may help to imagine God as the entire spectrum and that angels exude essences of God energy, both immaterial and corporeal.

While many might believe in the validity of this, Aquinas is not among them. He does not believe that angels slide from one form into another. He does not believe that "anything corporeal (as we know it) ever existed in them."[29] In other words, an X-ray will not suddenly morph into a microwave.

Not every theologian agrees with this. The Zohar offers this explanation of angels in human form. "He makes his angels spirits . . . but when they descend, they put on the garment of the world. If they did not put on a garment befitting this world, they could not endure in this world and the world could not endure them."[30] Human forms, however, aren't the only forms that angels take. Sufi theologian Shaykh Kabbani suggests that: "Angels can come as birds, as human beings, or a form of light like a rainbow adorning the sky."[31]

Our longing for God and the desire to know why we exist seems to be the most ineffable and sorrowful of mysteries. Humans crave certainty that their lives matter, although discerning the spiritual purpose is difficult. We feel bereft, as if we were unable to reach our God—the creative intelligence of the universe—because of these bulky, fleshy clothes that we must wear. For this reason we need angels. Angels offer us a glimpse into the spiritual world and the nature of God. Unity minister Eric Butterworth has said that "all religions begin with a first-hand experience of God"[32] and that may be so, but that first-hand experience often necessitates a message delivered in person by an angel.

Messengers of God

Biblical messengers of God often appear in human form. Three very corporeal angels visited Abraham in the heat of the day as he sat in his tent under the oak trees. Legends identify them as archangels Michael, Gabriel, and Raphael in human form—definitely not winged. They refreshed themselves with cool water brought for them. They ate cheese and the meat that Abraham's servants prepared for them; they ate bread baked by Sarah, Abraham's aged wife. That's as corporeal as it gets. Immediately after their repast, "the Lord" overshadowed one of them, revealing him as an angel who then prophesied, "I will surely return to you at this time next year, and your wife Sarah will have a son!" (Genesis 18:1–11 The Berean Study Bible). For the barren Sarah and Abraham that seemed like ridiculously blessed news.

In the next moment, however, the angel brought a dire warning. Yahweh, Abraham's god, planned to destroy the wicked cities of Sodom and Gomorrah where some of Abraham's relatives lived. Apparently angels don't sugarcoat their pronouncements; their job is to tell the truth and leave. This angel, however, seemed willing to bargain with a good man. Should Abraham reveal to him at least five worthy occupants of the city, the angel said they would not destroy Sodom and Gomorrah. The message having been delivered, the first angel disappeared.

The two remaining angels traveled on to Sodom, where Lot and his family lived. Lot greeted the beautiful angels and quickly took them into his house for the night to protect them from the rabble-rousers of the city. Yet the rowdy townspeople had seen them. Incited to lust by the very corporeal beauty of these male visitors, a crowd insisted that Lot turn them over to their doings for the night. For some reason, Lot offered in trade his two beautiful daughters, perhaps knowing that to Sodomites women would be no bargain. However, the bargaining only angered the crowd. They threatened Lot to the point that the angels had to drag their host back inside, seal the door, and render the crowd blind so that they could not break into Lot's home.

This raises a question as to whether the angels actually had any control over the situation or—even though they said they did—whether they could choose to save the city or destroy it. Apparently, however, because God said he would destroy Sodom and Gomorrah, the angels already knew how it all would unfold. They helped Lot and his family escape, telling them not to look back, not to regret their decision to leave. Fire and brimstone rained down on the cities and, of course, Lot's nameless wife looked back, turning into a pillar of salt. Angels did not cause these events. They merely announced the predictions and allowed the consequences to follow.

Hierarchy Describes Bands of Energy

Among his theosophical investigations into the nature of all things spiritual, Manly Palmer Hall presented a treatise on the hierarchies of angels. He agreed with Thomas Aquinas that "God is the primary (progenitor) and these angels are the secondary cause of all visible effects. Everything is done by the Logos . . . " All things in the universe begin, as it does in the Gospel of John, with a resounding divine thought or Word. Whatsoever happens in life, Hall says, "is the outcome of natural forces working under cosmic laws; but do not forget that behind every force is its administrator, an Intelligence directing and managing."[33]

Angelic hierarchies operate in separate realms on a continuum that describes the density of the energy pattern as it coalesces into form. Hierarchies are not about degrees of power, but rather degrees of energetic operation. Looking at the light codes sent out by our sun and the unseen impulses of the exploding big bang, we observe that form follows energy. All spiritual evolution, whether falling from grace or ascending to heaven, is engaged in the same hierarchal structure of energy forms. From ferns to archangels, all unfold through process. At its deepest levels, Creation is about the divine process of unfoldment.

Every world tradition created hierarchies of spiritual beings and identified the planes they inhabit. In many cases the hierarchies of the Eastern and Western traditions overlap. The more we hear from people having near-death and out-of-body experiences, the more we discover that consciousness is not limited to a particular etheric locale. Esoteric sciences, including those based in Buddhism, Hinduism, Kabbalah, and Theosophy, for example, ascribe to the idea that we do not possess just one body, but many energy bodies. One physical and material body contains finer and finer degrees of substance the further into it we look. We exist simultaneously in etheric, astral, mental, and spiritual planes. Angels similarly exist in varying forms and within varying hierarchies.

Spiritualist medium Rose Vanden Eynden offers a workable analogy of the hierarchy of angels to the rings of Saturn, with Saturn playing the pivotal role of progenitor. We find three levels or operating bands of angels. In the first band, the cherubim, seraphim, and thrones hold the keys to how God's power operates throughout the universe. In the second band, the dominions, powers, and virtues keep order and maintain the cosmic patterns that hold the cosmos together. In the third band, the principalities, archangels, and angels involve themselves with the operations of humanity. Within their planes every angel holds a particular job relative to his plane. The purpose of every angel is to create a workable flow of energy throughout all the planes.

Angels of the First Plane

Seraphim	Create positive energy, which carries through all realms
Cherubim	Offer divine protection for all spiritual purposes
Thrones	Help smooth interactions between large groups of humans

Angels of the Second Plane

Dominions   Integrate material and spiritual energies; oversee leadership roles and issues

Powers   Dispense justice in loving ways; record human history and oversee governments and religious institutions

Virtues   Move spiritual energy to human consciousness; serve as "miracleangels" and angels of nature

Angels of the Third Plane

Principalities Serve as guardians of large groups of people, such as countries, and work toward reforms for humanity

Archangels   Work as mediators between divinity and humanity

Angels   Are assigned to work with a particular person for matters of physical and divine manifestation[34]

Hierarchies give us metaphors for the planes of existence stacked one upon the other to depict the symbolic height of God's universe. What about its breadth? How vast is the kingdom of God? The Islamic tradition offers a story about the angel Harquaeel to whom God gave eighteen thousand wings. He desired eighteen thousand more so that he could fly all the way around God's throne. Given those wings, he flew for three thousand light years, but tired, and then asked for eighteen thousand more. Given those wings, he flew another three thousand light years and kept flying and flying.

Now Harquaeel asked God how many times he had flown about the throne.

God said that although he had flown nine thousand light years he had not reached even one pillar of the base of God's throne. Then he learned that even if he flew incessantly up until the day of resurrection, or the end of time, he would not even know the height of the first pillar of the divine throne. "No-one can know the unknowable except by My favor and My grant," God said.[35]

Yet scientists, physicists, mathematicians, and angelologists continue exploring deeper and higher, trying to understand the universe and to map the mind of God. Despite the fact that most of it lies beyond our ken, the mysteries of God's cosmos continue to bloom somewhere out in deep space and within the mind.

In Colossians 1:16 the disciple Paul suggested that God created all of the thrones, powers, rulers, and authorities of heaven at the same time. Human beings and other mammals incarnated in pairs—male and female; they exist for a time, then die. Angels neither die nor propagate, and thus their multitudes manifested simultaneously. As God's manifested thought, the angels move about in constant motion on Earth and in heaven. No angel receives God's permission to sit, except for the scribe angels who write in the books of the living and in the books of the dead. Metatron tracks all the work of every angel as well as the commands of God. Seated beside the Creator, Metatron, again, is viewed as the Lesser Yahweh, a deity second only to God.[36]

The Archangels

In the kabbalistic tradition the four most exalted angels surrounding the throne of heaven are Raphael, Michael, Gabriel, and Uriel. The names that describe the angelic qualities often end in *el* or *yah,* which indicates that these are the names of God. Thus they carry the essence and imprint of God.[37] Raphael means "God has healed"; Michael means "He who is like God"; Gabriel means "Strength of God"; and Uriel means "Flame of God." These four angels who are in protective guardianship of the four corners of the Earth and stand at the foundation of great cathedrals are Raphael in the east, Michael in the south, Gabriel in the west, and Uriel in the north.

It would be impossible to detail every angel in the monotheistic traditions. In the kabbalistic tradition there are seventy-two letters in God's sacred name, and seventy-two named angels who manifest as his divine breath. Five angels appear by name in the Bible. Gabriel and Michael represent the light of the world, but Lucifer, Beelzebub, and Abaddon represent the fallen angels. Only Gabriel and Michael make an appearance in the Qur'an. Sufi Shaykh Muhammad Kabbani believes that the angels are all represented in the seventh heaven where God has created a tree.[38]

Every angel has multiple attributes and jobs to perform; its nature isn't always clear. Angelic powers can run along lines of positive or negative force. When they appear on Earth, their pronouncements may suddenly penetrate our consciousness and often foretell events with major consequences. In monotheistic traditions the messenger Gabriel initiated three great religions. He made a covenant with Abraham, father of the Jews. To Mary he announced the immaculate conception of the Christ child. To Mohammed he dictated the holy Qur'an. Yet the peaceful Gabriel, also an angel of fire and of war, sent Daniel a vision of a cataclysm for the Jewish kings that would give rise to an Antichrist, or demonic figure.

Raphael, known primarily as the angel of healing, doubles as the Prince of Hades, but his work there isn't all negative. In the apocryphal book of Tobit 3:1–17, Raphael overpowers the demon Asmodeus and shows himself as the ultimate healer. He protects the innocent through his gift as messenger. When the woman Sarah was to marry Tobit's son Tobias, Tobit listened to the gossip of others and set himself against the marriage. Sarah had been married seven times and seven times her husbands died. Rumor had it that she murdered her husbands. But before the couples had consummated their marriages, Asmodeus, the demon, took Sarah's husbands from her; and yet people talked. The angel Raphael battled and bound Asmodeus, then removed the scales from Tobit's eyes. At this point, Tobit allowed Sarah and Tobias to marry. In the act of binding Asmodeus, Raphael healed a man of spiritual blindness, and he healed the broken heart of Sarah.

The work of Michael, the angel of mercy, healing, and prayer, overlaps with that of Sandalphon, the angel of prayer. Metatron, chief archangel, overseer and highest of all angelic realms, receives the human prayers that Sandalphon delivers. While angels and humans are different species, Metatron and Sandalphon have a special association with humans. The prophets Enoch and Elijah rank among the few mortals who never died; thus, they entered the lineage of angels and became subsumed into Metatron and Sandalphon, respectively.

Whenever he appears in the Hebrew scriptures or the Qur'an, the prima messenger Gabriel foretells momentous events that will change the face of religion. The Bible simply identifies Gabriel as a messenger. Most often the Bible's authors describe him as a man. To Daniel, however, he revealed himself in swift flight, so one is led to believe that Gabriel has wings. He appeared to Zacharias and Elizabeth to announce the birth of John the Baptist; he approached the maiden Mary to announce the virgin birth of Jesus. To Joseph, the future husband of Mary, he appeared more than once. Each time Gabriel appeared, he prophesied not only history-shaping events, but transformations in worldly consciousness. Christian scriptures name Gabriel as God's most frequent messenger.

Overall, eighteen angels appear in the Christian scriptures. Unnamed healing angels, perhaps emissaries of Raphael, ministered to Jesus when he entered the desert to fast and pray. They comforted him in a moment of doubt in the Garden of Gethsemane. Angels appeared to the blind, lame, and crippled at the pool of healing water in Bethesda. After the death of Jesus, unnamed angels showed themselves at the tomb. When Jesus ascended into heaven, he did so flanked by two angels and before the eyes of his disciples. Guardian angels even unlocked the prison gates and told the freed apostles to go and spread their story. They offered messages of hope and persistence to Peter, Paul, and Cornelius the centurion; but to Herod, an angel brought a message of death.

Unnamed angels frequently accompany biblical prophets. Two such angels unveiled themselves before the prophet Daniel, whose vision included the two messengers speaking to one another. They showed the prophet sweeping apocalyptic visions of the future. In the associated wars, mighty rulers fell, and subsequently demonic energies arose. The angel Gabriel appeared yet again to explain to Daniel these visions (Daniel 8:15–27). The angel so frightened him that he fell facedown and the terrifying visions left him sick and weak.

The only other angel to appear by name is the archangel Michael, who battles Lucifer in the book of Revelation. In Revelation 12, a woman crowned with stars appears ready to give birth, but a dragon threatens to eat the child the minute he is born because ancient prognosticators foretold that he would rule the world with an iron scepter. The unseen and hidden God sweeps up the child to safeguard it, and he sends Michael to battle the dragon. Michael is not your average fluffy, curly-headed angel. "Then war broke out in heaven. Michael and his angels fought against the dragon, and the dragon and his angels fought back. But he (the dragon) was not strong enough, and they lost their place in heaven. The great dragon was hurled down—that ancient serpent called the devil, or Satan, who leads the whole world astray. He was hurled to the earth, and his angels with him" (Revelation 12:7–9 NIV). This story bears a similar theme to the Egyptian Isis birthing her child Horus, the future ruler of the kingdom. The child is in danger of slaughter by her brother Set (Satan) who is trying to seize power.

Michael the archangel not only fights on behalf of heaven, he fights for the individual. In the enigmatic story in Jude 1:9 we hear that he battles Satan over who had the right to claim the body of Moses after the prophet's death. No other mention of this event appears in the Bible, and it leaves one to wonder why Michael had to fight for the body of Moses. Perhaps this alludes to the Exodus story in which Moses murdered an Egyptian and hid the body to avoid punishment. Michael is not the judge, but the defender of Moses. The overarching power of Michael is so great that no other angel in the Christian scriptures or the Hebrew scriptures bears the same title he does: *The* Archangel.

Angelic Appearances

When the angels of the Christian and Hebrew scriptures appear to humans, they seem alien and terrifying. Their first words are "Fear not!" because the initial human reaction is not joy or wonder but terror at the irruption of the invisible world into the visible.[39] In the presence of God, and in stark awareness of his own imperfect state, the prophet Isaiah shrieked. When he saw the seraphim surrounding the Lord upon his high uplifted throne, fear filled Isaiah. Each angel had six wings.

Two wings covered their faces, two covered their feet, and two more wings allowed them to fly. They surrounded his throne, crying, "Holy, holy, holy is the Lord of Hosts: the whole earth is full of his glory." Rather than feeling overcome with joy, Isaiah swooned as if he stood on the brink of annihilation, but an angel came to him and stood between heaven and Isaiah to help him overcome his feelings of unworthiness (Isaiah 6:1–7 King James Version).

Winged seraphim showed themselves to the prophet and priest Ezekiel, perhaps appearing with a different vibration. One day in 597 BCE on the banks of the river Chebar, the heavens opened, and Ezekiel saw a vision delivered to him by "the hand of the Lord." In a storm cloud of fire, blazing light the color of electrum streamed toward him. Inside the cloud four creatures appeared; each had four faces and four wings. The soles of their feet he described as an animal's hooves that sparkled like burnished brass. Under their wings, human hands extended on all four sides (Ezekiel 1:4–9). These beings resemble those creatures who guard the gateways in Assyrian and Babylonian temples that Ezekiel knew to be similar in appearance to those that guarded the temple of Solomon.

After these creatures manifested, Ezekiel observed the wheels within wheels that appeared first, emerald in color, "then a sapphire throne [appeared], more fire, electrum and a rainbow brilliance" (Ezekiel 1:26–28 Evangelical Heritage Version). Those things appearing to him in this vision bore likenesses to things with which he was familiar. After these visions, a man appeared seated upon a throne, and Ezekiel heard a voice speaking, delivering a message about the trials to come. Then, "a curious event happens," as author and esoteric scholar Valery Rees says.[40] In Ezekiel 3:3 (New English Translation) we learn that the visionary prophet is shown a parchment scroll and a voice commands him to eat it and then recite what is in the scroll to the exiled Israelites.* The scroll, we are told, tastes like honey. We do not know

---

*The recitation of sacred text delivered from the hand of a spiritual being is similar to the recitation that Gabriel (Jibrīl) commands of Mohammed.

if this voice emanated from the seated figure, but it seems to represent God rather than an angel. The text identifies them simply as "living creatures," yet none of these creatures seem to resemble either angels or God. Later writers identified them as angels because they carried out God's bidding and delivered powerful messages.

Often angels of medieval rabbinical literature take on forms with multiple eyes, multiple wings, and frightening visages. Authors of the Christian scriptures tended to describe angels with radiant human forms—often glowing, sometimes winged, usually entirely disguised in flesh. The variableness of appearance is not due to a fallacy of description, but to the changing forms in which angels appear. Indeed, their appearance is part of the message.

Among Sufis, angels partake of a changeable nature. Shaykh Muhammad Hisham Kabbani said: "Angels are like water, becoming either steam or ice; [they] may take any form they wish."[41] Lest one think that these insubstantial forms are not important, Kabbani reminds us that the belief in angels is one of the five pillars of the Islamic faith. "God requires every person to believe in angels as equally as they believe in His Divine Self."[42]

Perhaps God made angels not for humankind to believe in them, but for the angels to believe in us—to believe in us, to protect us, to help us to develop our capacities. God imagined a Creation made in all manner of forms, and these human forms contained the capacity to hold all of our varied human experience. The great German theologian Meister Eckhart believed angels and all creatures held a sacred contract. Citing Aristotle, he said: "[A]ll creatures with their ideas and forms are grasped intellectually by the angels. The angels intellectually understand each thing in itself. This affords great joy to the angels and it would be a miracle for them not to have received and enjoyed this intellectual vision."[43]

The Judeo-Christian ordering of angels differs from the descriptions of angels in other religious traditions. There is much more ordering of angels, naming of angels, and defining the rankings of angels. In Colossians 1:13 we learn that God created all things seen and unseen, in heaven and on Earth—including spiritual powers, princes, lords, rulers, and authorities. The angels through whom God orchestrates the mysteries of the whole universe (for his own reasons) often are compared to military officers. Legions of angels exist. Some angels appear more commanding than others, but each has its pedigree and purpose: watchers, guardians, soldiers, protectors, defenders. The conundrum is that angels are described as warriors in battle, yet their purposes coalesce around God's love. God's love has conditions, however, and both humans and angels suffer, apparently, if either willfully breaks commandments.

I marvel at the way Judeo-Christian traditions have tried to define the ineffable, the mystery of creation and experience. Perhaps more than any other religions, Jews and Christians think perhaps obsessively about angels; they categorize and rank them in order to understand their purpose and function. There is a distinction between understanding the angels so that we may understand our purpose or, on the other hand, so that we may understand how to use their energies for both spiritual and earthly purposes. The latter will put us onto tricky ground.

Except for the numbers of angels that overwhelmed John of Patmos as he composed his book of Revelation, the Christian scriptures do not dwell upon the angelic messenger. Perhaps that is so that Jesus, the embodied messenger of God's love, was not overshadowed by the angels who announced his coming and going. When the armed men of the Sanhedrin came for Jesus, he assured his disciples that he could have called upon legions of angels to defend him, yet he did not, having just previously prayed, "Not my will, but Thine." That detail alone suggests that we might contemplate the efficacy of calling on angels before we examine the will of God.

Modern Angelic Prophesy and Appearance

Lest one think that angels are a new age fad or an archaic superstition, we can find many prominent and influential thinkers whose life work has been influenced by the appearance of angels. For forty years Edgar Cayce, the renowned clairvoyant healer, provided more than fourteen thousand recorded messages from Spirit. He maintained trance contact with the angels, primarily the archangel Michael who first appeared in 1928 to speak through him in trance. This angelic conversation continued for the next fifteen years as Cayce delivered messages to the newly formed Association for Research and Enlightenment (A.R.E.). At his first appearance, the archangel Michael, the head of the divine army of angels, predicted a time of trouble, a world filled with unrest and death. Michael the angel identified those listeners as the "chosen." He incited them to build up their strength in meditation and prayer so that in the days to come they might lead.[44]

For a brief time, Cayce and his study group also received messages from the angel Halaliel, who called himself the "Lord of the Hard Way." The information provided by this angel, however, offered apparently darker prophecies. Halaliel suggested an apocalyptic scenario in which Earth's poles shifted, causing earthquakes, volcanic eruptions, and rising seawater. Nefarious leaders rose as well. Halaliel identified himself as the Angel of Karma. Cayce's alarmed group asked him to stop transmitting Halaliel's messages and, rather, to continue his work with the Christ Consciousness, which he did.[45]

Perhaps in 1935 the dark truth receded into the unconscious mind because others could not bear to hear such a message. Angels do not simply tell us what we want to hear. Some of Cayce's members believed that he had somehow come under an evil influence. It is my belief that both angels offered accurate prognostications, but the appearance of Halaliel remains mysterious. His presence in the pantheon of angels was not previously known. To this day, angelologists try to discern the appearance of an angel who has no known presence in the Bible and yet whose predictions, for the most part, proved spookily accurate.

Rudolf Steiner, known primarily for establishing the Waldorf schools for children, became a leading thinker of the Anthroposophical Society, an offshoot of the Theosophical Society. He attributed his life's work of educating the soul of man to the influence of the angels. While Steiner named many of the angels, identifying the main angelic workers as Raphael, Gabriel, and Michael, he went on to say: "We can give such names to these spirits, although it is not the names that are essential.

We name them just as we name other things."[46] He did believe that Gabriel could be classified as the most prominent messenger of the last age of man because Gabriel prominently appears in biblical literature.

In an address to his Waldorf teachers at a May 1913 congress, Steiner said that while all angels partake in developing human spiritual understanding, the archangel Michael "will become a leading Spirit of the Times, the spirit who guides the whole of mankind." He commissioned these teachers to the influence of the angel Michael. He believed that by advancing our spiritual understanding, "we shall come to know what the anthroposophical world view means for individual souls, and we shall have a sense of what evolution means for mankind. We are privileged to become participants in something very significant."[47]

While rational-thinking individuals of the modern world might put aside the idea of angels influencing our world, the angels, apparently, have longer memories and have not forgotten about us. The angels are still here influencing the modern age, and they are available to us. In what way do the angels make themselves available? Gary Lachman, biographer of Rudolf Steiner, suggests that Steiner could answer that question. "It is through our own minds and our power of thought that we gain access to the spiritual world. Steiner would later tell his students that if they wanted to have a conscious experience of the spirit world, they first must learn how to think."[48] Lachman believes this is one of Steiner's most important insights.

In other words, it may be necessary to take angelic contact out of the mushy feel-good category and elevate it to work on the mental planes with mind-to-mind, spirit/angelic contact. That said, we must bear in mind that angels are messengers. They bear the message; they are not causal. Neither sender nor receiver, angels are the conduit between heaven and earth.

ISLAMIC ANGELS

Abraham the patriarch provides the link between the Judeo-Christian and Islamic traditions. Jews and Muslims share many of the same early prophets and angels. While delivering messages from God is the primary work of angels, one iconic story of Gabriel (Jibrīl) testing Abraham appears in both the Qur'an and the Jewish Midrash (but not in the Bible). Gabriel asked God to show him his most beloved servant; God sent him to Abraham. Gabriel tested Abraham's generosity by asking for all his sheep. Abraham played along because he knew it was an angel who was bargaining with him. Even after Abraham discovered the angel's ruse, he would not take back the sheep he had given away because he believed it was wrong to take back a gift.[49]

In the Islamic wisdom tradition steeped in the Qur'an, angels take on a primarily prophetic or revelatory wisdom. Shaykh Kabbani assures us that "only angels can bring that kind of knowledge."[50] Because angels are respected in the heavenly realm, they must be obeyed in the earthly world. They prove themselves trustworthy in receiving, keeping, and delivering the revelations to which God gave them access. The angel is made of "sublime luminescence [and] his knowledge is perfect and complete because he knows the secret of the unseen and is acquainted with the hidden secrets of creation. His knowledge is real, active, and continuous."[51]

According to Sufi Shaykh Kabbani, the early prophet Moses received secret alchemical knowledge from the angels when the Ten Commandments appeared. When Yahweh informed Moses that he had to write the Torah on tablets of gold, Moses asked where he might find gold. God sent him the archangel Gabriel and ninety-nine other angels. Each of these angels represented an attribute of God that relates to one of the ninety-nine sacred names of Allah. The angels "taught Moses one hundred and twenty-four thousand words. . . . Then Gabriel poured into his [Moses's] heart the heavenly knowledge meant to be consigned in the tablets [and] he taught him the chemistry of gold."[52]

In addition to teaching Moses alchemy and the names of Allah, Gabriel instructed Noah to build the ark with one hundred twenty-four thousand planks, each one inscribed with the name of a prophet, beginning with Adam and extending to the end of time. God dispatched one angel each to safeguard the plank that bore a prophet's name.[53]

The story of Hagar appears in both the Judeo-Christian Hebrew scriptures and the Qur'an. Angels safeguard the mothers of prophets: Sarah the mother of Isaac in the lineage of the Jews, Mary the mother of Jesus in the lineage of Christians, and Hagar the mother of Ishmael in the lineage of the Muslims. The elderly childless couple, Abraham and his wife Sarah, kept a dark-skinned female slave named Hagar (stranger). Sarah urged Abraham to sleep with Hagar in order to conceive an heir, even though it was not her own child. However, after Hagar delivered Ishmael, Sarah grew jealous. She began to mistreat Hagar and the child. So Hagar left her employers and ran away into the desert. There an angel appeared to her and told her to return to Abraham and Sarah.

Not long after, Sarah miraculously became pregnant. She feared that Isaac, her child and the second son of Abraham, would be overlooked in favor of Ishmael, the firstborn son of Abraham. So Sarah asked Abraham to take Hagar and Ishmael into the desert and abandon them with few provisions, which he did. They soon became thirsty. Hagar climbed several mountains, trying to see which way to go for help. She heard a faint yet persistent voice, which she ignored until she could no longer dismiss it. She said to the angel in the desert, "You have made me hear your voice, so give me water, for I am dying, as is the one with me."

The angel took Hagar to a place in the desert called Zamzam. There, he stamped his foot, and a spring gushed forth from which Hagar filled her waterskin. "May God have mercy on the mother of Ishmael!" the angel said.[54]

The Angelic Visions of Mohammed

The Islamic religion began when the angel Jibrīl broke through the meditations of the devoutly praying Mohammed (born 570 CE), a descendent of Ishmael. It would seem the destiny of becoming a prophet made itself readily known in Mohammed's infancy. One remarkable story tells us that on the night of his birth, all of the eternal fires of Zoroaster in every temple suddenly extinguished themselves. When he was but a toddler, the angel Jibrīl appeared, filling the room with his seventy wings. He cut open the boy and withdrew his heart to cleanse it of every "black drop of original sin" since the time of Adam. Then the angel returned this purified heart to the young boy's body.[55]

At age forty Mohammed had decided to emulate the Nestorian Christian monks whom he had met on his travels. Year after year, he came and went on spiritual retreat. This time he climbed the rocky, desolate slopes of Mount Hira (now called Jebel Nur, or the Mountain of Light). Walking toward the cave with his few provisions, he heard a voice clearly say "Peace be on thee, O Messenger of God," but when he turned toward the speaker, he saw only a tree or stone.[56]

He entered the mountain alone to meditate. In a darkened cavern, the merchant hoped to find the spiritual enlightenment experienced by the mystics and holy men he had met on his travels. During his meditations Mohammed asked God to reveal anew "the pure religion of Adam, that spiritual doctrine lost to mankind through the dissensions of religious factions." As he lay upon the floor of the cavern, wrapped in darkness and in his cloak, "a great light burst upon him. Overcome with a sense of perfect peace and understanding in the blessedness of the celestial presence, he lost consciousness. When he came to himself again the angel Jibrīl stood before him, exhibiting a silken shawl with mysterious characters traced upon it."[57]

Jibrīl unfurled two green silken shawls brought down from heaven for him. "One . . . was decorated with all kinds of precious stones from the earth, and the other with precious elements from heaven."

The angel commanded the illiterate prophet to read.

"Read what?" Mohammed protested. He explained that he could neither read nor write.

The angel directed Mohammed to sit on top of the first silken scarf, then undeterred, the angel unfurled the second green cloth that floated down from heaven. Mohammed heard the angel command again, "Recite!" The cloth unfurled in his lap, revealing a brilliant script with shining letters made of light. This sacred cloth contained the entire holy Qur'an written with its words of light. It revealed the secrets of the tree in the seventh heaven.[58]

Thus begins the Islamic faith, first delivered from the lips of an angel, and subsequently from the lips of every prophet who has memorized the Hadith and suras from the Qur'an. Memorization keeps the oral tradition alive. To this day, imams deliver to the masses the same verses of Mohammed just as the words of the prophet emerged from his lips and the lips of Jibrīl in the beginning.[59]

Jibrīl promised the prophet that for every letter of the Qur'an he recited, God would plant a tree for him in paradise.[60] From these characters Mohammed gained the basic doctrines later embodied in the Qur'an. In a clear mellifluous voice, Jibrīl spoke, declaring Mohammed to be the prophet of a living God.

Mohammed described it to his disciples thus: An angel in the form of a man appeared and said to him, "'Recite!' Mohammed said, "I am not a reciter," whereupon, as he himself told it:

> [T]he Angel took me and whelmed me in his embrace until he had reached the limit of mine endurance. Then he released me and said: "Recite!" I said: "I am not a reciter," and again he took me and whelmed me in his embrace, and again when he had reached the limit of mine endurance, he released me and said, "Recite!" and again I said, "I am not a reciter." Then a third time he whelmed me as before, then released me and said: "Recite in the name of thy Lord who created! He createth man from a clot of blood. Recite; and thy Lord is the Most Bountiful, He who hath brought by the pen, taught man what he knew not?"[61]

Mohammed told his disciples that after the angel introduced himself as Jibrīl, he tried to look away, but no matter which direction he looked—north, west, east, or south—the angel stood in front of him. At last the angel took its leave. Full of misgivings and fearing that evil magicians had conjured the vision, Mohammed hastened home to Khadijah. There, bursting through the door, he collapsed on the couch, begging his wife to cover him and hide him. In a halting voice he finally revealed what had happened—that the greatest of *nāmūs* (revelations) had come upon him. She assured him that his own virtuous life would be his protection.

For the Sufi and other People of the Book, the mind or intellect of God creates the story of the world—and in that way, we have seen, the angels become the words themselves sitting on the leaves of the Tree of Knowledge that is the Book of Heaven. The authorship of the sacred text is God/Allah. When the illiterate Mohammed asked the angel about the pen of which it had spoken, Jibrīl advised him: "The first thing God created was the pen. He created the tablet and said to the pen: 'Write!' And the pen answered, 'What shall I write?' He said: 'Write my knowledge of my creation till the day of resurrection.' Then the pen traced what had been ordained" (Hadith 2).[62]

After this great start, nothing happened. Mohammed awaited further angelic visitations, but when these did not come immediately, anguish filled his soul. In the throes of great despair he decided to throw himself over a cliff. Jibrīl himself reappeared in order to stop him. The angel assured Mohammed that the revelations his people needed would be given in due time. At the same time many people began to gather in Mecca, drawn to Mohammed by visitations in dreams or by hearing a voice speaking in the wilderness. In all these ways, the faithful found Mohammed.

In the meantime, Mohammed became subject to ecstatic swoons. When asked how the revelations came, the prophet said in two ways: sometimes he would hear the reverberations of a bell and, when the sound stopped, he became aware of the message. At other times the angel simply appeared again in human shape and spoke. Each time Jibrīl suggested that when the "day of anguish" approached, the trumpet would be blown, and Mohammed must arise and prophesy.[63] Jibrīl himself taught Mohammed to greet his wife and followers with the peaceful words known throughout the world: *Salam alaykum,* "Peace be upon you."[64]

Whenever Mohammed dictated the various suras, he fell unconscious and lay shivering, covered in blankets and beads of sweat in an apparently unconscious state. Yet he clearly dictated various passages to this small circle of trusted friends. These verses his friends either committed to memory or reduced to writing. "Quietly, but industriously, Mohammed promulgated his doctrines among a small circle of powerful friends. When the enthusiasm of his followers finally forced his hand and he publicly announced his mission, he was already the leader of a strong and well-organized faction."[65]

The Night Journey

One majestic story described an ecstatic night journey. In it Mohammed fell asleep in the mosque at the Kaaba when Jibrīl appeared, kicking him three times to awaken him. At last he lifted him up by the arm and walked him outside to where a white winged donkey stood. Some stories say that the donkey had the head of a woman and the tail of a peacock.[66] Mohammed climbed on its back and the donkey flew with great strides alongside the archangel until the three reached Jerusalem. The prophets Abraham, Moses, and Jesus met Mohammed there; they entered a temple and prayed together. Angels offered him wine or milk; Mohammed chose the milk for it was the righteous path. "Then, as had happened to others before him—to Enoch and Elijah, Jesus and Mary—Muhammad was taken up out of his life to heaven."[67]

The winged steed carried him far. Flying beyond earthly space, he passed through the seven heavens. Again he saw the prophets, but not as they had appeared on Earth; now they inhabited their transfigured celestial bodies. Joseph's countenance shone with the splendor of moonlight and Aaron's countenance appeared exceedingly beautiful. "Everything he now saw, he saw with the eye of the Spirit; and of his spiritual nature, with reference to the beginnings of all earthly nature, he said: 'I was a prophet when Adam was yet between water and clay.'"[68]

In his book *Angels Unveiled*, Shaykh Kabbani details the glories of the seven heavens. The angels Israfil and Ishmael greeted Mohammed and showed him a ladder reaching into the upper planes of heaven. More and more, this metaphor of the ladder serves as an image of the shift in consciousness as one climbs higher in meditation toward the celestial realm. "O heavenly stairs show yourselves and descend!" the angel

Ishmael called. Before his eyes a ladder to heaven materialized. Two streams of heavenly light were its sturdy rails, and its polished steps were made of red amethyst and green jasper. "Every believer is going to see the ladder and climb on it. It has one hundred steps, and it goes from the Temple [of Solomon] to the first heaven."[69]

Mohammed's ladder does not differ substantively from the ladder on which Jacob observed angels ascending and descending. In like manner, the kabbalist sees a multitude of angels occupying and flowing up and down along the branches of the Tree of Life, whose furthest reaches are beyond the veil.

On each step of his ladder, Mohammed saw the shining subtle bodies of angels encouraging him to keep climbing. On each step, a world of angels "that had no beginning and no end" appeared. *How many angels are there?* Mohammed wondered. An angelic voice told him: "If the skies and the earth and the moon and the sun and the stars and galaxies were crushed into dust and were all piled up, their dust particles would not be one tenth of the angels of this [one] step of the ladder of Paradise."[70]

After ascending to the fourth paradise, Mohammed encountered Idris, whom the Jews knew as the prophet Enoch on Earth and who in heaven became the angel Metatron. Kabbani, however, simply identifies this angel as Idris the prophet. As the keeper of the Akashic Records of all human deeds on Earth, Metatron could be found "leaning against the books of human beings in which were inscribed all their deeds." Idris thanked Mohammed, telling him that after his earthly life he had not been allowed to pass into paradise because the closed door bore a sign that read: "'Beyond this door none may enter before Muhammad and his nation.' And I asked God, 'For the sake of my grandson Muhammad, let me in.' God let me in, so now because of you I am in this place.'"[71]

The fifth heaven contained the beautiful garden where the great mothers of the world reside: Eve, the Virgin Mary, Yukabid (Moses's mother), and Assia (pharaoh's wife). Since her tragic death, which immediately followed her father's, Fatima, Mohammed's youngest daughter "to whom the angels speak," also resides in this fifth heaven. Legend says that three of the great mothers of the world attended Fatima's birth: Mary, Yukabid, and Assia.[72]

Jibrīl tells Mohammed that God created this particular level of paradise to reflect the perfection of women because women carry the secret of creation in themselves. God looks upon their wombs as the depository of his secrets and covers it with "three protective layers to shelter it—the first is a layer of light, the second a layer of love, and the third a layer of beauty. There he fashions and creates human beings after His likeness."[73]

Mohammed continued to move up through the seven heavens, talking with angels, learning truth, and witnessing great beauty. At last he saw the Lote Tree rooted in the Throne of God, described with details similar to the kabbalistic Tree of Life. Here the divine light descended upon the tree and enshrouded it. On each leaf of that tree appeared one letter of the Qur'an, and each letter represented an angel seated on a throne. Each angel held the key to a different, endless ocean of knowledge. The diver into this ocean was Jibrīl, who retrieved the messages like pearls of wisdom.[74] So great is the mystery of God that no prophet, nor any archangel, can peer beyond this veil without risking annihilation. This hidden mystery is known to God alone. Yet Mohammed received permission to go because he was a lantern and a light to his people.[75]

When Mohammad returned on the winged steed to Earth he awoke as if he had slept but one earthly night. That morning he appeared in the mosque, telling the story of how he went up into the heavens and came back. Very few believed him except for his faithful followers, to whom he told the details of his night journey little by little over the years.

Mohammed's growing group of followers aroused anger and fear in certain people in Mecca; murderous plots against the prophet sprang up. Forewarned by spirit, Mohammed eluded his enemies and joined his followers, escaping to Medina. Even though conspirators watched his house, angelic beings overseeing his *hegira,* or flight, enabled him to slip away in the night unseen. Eight years later he returned, entered the Kaaba itself, cleansed it of its idols, and rededicated the structure to Allah. Then he granted amnesty to all who had attempted to kill him. And still the unfaithful tried to poison him. He survived their attacks, albeit severely weakened.

Mohammed eventually died in 630 CE. The old poison he ingested during the previous assassination attempt had taken a toll on his health. One night during his last sickness, he visited a burial ground on the outskirts of Medina. He told an attendant he met there that "the choice had been offered him of continuing his physical life or going to his Lord, and that he had chosen to meet his Maker."[76]

On his last day, seated in the courtyard, he delivered his final lecture in a powerful, clear voice. After that his attendants carried him into the house and laid him upon a pallet on the bare floor. Two hours later, he called for water. Feeling death upon him, he prayed: "'O Lord, I beseech Thee, assist me in the agonies of death.' Then almost in a whisper he repeated three times: 'Gabriel, come close unto me.'"[77]

JACOB AND HIS ANGEL

The story of Jacob wrestling an angel appears in all three monotheistic traditions, and it seems important to include it here because of its similarity to the seven-layered heavens of Mohammed. In addition to the famous painting by William Blake, a number of artists have undertaken attempts to capture the transcendent nature of Jacob's vision of angels. More modern artists depict the angels climbing along a ladder of DNA.

In the chapel at Camp Chesterfield in Indiana is a painting of Jacob sleeping with his head on a stone while myriads of angels ascend and descend the ladder. I'm fascinated by the powerful visionary quality of that figure, the one who slept with his head on a stone in the wilderness and dreamed of angels. When this same flawed man wrestled with an angel later in the Genesis story, he could not say whether he had truly wrestled with a man, an angel, or God. So full of conflicted desires was Jacob—the deceiver, the betrayer, the scoundrel—that he completely embodied the meaning of the Spiritualist Principle 8: "The door to reformation is never closed."[78]* And God never gave up on the visionary Jacob. No wonder so many artists have painted visions of Jacob and his visiting angels.

This encounter with the angel wrestler near the river Jabbok is not narrated as a dream; it is told as an actual event. Why does this wrestling match matter? Human in his fallibilities, Jacob, the second-born twin, will do anything to gain his father's blessings. He even wrestled his twin brother Esau in the womb, but Esau was firstborn, and Jacob came out of the womb clutching his brother's heel. As a grown man, he cheated his brother Esau out of his inheritance by disguising himself and tricking his blind elderly father into giving Jacob the first and favored son's blessing.

Isaac sent Jacob to his uncle's home to find a more pleasing wife than Esau's idolatrous wives. On the road, Jacob first encountered the ladder of angels in a dream. He saw them ascend and descend. To honor the blessing of this dream, he called the place Bethel, meaning "house of God," where he vowed to build a temple. He spent twenty years away from his homeland in order to win a bride from his uncle Laban. To marry the beautiful girl who caught his eye at the well, he first had to marry her older sister Leah who thereafter conceived the first son of Jacob. Jacob believed his beautiful Rachel was barren, but eventually she conceived, and so Jacob's tribe increased.

Deciding at last to return to his own family, Jacob tricked his father-in-law into giving him the best sheep in the herd as part of his wages. Then he stole them away in the night, along with his wives Leah and Rachel. Fearful of meeting Esau, his brother, whom he had cheated, and his army of four hundred, Jacob sent a bribe ahead for his brother.

---

*According to the National Association of Spiritualists, the eighth Spiritualist principle states: "We affirm that the doorway to reformation is never closed against any human soul here or hereafter." In other words, we may make amends for past mistakes on Earth and even after the change called death. There is no eternal punishment for mistakes made in this life. Ultimately, every soul will reunite with God. Refer to the National Association of Spiritualists website.

Trying to bargain his way out of his brother's retribution, he offered Esau half of his livestock—sheep, cattle, camels, donkeys, goats, and so on. In the meantime, Jacob's sentinels, his wives, and his children snuck away from the brewing battlefield by fording the river Jabbock. He stayed behind beside the riverbank to spend the night alone.[79]

Enter Jacob's angel.

Often the angelic messengers in the Bible appear in the mortal shape of a man, like the angel with whom Jacob wrestled. Genesis 32:24–28 details the encounter:

> So, Jacob was left alone, and a man wrestled with him till daybreak. When the man saw that he could not overpower him, he touched the socket of Jacob's hip so that his hip was wrenched as he wrestled with the man. Then the man said, "Let me go, for it is daybreak." But Jacob replied, "I will not let you go unless you bless me." The man asked him, "What is your name?" "Jacob," he answered. Then the man said: "Your name will no longer be Jacob, but Israel because you have struggled with God and with humans and have overcome." (NIV)

The Talmud (Chullin 91a, translated by Rabbi Adin Even-Israel Steinsaltz) goes into greater depths describing this clash of the titans as the two who "grapple with each other, casting up dust all the way up to the divine throne." The Talmud then identifies the divine wrestler as an angel who realizes he cannot overpower Jacob, so he "touches Jacob's thigh" and dislocates it.

The Zohar adds an extra detail, saying that as dawn approaches the angel must untangle himself from Jacob and beg for release in order to join his colleagues who daily sing God's praises. Jacob agrees, asking for one condition: an angelic blessing.

This point is important because for the first time, Jacob's earns this fairly from God's messenger, or maybe from God himself, as some say. It has not been an act of fraud but perhaps a true struggle with one's own shadow, or darker nature, to meet God on his terms. The angel does bless him.

While other narrators of the story (Hosea 12:4) identify the being as an angel, or mal'akh, the Genesis author says simply that he wrestled a man. Jacob himself must believe this superhuman strength means that the being is an angel. He demands that the being tell him his name, but the angel altogether ignores the plea. Because of the refusal to reveal his name at all, Jacob surmises later that he had wrestled with God, for God reveals His true sacred name to no one. That metaphysical concept appears in many religious traditions; if one knew the true name of God, one would either be destroyed by the sheer nuclear energy that the holy name would release, or else the knower might be able to assume the same divine powers as God himself.

Genesis 32:30 goes on to say: "So Jacob called the place (where he spent the night) Peniel, saying, 'It is because I saw God face to face, and yet my life was spared'" (NIV). He does not go unscathed in the fight, however, and thereafter limped because of his hip.[80]

The fourth archangel is sometimes thought to be named Peniel (or Phanuel), the angel who offers help in difficult situations—or as Gustav Davidson defines Peniel: "the curer of human stupidity."[81] Yet others identify the mal'akh as the archangel Michael, or even the second Yahweh, Metatron.[82] The Zohar identifies this nameless one with the angel Samael, the guardian angel of Esau, sometimes called "the accuser." Alternately, Samael the angel becomes identified as the tempter—either Lucifer himself or a member of the fallen tribe. His appearance here seems to be a real and grave portent of death.[83] Jacob's brother Esau waited on the other side of morning with an army of four hundred men. Jacob fully expected that Esau would murder him. He knew he might never see the next day's dawn. Yet before dying in the fight of his life on a dark and lonely plateau, Jacob sought his true, hard-fought destiny—this blessing from God.

Desperate to leave before the dawn, the angel perhaps relinquished his own name in an effort to get away from Jacob. Israel, some say, was the name of the angel, meaning either "May EL (God) persevere" or "May the angel triumph."[84] Jacob won his blessing after all, but still had to confront his brother, whom he feared. He even placed himself at the rear of the caravan in case an altercation erupted and he needed to flee. Dislocating his hip in the wrestling match, however, prevents him from escaping the inevitable; he must meet his brother. He must confront his own deceitful past in order to overcome it. The physical wound delivered by the angel heals the greater emotional wound. Harold Bloom translates the angel's declared blessing in the *Book of J:* "Not anymore Jacob, heel-clutcher, will be said in your name; instead, Israel, God-clutcher, because you have held on among gods unnamed as well as men, and you have overcome."[85]

Still we ask ourselves, what exactly is an angel? And why does it wrestle with a prideful mortal all night? Is this being mortal like Jacob himself? Is it a deity, a psychological archetype, or some other class or species of being?

Thinking metaphorically, I do see this angel as Peniel, the one who allows mere mortals to conquer their human stupidity. The angel will not tell Jacob his name because in reality he is but a mirror of Jacob's fear and ignoble desires. In wounding him, the angel makes sure that Jacob cannot run away from confronting his truth. Doing so will change Jacob's destiny, his name, and thus his spiritual mission. By defining Jacob's own lower nature (heel-clutcher), the angel offers a vision of his higher nature, his spiritual promise (God-clutcher). Let us imagine that this is a metaphor for the destiny he dreamed. A ladder of heaven extends above and below, resting in the Earth and anchored within ourselves.

The Muslim dream and the Islamic vision quest point in similar directions: spiritual ascension through the planes and upward along the Tree of Life—whether we are Mohammed on his night journey or Jacob in his dream—is another way of alluding to the fact that we may find the angels and devils extant within ourselves.

2

Eastern Traditions

The moment an angel enters a life, it enters an environment. We are ecological from day one.
JAMES HILLMAN, THE SOUL'S CODE

HINDU DEVATA

Many different angels move through the seven heavens of the Western traditions. In the East, diverse celestial beings swirl through the planes and heavens of the polytheistic spiritual traditions. Whether we call them angels or devata (plural of deva), those spirit beings who fly up and down the ladder of existence take on various forms, creating diverse hierarchies or families. All in all, these divine entities enter and exit under the command of the Great Mind of the Universe, the Ultimate Reality.

In Western monotheism, one god—called either Yahweh, Allah, or the Christian God the Father—creates and orchestrates all other spirit beings. Any celestial being is an angel of one variety or another. All bow and subject themselves to the will of their Creator. In Eastern traditions, however, these celestial beings—devata—demonstrate what appear to be competing interests.

Some of the oldest Sanskrit texts, the Puranas, contain a cosmogenesis that narrates a history of the universe from its creation to its destruction. This oral story, which later appeared in script, might have originated as early as 3100 BCE or as late as 300 CE. In other words, the sacred texts of both Eastern and Western traditions may be contemporaneous, and it would not be unusual to find traces of one traditional story in another tradition. Depending on their true origins, competing cosmologies may exist within the same text. That makes for an adventurous quest after our angels and devata.

According to the Puranas, Prajapati, Lord of Creation, allowed the ancient rishi Kashyapa to marry his thirteen daughters. Because of this marriage, Prajapati became grandfather to everything that existed. That includes all the devata, the celestial denizens of paradise; the Asuras, those supernatural beings often seen as dark; and all of the *manavas,* the sentient beings that include humans and animals. The oldest of the Vedas, the Samhita, names thirty-three devata in the three created worlds of heaven, Earth, and the "midair" between.[1]

The *Brihadaranyaka-Upanishad,* chapter 5, tells the story of Creation this way:

> Three groups of beings—the devata, the manavas, and the asuras— studied at the feet of Prajapati. At their final teaching, each group approached their Creator one at a time to ask for a final teaching. To the devata Prajapati said, "Da." Then he asked, "Do you understand?"
>
> "Yes," they answered. "It is Daamyata, which means 'Control Yourself.'"
>
> When the manavas approached and asked for a final teaching, he said, "Da." Then he asked, "Do you understand?'"
>
> "Yes," they answered. "It is Datta, which means 'Be Charitable.'"
>
> The Asuras approached Prajapati and asked for a final teaching. "Da," he said. "Do you understand?"
>
> "Yes," they answered. "It is Dayathvam, which means 'Be Merciful.'"
>
> Then in a loud voice of thunder they heard "Da Da," which reflected in the minds of the devas, manavas, and asuras the mantra

"Daamyata, Datta, Dayathvam." Thereafter thunder always speaks of self-control, charity, and mercy.[2]

The one Creative Spirit shows three faces: Brahma, Vishnu, and Shiva, who are the main devata of cosmic creation, order, and evolution.* Lesser devata are the demigods of Hindu and later Buddhist traditions. The devata carried occasional appellations, such as "Lord of . . . " (this or that). Some devata represent ideological and moral concepts. For example, the Hindu Lord of Intelligence is Ganesha, and the Indo-Iranian Lord of Harmony is Mitra (Mithra) who appears as a sun god in his chariot. Devis are female or goddesses. Other devata materialize as forces of nature. Vaya is Lord of Cosmic Creation, Order, and Evolution. Agni is Lord of Fire, and Indra, the king of deities, shows himself as Lord of Thunder. Handsome and stately, with wry, knowing smiles, the devata often resemble royalty. The term *deva* began as a derivative of the Greek word *deus*, or god, sometime around the third century when the two cultures met. Deva and deus carry a similar polytheistic energy.[3]

The Hierarchy of Devata

Seekers from the West traveled to the East mining the culture for spiritual gold. Theosophists like Helena Petrovna Blavatsky, Annie Bessant, Alice Bailey, and their community found rich similarities in Eastern and Western mystery schools. Appropriation of Oriental philosophies gleaned from mystical, sacred texts has created a modern adaptation of the world's oldest living ancient wisdom. In the late nineteenth and early twentieth centuries Blavatsky used the term *devata* to define spirit beings who respond to our human affairs more or less as soul-building angelic beings. "Power, light, life; these are the gifts which companionship with the angels (devas) shall place in human hands. Power that is limitless; life that is inexhaustible; light before which all darkness melts away."[4]

---

*The powerful shakti of creation and destruction likewise includes three Hindu goddesses: two forms of Kali and one of Durga.

Devata enacting the bidding of higher energies function more or less as angels do. They inspire the individual to grow mentally and spiritually, to prosper as they meditate, and to become one with the universe. Resurrection, ascension, and final liberation are the highest goals of Spirit on behalf of which Western angels operate. These celestial beings identified by Blavatsky as the three spiritual fires—Indra, Soma, and Agni—appear throughout the Hindu spiritual classic the *Rig-Veda*. Heavenly, divine, and excellent, these immortal devata appear prominently in the one thousand hymns of the classic text. Indra, the benevolent leader of the devata, must slay the dragon king of the demons; Soma is the deity of the intoxicating drink that initiates one's vision quest; and Agni, the fire of Spirit, assists in recycling matter and spirit through his crematory.[5]

In *The Secret Doctrine*, Blavatsky likens Indra, the dragon slayer, to the archangel Michael. She further connects these two through the astrological patterning of eclipses, known as Rahu and Ketu, or solar and lunar eclipse nodes. These points interlink with the spiritual initiations that one undergoes during incarnation as part of clearing one's karma. The hosts of heaven in the Roman Catholic Church become the Theosophists' devata (angels and archangels in charge of spiritual development). She further likens Sanat Kumara, the architect of planetary evolution, to the archangel Michael, who oversees the angels. Even Thomas Aquinas considered that "the celestial bodies are guided by some intelligence, either directly by god, or by the mediation of angels."[6]

Of course, the early church saw the devata as idolatry; the disciple Paul condemned the worship of angels as also being idolatrous. But the playbook of devata and angels rhymes. In a description of the planes of existence, Blavatsky points to the hierarchy of creative powers that she identifies with the twelve constellations and the seven visible planets. "All this," she says, "is subdivided into numberless groups of Spiritual, semi-Spiritual, and ethereal Beings."[7] She goes on to quote innumerable sources from the Kabbalah, Christian mystics, Greek philosophers, and Hindu and Buddhist thinkers.

Beneath the supernal beings of Indra, an array of demigods and goddesses, devata, migrate between heaven and earth. Their interactions with earthly humans fall under the direction of the master deity Indra. Their domains are somewhat similar to the hierarchies of the Western tradition. In this way we might recognize these lesser, albeit high functioning, spiritual beings as equally angelic presences based on their appearances and activities. All life, Paramahansa Yogananda says, is controlled by these inner or astral deities. These cosmic angels labor sleeplessly for the universal good, and every man should seek to attune with the "shining ones." These astral angels are the God-consciousness governing both the microcosm and the macrocosm.[8]

The Roles of Devata and Asura

Hindu myths richly personify the intercessory influences of the devata. In the earliest Vedic texts, devata and Asura appear as dynamic cosmic forces. Each devata pairs with an opposing Asura, creating dual, polarized states of being. Only Indra, the highest ranking being of light, rules over all of them. Post-Vedic texts split the celestial beings into camps of good and evil: the devata hold celestial goodness and the Asuras hold more demonic qualities. In the oldest pre-Vedic text, the creation of Asuras precedes that of the devata. As the mythology developed in the early Vedas, however, one finds that each potentially may overpower the other.[9]

Early Vedic texts drew heavily on the dualism of the Zoroastrians. Indian mythology transmuted Ahura Mazda, the Zoroastrian supreme deity, into an Asura.* In the *Rig-Veda* we find the angels and devils switching sides as battles between light and dark wage on. The earliest Vedas of the Hindu scriptures speak of the virtues of the Asuras as just, good, and equally as powerful as the devas. Both devas and Asuras demonstrate powers enough to create wonders, including life itself.

In the *Rig-Veda,* the word *sura* indicates any spirit. Asuras preside over moral and social phenomena; suras preside over natural phenomena. However, due to tribal clashes, by the time the written texts appeared,

---

*One clue is the similarity in the names Ahura and Asura.

the character of the Asuras turned negative. The Satapatha Brahmana cites that "the gods and asuras, both descendants of Prajapati, obtained their father's inheritance, truth, and falsehood."[10] The proud Asuras envied the happy Earth-loving devas. On Earth lived a noble humanity and an ignoble humanity, heroes and antiheroes; in the heavens dwelled gods and antigods. The divinities of the new culture consume and devour the divinities of the previous culture, turning the story of great spiritual destinies on their heads. French historian and Indologist Alain Daniélou explains it thus: "[I]t was not for their sins that the anti-gods were destroyed but because of their power, their virtues, their knowledge threatened that of the gods . . ."[11]

Because of this connection to the lost Zoroastrian suras (beings of light), some modern authors say that stories from the Mahabharata suggest that Asuras can become devas if they do good deeds and are helpful to mankind. The actions of any spirit being create karma for good or ill.[12] And vice versa . . . "In the course of time, on account of their change of heart, I saw that the divine law had disappeared from them, who are animated by passion and rage."[13] The transformative quality of these spirit beings differs from that of Western angels who appear to have no will of their own.

Their mutual presence in the celestial/terrestrial/midair worlds is neither polytheistic nor monotheistic, but henotheistic—that is, the individual and the community may make offerings to one deva or devi while acknowledging the presence of others. Henotheism is likened to the dueling natures of the Greek and Roman divine families.[14] Tamil metaphysician and historian Ananda Coomaraswamy applied that Olympian analogy to the battle between Asuras and devata. The conflict between forces of light and dark, he said, exists as "an eternal dance" within every human psyche.[15] Other Hindi scholars, however, argue that psychologizing the devata and Asuras occludes their true power.

God's Cosmic Agents

Yogi Paramahansa Yogananda described the devata as "God's cosmic agents."[16] *Devata* means literally "shining ones." Like the angelic hosts, thrones, dominions, cherubim, and seraphim of the Jews and Christians, the supernal devata and *apsara* resemble angels by also appearing in a kind of celestial ranking. Rather than being divided into planes and hierarchies of existence, however, the devata align with areas of expertise. The idea of separating devas into planes of existence seems foreign at first until we remember the analogy of the hierarchical pattern for Christian angels: the rings of Saturn.

For the hierarchy of devata, let's use the analogy of the periodic table. If we understand the way chemical elements align in a hierarchy of atoms, we might see how angels and devata work invisibly behind the scenes of all matter. William Bloom, in his book *Devas, Fairies, and Angels,* created this description of energies as analogous to atomic theory and the dance between minute electrically charged particles in motion. He says, "Devic essence bridges between the constantly moving electric charges to produce the matter we can see and touch . . . Without devic essence there would be no coherence to manifest life— just an ocean of unconnected electric charges. All form is a mixture of a relationship between, devic essence and atomic electric charges."[17]

Numerous devata orchestrate all life. They enter as the protective spirits of nature and of the forest, which are called *vanadevata;* of villages, which are called *gramadevata;* of families, which are called *kuladevata;* and of households, which are called *vastudevata.* Some devata specifically protect river crossings, mountains, and caves.[18] Just as medieval alchemists observed multitudes of angels at work and in charge of every human action, so the devata watch over all deeds and human interaction in the Hindu tradition. They are said to be the many aspects of Brahman in action.

An *ishta devata* is one's chosen deity, a personal angel if you will, who is intimately connected to one's higher self and developing consciousness. Vedic astrologer and Hindutva activist David Frawley succinctly defines the concept by saying, "The vision of the Ishta Devata arises from studying the Divinity inherent within us, our own inner God or Goddess that is our deeper nature." A true guru will awaken the devata within us so that we may perceive our inner divinity.[19]

All things—ourselves, our gurus, and our deities—have an ishta devata. The monkey-faced lord Hanuman mentioned in the Mahabarata is considered the avatar of Lord Shiva and his ishta devata. Among his many skills, Hanuman wrestled demons and transformed himself to fit the needs of the particular circumstances against which he fought. In the Ramayana, he does all these things for Rama with unwavering devotion. Ceremonial rituals for the deva may be personal or communal. For example, pujas dedicated to Hanuman are held every Saturday in August in the region of Konkan. People fast all day until the evening, eating only after offering Hanuman his portion of rice and cakes.[20]

Many devata make themselves available for conversation and a deeper relationship. Enlightenment comes when one commits to a single deva or devi, then following that devic path in the world and within the self. Each deva/devi expresses a particular form, arrives in a particular vehicle, manifests particular symbols, and responds to particular yantra, mantra, and rituals. Meditations on a deva and his or her cosmic meanings reflects all levels of human existence. A yogi, then, is one who practices these techniques of honoring the devata for God-realization.

This God-consciousness, Yogananda says, governs the macrocosm and the microcosm. Devata play instrumental roles in determining how the greater and lesser worlds operate to maintain harmony, and in keeping an orderly universe according to the laws of nature. He explains the many devata as: " . . . the countless beings born out of the one Spirit, even as one mass of dynamic current can manifest itself as millions of little electric lights."[21] Similarly, the one soul, as the ego, manifests itself in the multifarious activities of physical man.

Seven Highest Devata

According to Yogananda, "Spirit, as God the father of creation, differentiates itself as seven principal angels who govern all creation: the macrocosmic and the microcosmic ideational, astral and physical universes."[22] He further identifies the seven highest devata as being similar in quality and action to the seven flames before the throne of God who defend the Judeo-Christian religion. He names them as follows:

Virata, the divine cosmic builder of the material universe;

Vishva, the aspect of the soul who creates and maintains the miniature universe and man's physical body;

Hiranyagarbha, the "lifetronic engineer" who creates and sustains the macrocosmic universe;

Taijas, the aspect of the soul who creates and maintains the astral body of man;

Ishvara, the divine cosmic architect of the cosmic ideational (mental) universe;

Prajna, the aspect of the soul who creates and maintains the ideational body of man.

"These six deities," Yogananda says, "are a transformation of the supremely guiding seventh 'angel,' Maha-Prakriti, the active expression of the *Kutastha* Intelligence, which is the pure reflection of God in creation."[23] Kutastha indicates the imperishable, immortal Mind of the Universe.

Devata live on a higher astral plane than humans; they guide, guard, and protect all other living beings, including animals and plants. By connecting with the atman, or divine spark in each person, these angelic beings instill in humanity higher levels of consciousness to assist them in making life changes via various reincarnations. Through special fire ceremonies, chants, and oblations, the two worlds draw nearer. The Bhagavad Gita 3:11 assures the reader that if one thinks and meditates on these world guardians, "those devas will think of thee; thus, communing with one another, thou shalt receive the Supreme Good."[24]

Consider them guardian angels that assure better outcomes to the decisions we make. Many Hindus believe that planets and stars have angelic connections and links within the cosmos. I am not surprised to know this. As I mentioned before, I too, like Jacob, beheld angels in my dreams, and we created my astrological chart.

In the East, an astrological consultation is akin to conversing with the devata. In other words, devata or angels govern the stars, and all is governed by the mind of God.[25] Among the Sufis there circulates a similar idea: that angels are more than simple messengers and beings of light. They appear equal to stars, planets, and the cosmos itself. "They are sublime luminescence," says Shaykh Kabbani, "with complete knowledge of all that is seen and unseen. Angels inhabit the seven visible planets, the pole stars, and the fixed stars, and the planets that orbit these fixed stars are likened to their bodies. Signals from these light bodies even millions of light years away from us affect the states of human nature."[26]

On a cosmic scale, the mass karma of planet Earth can be attributed to particular racial groups or nations that the devas or angels oversee. Well-acquainted with biblical tradition, Yogananda referred to foreknowledge about the birth of the Christ child as foretold by the stars and angels.[27]

What common qualities do angels and devata possess? One clue may be found in the early Vedas. Like the Jewish angels, their names describe their divine qualities. For example, the deva Krīdā is known for the quality of playfulness; and *krīdā* means "to play." Yogi and musicologist Alain Daniélou defines the devata in the Vedic poem from *The Myths and Gods of India* that follows. Again, I remind the reader that devata function with the qualities of demigods or angelic beings who are the embodiment of the divine creative force.

> *The gods play. The rise. Duration and destruction*
> *of the world is their game.*
>
> *The gods conquer. They destroy the power of the*
> *antigods, as well as sorrow and sin.*
>
> *The gods are the source of all activity. In a world*
> *where all is relative, they are the links which unite*
> *the moving to the unmoving, the subtle to the*
> *gross world, spirit to substance.*

*The gods are the inner light of knowledge and the
outer light which reveals the world.*

*The gods deserve praise; the whole universe sings
their glory.*

*The gods enjoy all things. It is divinity hidden
within us that enjoys all our pleasures.*

*The gods intoxicate the mind, make us forget the
agitation inherent in attachments.*

*The gods are subtle beings corresponding to the
state of dream.*

*The gods ever shine. Their splendor illumines the
worlds . . .*

*Their nature is movement. Their substance is
knowledge.*[28]

Heaven and Earth

Indologist Daniélou goes on to describe the devata in angelic terms, saying that they move in high spheres of space, they dwell in heaven, they
descend to Earth. As they appear before mortal eyes, they do not blink,
they do not sweat! Their feet do not touch the ground. "They always
wear fresh wreaths and have no shadows."

Their meeting place is Mount Meru, sometimes called Mount
Sumeru, which is located on Earth, high in the Himalayas. This central
world mountain arises layer upon layer, like the Tower of Babel in the
ancient land of Sumer, connecting earth and heaven. The Mahabarata
describes the mountain of Meru as "round like the morning sun" with
a flame that does not smoke. It is three hundred fifty thousand miles
high and just as deep. Its birds are beautifully plumed, and its gardens

filled with fruit and flowers. Everywhere, in palaces of gold, live devata and Asuras—gods and genies. Demons live here, too, but also celestial musicians and heavenly nymphs.[29]

The Theosophists borrowed the concepts of Hindu devata pertaining primarily to the spiritual essence of nature beings who control the manifest world. Not only do the devata of the natural world operate according to the natural laws of the universe, they also oversee and protect these physical domains. They also "are responsible for building up forms on inner planes as well as on the physical plane."[30]

According to this theory, two distinct pathways of evolution are set in motion. The first evolution arises in the natural world and moves from the mineral, through the animal, to the human and beyond; the second evolves from elemental spirits, through fairies, to angels (devata), and on from there. Not only do Asiatic cultures work with devata who offer their divine energy for the agricultural community, but they have been summoned by Peter and Eileen Caddy and Dorothy Maclean to send their energies to the human community. The Caddys, the founders of Findhorn in the early 1970s, were joined by Maclean later. Together they built an intentional community in an unlikely spot near the Arctic Circle on the northern Scottish coast. All of their work was based on direct instructions from their guides and angels. Clairvoyant mediums Peter, Eileen, and Dorothy believed that "devas hold the archetypal pattern and plan for all forms around us, and they direct the energy needed for materializing them. . . . [A]ll energy is brought into form through the work of the devic kingdom."[31] In this way—under the direction of Spirit—the plant devas helped the Findhorn community gardeners produce incredibly large cabbages and other vegetables in the cold, sandy soil.

Apsara—Hindu and Buddhist Angels

Apsara are spiritual beings often depicted in physical form escorting into heaven those brave Hindu warriors killed in battle. These beautiful apsaras resemble Shaykh Kabbani's descriptions of angels as graceful, floating, and dancing; the apsaras' bodies flow with the liquidity of water. In the Cambodian temple of Angkor Wat, the sculpted young maidens who dance across the wall appear with flames or serpents in their hair. In the Buddhist Yulin Caves of China, the painted images of *gandharvas,* the apsaras' husband musicians, float through the air while playing flutes and trailing ribbons of discreet outerwear. The Chinese call them *feitian,* named after a Hindu goddess.

Apsara waft in the wind and float on the waters under the bodhi tree. The beautiful bodhi tree under which the Buddha sat meditating when he attained enlightenment resembles the Tree of Life upon which Jewish kabbalists meditate to attain visions of cosmic truth. To deliver messages and light to humankind, both angels and apsara move up and down the branches of the sacred tree, or ladder to heaven.

As one travels further east on the Asian continent, the apsara begin to exhibit a more severe countenance. Like the angels of death or the Norse Valkyries, apsara scoop up the bodies of slain war heroes and carry them off to heaven. As servants of the deities, they do the bidding of the gods, often waiting on them as attendants. Similar to the angels in Ezekiel's vision, they can appear as shape-shifting beings.[32] They also can be invoked for use in fertility rites in the human, animal, and natural worlds.

Beautiful as they may appear at times, these apsara are not always helpful to humankind. Sometimes they lead us astray. They test our spiritual commitment by offering tempting foods, magical powers, and sexual favors, as fallen angels sometimes do. The Mahabharata, which had been called as one of the greatest mythic/spiritual texts of all time, describes the beautiful apsaras. They live in the gardens called Nandana. The apsaras' slim waists and deep bosoms tempted the guru in meditation. Their hypnotic eyes resembled lotus leaves as they "enticed the hearts of those persons practicing rigid austerities."[33] The poetic detail of Arjuna lost amid the apsara in the land of Nandana feels much like a retelling of the Homeric hymn describing Odysseus in the land of the lotus-eaters.

In one well-known story of spiritual temptation, the great god Indra sent two apsaras to visit Nara-Narayana, a holy man deeply meditating in his cave high in the Himalayas. Indra wanted to distract him from his task in order to prevent him from acquiring divine powers through meditation. Not to be thwarted, Nara-Narayana struck his own thigh and created a woman more beautiful than both apsaras. Her name, Urvashi, meant "one who controls the hearts of others." After his meditation, the holy man sent Urvashi to live with Indra in his heavenly court.[34]

In a second story, Indra sent the beautiful Urvashi to seduce the mortal king Pururavas. She fell in love with him, married him, and conceived a child. One evening, however, she woke with a fright, thinking that the other gods had tried to steal her son from her. She shrieked, waking Pururavas. Her husband sprang from the bed naked. Affronted by his humanness, Urvashi vanished, leaving him in a blaze of light along with the other nymphs who had accompanied her all this time in their shape as waterbirds.[35]

In Java the Buddhist and Hindu religions mix and transform. The apsaras become known as *hapsari*; the story of the celestial maidens becomes the narrative of such Balinese court dances as the legong. When Islam came to the Malay Archipelago through Arab spice traders, the idea of the hapsari became the idea of the *houri*—those "forbidden pearls of heaven" whom God offers as celestial wives to men who have been pious and holy in the physical realm.[36]

What we have come to know of these devas, apsaras, gandharvas, and the like is that in the later centuries their talents and protective influence have become more attached to the physical world. They give the appearance of etheric beings of entertainment and seduction, what the masters of Theosophy would call "the glamours of the world." It almost seems too difficult for the modern sensibility to translate etheric beauty into something otherworldly. Didn't the Renaissance painters "fleshify" their angels and cherubs, giving them definite sexual and sensual attributes where nothing of the like had existed before? Perhaps human imagination itself limits what can be brought down from the spirit world, making the etheric something sensory and tactile, rather than attempting to lift up the physical world into the more etheric spiritual domain.

BUDDHIST SPIRIT BEINGS

Some will argue that Buddhism is nontheistic (without a deity), rather than polytheistic (with many deities), as Hinduism is. Yet within the Buddhist tradition resides an awareness of spiritual beings that are other than human. Their presence permeates the inner and outer landscape. Much of this derives from the childhood of Siddhartha Gautama. Seven days after his birth, his mother died, which the Hindu astrologers took as a sign that he would become a powerful, enlightened religious leader. A royal Hindu family raised him. Long before he sat beneath the bodhi tree he had been immersed in the religion of Buddhism. And long before that, some believed, he had experienced five hundred and fifty births prior to becoming the enlightened being Gautama Buddha.

The Jātakas is a body of ancient religious literature that details the emergence of the Buddha (it's also known as the Jātaka Tales). This work recounts stories of the Buddha's human and animal lives.[37] In these stories we find appearances of devata, nature spirits, apsara, and Asura, because these come from the Pali and Sanskrit lineage from which the Buddha springs. Equivalent devas or spirit beings appear in Buddhist thought. Lord Matrireya Avalokiteshvara, the most venerated deity of compassion in the Hindu tradition, appears as a bodhisattva in Mahayana Buddhism. Avalokiteshvara protects against shipwrecks, fires, wild beasts, and other disasters, and is considered the creator of the fourth world. The eleven-eyed Lord of Compassion gazes down upon humanity and pledges to use his thousand arms to relieve the suffering of every sentient being on Earth. This includes every being within his gaze—including the deva world, or world of the gods; the Asura (Titan) world; the human world; the animal world; the world of *pretys* (tantalized ghosts); and all those beings in the hells. From the two tears that fell from his eyes as he witnessed the dilemmas of suffering, twin goddesses were born: the White Tara and the Green Tara; and the goddesses swore to assist Avalokiteshvara in his sacred work. He put off his own Buddhahood until that goal has been accomplished. To the Chinese, the female bodhisattva Kwan Yin embodies the role of angel, enacting the duties of spiritual mother.[38]

Hierarchy in the Buddhist Tradition

In Theravada Buddhism, beings may be reborn into one of thirty-one planes of existence during their long wandering through samsara (reincarnation). Eleven of those realms are dominated by sensory experiences; the animals, asuras, hungry ghosts, and true demons occupy the four lower levels. Above them is the human realm, which opens into the *kama loka* or sensuous world that is occupied by humans and lesser deva. Beyond humans exist realms of tree spirits, earth spirits, and musicians; the *tavatimsa deva* or thirty-three gods; the air beings or *yama deva*; the contented deva; the delighted deva; and finally the devata who wield power over the creations of others. Mara, personified delusion and desire, lives here.

Once we pass the plane of Mara, we move into an even more duplicitous realm, the three planes of Brahma, spending time first in his retinue, then with his ministers. Next there is Maha Brahma, a deity who, according to Buddhist ideology, deludes himself into thinking that he is the all-powerful, all-seeing Creator of the universe.[39] The idea that Brahma's creations are delusions contrasts with what we understand about Brahma in Hindu theology.

Competing theologies often demonize each other's deities. The Hindu/Buddhist understanding of Brahma is a case in point. The enigmatic Angkor Wat temple exemplifies this conundrum. This beautiful, sensual delight of a Buddhist temple owes its architectural splendor to the Hindu devata and the god Indra, who many claim built it in a day. The Buddhists say that Indra's net is a metaphor for the emptiness of all things. Emptiness, it turns out, is the primary component of all forms.

In the Hindu cosmos, Brahma is the creator, Vishnu is the sustainer, and Shiva is the destroyer. Although Brahma can only create a universe that lasts one day, his day is four hundred thirty-two billion Earth years. But no worries! After he breathes out, he breathes in again, and the world vision reignites itself. How does he create? He is lonely and desirous of another, and splits himself in two. Thus the polarities of the devata and Asuras are built into the creation of the world. "There can be no creation without the relation of opposites. There could be no creation from Shiva alone or from Nature [*Prakrti*] alone. The union of a perceiver and a perceived, of an enjoyer and an enjoyed, of a passive and an active principle, of a male and a female organ, is essential for creation to take place."[40] The Upanishads offer a look at how the pluralistic universe arises from a sole being's creative impulse—a divine lust to become Other. "He desired, 'Let me create. May I be many.' He performed austerities. Having performed austerities, He created all this—whatever there is. Having created all this, He entered into it. Having entered into it, He became both the manifested and the unmanifested, both the defined and undefined, both the supported and unsupported, both the intelligent and the nonintelligent, both the real and the unreal. The Satya became all this: whatever there is. Therefore, call It the True."[41]

Now back to our thirty-one planes of existence: beyond the plane of the self-important/omnipotent creator Maha Brahma lie three planes of radiance in which at each level the devas brighten more significantly than they did in the last. Then follow three planes in which the devas exude increasing bliss and glory. Beyond that arise more subtle planes in which there is no experience that we would recognize because the body has dropped away; then individual mind drops away, entering finally into infinite space, infinite consciousness. Then, at last—nothingness.[42]

Neither heaven nor hell are permanent planes of existence. Neither do devata and rakshasas (Asuras) remain the same. All is fluid, migratory, and in process. Spiritual beings descend and transcend, moving up and down through the planes of incarnation, a Buddhist version of Jacob's Ladder. Positive actions beget positive rebirths, and vice versa. One of the rules for enlightenment in Buddhism is not to take refuge in the idea of a deity who has not yet transcended his samsaric plane of existence—that is, his endless cycles of birth and rebirth.[43] For this reason Buddhists place their faith in the teaching of Buddha, who has awakened to his true self and transcended this samsaric life with his five hundred and fifty incarnations.

Communing with Devata

Buddhists neither pray to deities nor invoke angels. In Vajrayana Buddhism the deva is not a god, but rather an enlightened, fully realized being. A Buddhist would say the deva is still a created being and therefore mortal. This deva operates like an archetype of our deepest nature. In meditation we commune with it and interact with it through ceremony. The appearance of devata in personal practice aids one in attaining Buddhism's ultimate goal—liberation from the cycle of death, rebirth, and karma.

Some Buddhists still seek the assistance of devata who may appear in attractive human form, or as invisible spiritual forces. The equivalent would be like conversing with an older, wiser spiritual mentor. Unlike certain Abrahamic traditions that prohibit praying to angels (all the while citing hidden knowledge about how to work with them), both Hindu and Buddhist practitioners are encouraged to connect with the devata during designated monthly or yearly pujas (ceremonies). Mandalas made in a meditative way honor the forces of the creation by honoring the devata of the directions. Their elaborate, beautiful, colorful geometric shapes mirror the patterns of the universe. In the next turn, the mandala honors the impermanence of godly creation as all is whisked away.

Nearly all religions seek divine intervention for sustaining life on Earth. In the Mahayana Buddhist tradition, nature-loving devata, the *lokapala,* can ensure favorable weather for agriculture. In their most powerful aspects, however, they serve as wisdom protectors and defenders of the faith. According to Master Hua of the City of Ten Thousand Buddhas, the powerful energies of the lokapala can be harnessed for the protection and endurance of temples and monasteries, but they must be invoked and subdued. Unlike monotheistic angels, the lokapala have wills and minds of their own. For example, sometimes the lokapala allow earthquakes to occur. Monks need to exhort them to behave and settle down in order to protect the dharma and its practitioners.[44]

Protection from disaster and forces of nature form the most powerful angelic petitions in any tradition. Catholics, Jews, and Muslims alike will beseech the archangel Michael for protection against legions of demonic forces. Likewise, devotees in the Eastern traditions invoke the lokapala, although their qualities function more or less like temperamental Greek gods. These spiritual, often wrathful warrior guardians sometimes appear as rulers of the various domains they guard, taking on the role of deity. The locales they safeguard are specifically situated placements on the mandala.

Devata and Geographic Direction

Hindu lokapalas are known as the Four Guardians of the Directions. These protectors of the cardinal directions are fierce and not cherubic at all. Their representations sometimes frighten us as they fill the world with their awesome powers. Kubera, guardian of the north, safeguards the prosperity of Earth as well as individual financial wealth; Yama, guardian of the south, is Lord of Death and dispenser of justice and punishment; Indra, guardian of the east and king of heaven, oversees lightning, thunderstorms, rain, rivers, and war; and Varuna, guardian of the west, is Lord of Oceans, Sky, and Truth. Each brandishes a magical weapon.

Buddhist lokapalas stand in each corner of the universe, appearing as four muscular superheroes. Known as the Four Great Kings, they rule the cardinal directions and four seasons, appearing as heraldic animals in Chinese astrology—specifically the Black Tortoise of the north, the Azure Dragon of the east, the Vermilion Bird of the south, and the White Tiger of the west. In the Japanese Shinto tradition, eight lokapalas are linked to the Hindu deities who guard the world. They are Indra (thunder and rain, the east), Agni (fire, the southeast), Yama (lord of death, the south), Surya, (rainbow, the southwest), Varuna (ocean, the west), Pavana (wind, the northwest), Kubera (wealth, the north), and Soma (sacrifice, the northeast).[45]

The Four Great Kings are called by other names in various traditions; the Four Heavenly Kings and the Catamaharaja all represent the same beings. They figure prominently in the Golden Light Sutra as rulers of the chaotic underworld forces of nature. These Four Heavenly Kings promise to protect anyone who recites their sutra. An original Sanskrit text, the Golden Light Sutra recounts how the bodhisattva

Ruchiraketu dreamt of a great drum that radiates a sublime golden light—a golden light that symbolizes the dharma teachings of Gautama Buddha.[46] It was written that "They belong to the heavens, but they are in touch with the Earth, and they are therefore able to keep the powerful energies of the Earth under control and prevent them from having a disruptive effect on the human world."[47]

In the Tibetan Book of the Dead, the Four Great Kings guard the gateways into nirvana. In the Vedic tradition these four gods are called lokapalas; in the Buddhist tradition, they are known as the Maharajas. Known as the *catamaharaja* in the early Sanskrit these four kings act as armed generals. They form the foremost realm of devata, who guard the world in all four directions from the top of their heavenly mountain. Buddhists invoke these powerful guardian angels to stave off calamities, destruction, and epidemics, to eliminate worry, and to fulfill one's wishes.[48] In the Yajur Veda the Four Great Kings (Agni–east, Yama–south, Savitr–west, and Varuna–north) have shuffled around to different cardinal points, but still, they are the same beings. These same beings visited the Buddha, often at crucial times, to listen to his teachings. One key feature of the four kings in the traditional wisdom texts (Buddhist sutta and Hindu sutra) is to safeguard against misfortune stemming from the *yakṣas,* or the supernatural meddling of the nature spirits sometimes called *djinn.*

Their Pali names are Dhataaraṭṭtha, Viurūlhaka, Virūpakkha, and Vaiśravaṇa. Again, the names differ, but the responsibility for guarding the cardinal points remains the same. Like the seraphim of the Judeo-Christian tradition who guard the throne of the Divine, all of these elevated beings are wisdom protectors and defenders of the faith. These exceedingly great lokapala keep a constant equilibrium between creatures in the divine and human worlds.

Vaiśravaṇa, guarding the north, holds an umbrella; some call it a victory flag. On his lap sits a mongoose spitting forth jewels that symbolize wealth from an unlikely source. His name means "He who hears everything." A benevolent being, he bestows prosperity and gives Buddhists the freedom to pursue their spiritual goals.

In the east sits Dhataaraṭṭha (sometimes Dhatarāttra) as "Watcher over the land," who sits with a pipa, or lute, in his lap, overseeing a celestial band of gandharvas. He and they create the celestial music that vibrates the protective power of compassion.

In the south, Viurūlhaka wields a sword, guards growing things, and sustains the powers of potent, male sexual energies.

Virūpakkha guards the west, holding a stupa and a snake, protecting the nagas and water spirits.

Each of the Buddhist Four Heavenly Kings lives in one corner, or cardinal direction, on the legendary Mount Meru. They occupy the sixth or lowest level of the mountain, mediating the above and below. Indra, the god whose creative potency includes the evocation of rain, wind, and lightning, lives on a continent just beyond it.[49]

East/West Connections

When it comes to trying to sort out all the devata, asuras, apsaras, gandharvas, lokapalas, catamaharaja, yakshas, and such, our eyes begin to whirl in our heads. Indian philosopher and yogi Sri Aurobindo addressed the confusion that predominates the Western mind (and the mind of the Eastern student trying to find his tradition) by pointing to "the one and only Deva" as the world teacher speaking to his students. Writing in the voice of the Deva, he said: "It is I myself, says the Divine Teacher, who accept these sacrifices and to whom they are offered, I who give these fruits in the form of the gods since no men choose to approach me. . . . It is the ignorant who worship the gods, not knowing whom they are worshiping ignorantly in these divine forms; for they are worshiping, though in ignorance, the One, the Lord, the only Deva, and it is he who accepts their offerings."[50]

In *The Jew in the Lotus,* poet Rodger Kamenetz recalls a dialogue between His Holiness the Fourteenth Dalai Lama and Rabbi Reb Zalman, a kabbalist, during an interfaith conference held in Dharmsala, India, in October 1990.* The two shared religious

---

*I suggest reading the entire chapter on the conference in Dharmsala in Kamenetz's book, *The Jew in the Lotus.*

philosophies as they tried to understand each other's culture. At one point, Zalman told the Dalai Lama that each of the Hebrew letters represented "a realm of the spirit or consciousness" that comes closest to the devata "according to our tradition."

The Dalai Lama asked what he meant by *devata,* and the rabbi replied, "angels."

Most Buddhists have no personal attachment to a divine entity like God, but for many Tibetans, devata are akin to divine beings. Tibetans regard them as guardians of truth; still others see them as more or less symbolic, mental projections.

So, the Dalai Lama wondered.

Zalman assured him that angels were beings of such enlarged consciousness that the human mind could not contain their enormity. There are so many angels that each nation has one. The angels engage in dialogue with each other beyond this human plane. There are angels of families, of various groups, of cities and nations. "But on the highest level," Zalman said, "there is one who contains and represents the consciousness of the totality."

Zalman affirmed that every angel answered God's commands—even "the black one" (Satan), he said. "All are doing God's work. All is in oneness; nothing is outside of God.'" Negative angels may create positive outcomes. Like the *thangkas,* or the paintings of wrathful deities of Tibet, all beings operate in service to the cosmos, with their strength, fire, and severity. So, Zalman believed, some angels reward us, and others punish or test us.

Zalman described seraphim, the fire angels who fly with two wings, cover their faces with another two, and cover their feet with two more. He described the seraphim who praise God, some looking more like animals—a lion, a bull, an eagle—then like a man. Zalman described the angels called "wheels within wheels" because of their shifting energies.

"Are angels connected with the weather?" the Dalai Lama asked. There had been a small earthquake in Dharmsala that morning at 7:00 a.m.

Zalman assured him that not a blade of grass grew without an angel noticing.

A persistent student, the Dalai Lama participated in this teaching in the way most Theravedic monks are taught, by asking questions, so he continued to question the rabbi. Was the action by an angel ultimate? Did it have autonomy and authority, or was all of its activity under the Creator's guidance?

In seeking to adequately address these questions, Reb Zalman tried on a scientific discussion about the nature of vibrations, electricity, spiraling energy forms, and transformers, until he finally settled on a metaphor—for metaphors may be the only way we really can explain Deity. Finally he said, "Ultimately, there are no angels, ultimately there is only God. But the garment God wears appears to us as angels."[51]

That exchange, in a nutshell, suggests that angels (and devata) are formulated ideations, imagined and unimaginably complex. They are a philosophy. They are chimera—something that one might wish were true, but may, in fact, be nothing more than illusion. They operate like scientific principles, yet they frighten and baffle us. Are they adversaries or champions? Do they even exist?

3
Silk Road Traditions

Wanting connections, we found connections—always, everywhere, and between everything.

UMBERTO ECO, *FOUCAULT'S PENDULUM*

ZOROASTRIAN ANGELS

Across the mountains, moors, and deserts of Central Asia and around the shorelines of the Indian Ocean there runs an interconnected trade route known as the Silk Road. This ancient tapestry woven by traders in silk commodities connects the spiritual flowers of many cultures and links three continents. From Asia through Central Asia, to Africa and to central Europe, the merchants plied their trade by navigating sailing ships and ships of the desert. Their long sojourns carried stories of mystical meetings with holy men who offered them the secrets of their traditions—Hinduism, Buddhism, Yezidism, Christianity, Zoroastrianism, Manicheanism, as well as Kemetic and Islamic beliefs. The interconnections among the religions seem as striking as their differences. Spirit beings of every culture have been assimilated as shining angels. Major Silk Road religions and their angels may predate Eastern and Western traditions, rather than having been influenced by them.

Unlike Abrahamic People of the Book, the traditions of these cultures seem steeped in oral traditions. Few textual references appear.

What stories there may be sometimes run wildly off the traditional scripts, with narratives derived from divergent sources. The Silk Road, traveled by merchants from Asia to the ocean, connects Eastern and Western traditions. While these religions align with certain beliefs in the Judeo-Christian and Islamic monotheistic traditions, there is a fuzzy line between separating which parts of their beliefs are monotheistic, and which parts are polytheistic. And the more we look at angels in these religions, the fuzzier the line gets. In this section, we examine angels primarily in the Zoroastrian and Yezidi traditions.

Fundamentally, Zoroastrianism springs from the vision of a dualistic universe, but ventures into polytheism, with its many spirit beings ensconced in the armies of good and evil. Good and evil ultimately arise from one deity. The one god shows two faces—light and dark. Those splintered aspects of the one become angels and demons of the upper and lower worlds.

The three Abrahamic religions and many of their traditions arise geographically from the lower plateau of Central Asia. The original Zoroastrian traditions of Iran migrated toward the Mediterranean Sea, making contact with Greeks, Romans, Sumerians, and Egyptians. The faith likewise spread into the mountains of Pakistan, Afghanistan, India, and Tibet, influencing the Hindu and Buddhist traditions. Texts that document the Zoroastrian concepts along the Silk Road are fragmentary at best. The oldest and most well-known text is the Avesta. Among the younger texts are the Gathas, which mostly resemble texts found in the *Rig-Veda*.

At age thirty, the prophet Zarathustra (later Zoroaster) received a vision when he went to the Daiti River to draw water for a haoma ceremony. Haoma practitioners apparently had long engaged in ceremonies of ancestral communication and nature worship prior to the beginnings of Zoroastrianism. Herodotus, Plutarch, and other Greek writers cited Zarathustra's haoma ceremony as originating around the time of the Trojan War, or the eleventh century BCE. Other more conservative historians date its origin to about 1500 BCE, based on the dating of the earliest text.[1]

In the Zoroastrian tradition the absolute ruler of the universe, Ahura Mazda, commands both light and dark. All ordered Creation comes from his essence, and he is its benevolent ruler. As a deity who predates the Vedic Hindu devata and Asuras, it's no surprise that the first part of his name, Ahura, sounds similar to the contrarian Asuras of the Hindu tradition. Often at the expense of their predecessors, the deities of earlier traditions become demonized. As such, Zoroastrian religion suffered greatly at the hands of both Abrahamic and Occidental religions.

The older text, the Gathas, attribute to Ahura Mazda three children named Good Thought, Good Order, and Humility while early versions of the Avesta say that he created at least three hierarchies of life-giving, immortal angels with whom he lives in "the House of Song."[2] The first of them was Vohu Manah, whose name means "Good Mind." Like the Jewish archangel Metatron, Vohu Manah ranks as the highest angel of all; he sits in heaven beside Ahura Mazda. At the end of life, after the soul crosses the bridge between the worlds, Vohu Manah rises from his golden throne to welcome the righteous into paradise (Videvdad Avestan 19.31). One with his Creator, Vohu Manah emerges from the mind of God and is called Ahura Mazda's "Good Thought."[3]

Around 600 BCE interfaith wisdom philosophies from surrounding Mediterranean cultures flourished and comingled in the university halls and mystery schools of Alexandria. There emerged as part of these philosophies an archangelic force from the Zoroastrian tradition, which was already in circulation a thousand years prior. The archangelic beings were called the Spenta Mainyu. They combined with the energies of what the Greek philosopher Anaxagoras called the *nous,* which is to say that they engaged in a cosmic interplay between God and the world. Plato defined this energy as the *demiurge.* The book of Genesis refers to this as the Spirit of Yahweh, and Jewish philosopher Philo Judaeus combined these philosophic and theological ideas to propose the idea of Logos, the Word that is the firstborn Son of God.[4]

Ancient Egyptians held a similar idea that the world began with a god force called Heka, or "magical utterance," which existed before anything else in the universe. At any rate, we now see the supreme angelic forces as sprung from the mind of God, first as his thought, and then as his word. Entirely mental, these divine essences do not take on form as yet.

Zoroastrian Angelic Dualities

The Avestan texts show the demiurge Spenta Mainyu (the Holy Spirit) always in conflict with Angra Mainyu, his other half. They represent alternating energies and the contrasting forces of Creation—light and dark, above and below, good and evil, heaven and hell, and so on. Divine twin siblings in earlier pagan traditions throughout the region are, for example, Romulus and Remus of Greece; Inanna and Ereshkigal of Sumeria; and Gilgamesh and Enkidu of Mesopotamia. There is even the two-faced Roman god Janus. The biblical Esau and Jacob follow the pattern of twins ensnared in conflict. For Zoroaster, two divine beings—"Bright Mind" (Spenta Mainyu) and "Dark Mind" (Angra Mainyu)—held the conflicting energies of Ahura Mazda. Good and evil derive from one holy source, but without both, life is impossible. Perhaps God is not all-powerful, but he has within himself an ongoing vacillation. He is a bright light casting a long shadow. Therefore the battle for the triumph of good over evil can only be won by the actions of humans who have free will and can choose to work with the angels.[5]

The inevitable antagonism of dual principles gains its greatest importance in the battle between God and the Devil. They fight to gain supremacy over the world and to capture the souls of humankind for an eternity in either heaven or hell. Legions and armies are engaged in winning the soul and the world. The upper legion of angels, or six archangels called the *amesha spentas,* represent archangelic forces presiding over fire, metal, water, earth, and cattle. Now Zoroaster's cosmic impulses begin to appear in manifestation. Male and female divine beings emerge, and some of them appear simultaneously male and female. Perhaps twin souls are also twin flames. Each of these "shining ones" has the capacity to peer into each other's soul.[6]

The amesha spentas occupy the golden seats in the highest council of heaven. Without sleeping, day and night they work to protect all Creation, and bring about the restoration of the world (Yasht 19:96). One might say they are *asha* (guardians of Truth), or the cosmic plan that Ahura Mazda set in place. Human prayer and offerings to the amesha spentas fills their hearts with joy, and inclines them to provide benedictions and prosperity, such as glory, riches, swift horses, and good sons, as well as to protect them from harm.[7]

The names of all Zoroastrian angels and demons illustrate the mental and emotional vitalities they exhibit. Bhagavan Das, a Vedic interfaith scholar, suggests that "One is tempted to think that the English word *anger* is connected with this Zend word *'angra'* and the Sanskrit *'angha'* to blame, and *'agha'* to sin." In later popular culture, these twin aspects of the one deity hardened into their two forms, resulting in Spenta becoming Ahura Mazda himself, and Angra Mainyu becoming the arch demon Ahriman.[8] The names of the seven Holy Immortals, or the Amesha Spentas who are Zarathustra's angels are:

Ahura Mazda, "Wise Lord," creator; his specialty is humanity;
Vohu Manah, "Good Mind," imparts enlightenment; his specialty is animals;
Khshathra Variyu, "Wished for Kingdom," offers wealth, abundance, heaven on Earth;
Asha, "Righteousness," confers spiritual wealth, health, spirit of fire;
Spenta Armaiti, "Holy Devotion," fosters human love, goodness, spirit of Mother Earth;
Haurvata, "Perfection," and Ameretat, "Immortality," usually invoked as a pair, in charge of strength in this life and hereafter; their specialties are plants and water, respectively.[9]

Because these archangels are primarily intellectual concepts—like Wisdom, Righteousness, and Perfection—they are invisible as beings. They have their counterparts in the world of demons ruled by a Luciferian being. Because they are concepts, they become unseen combatants and are, therefore, trickier to battle. For example, each archangel has his/her equivalent demon:

Angra Mainyu, "Evil Spirit," purveyor of death, battles Ahura Mazda;

Aka Manah, "Evil Mind," bad attitude, battles the good thoughts of Vohu Manah;

Druj, "Deceit," rules an entire class of female tricksters called *druj* who fight Khshathra Variyu, who attempts to place heaven on Earth;

Saurva, "Scorn," battles the health and righteousness of Asha;*

Taromaiti, "Heresy," who screams when she hears people pray, battles the holy devotion of Spenta Armaiti;

Taurvi and Zairicha, twin energies known as "Fever" and "Thirst," battle the twin beings Haurvata and Ameretat, "Perfection" and "Immortality."

The number of demons equals the number of angels. Seven angels represent holy virtues, and seven demons are seven deadly sins. Zoroastrianism teaches us that our thoughts create the reality we seek and, often, the reality we get. It is not just what we do, but what we *think*. Negative thoughts of anger, jealousy, greed, lust, deceit, and so on are the deadly sins that keep one from attaining peace and happiness. Remember the story of Jesus exorcising seven devils from a woman possessed (Luke 8:2)? (Some believe that woman to be Mary Magdalene.) Jesus then replaced those seven sinful/demonic thoughts with virtues.

This biblical story has a Zoroastrian component—or perhaps a Manichean one. How interconnected the Middle Eastern religions are! And how complex and powerful is the human mind!

In the Zoroastrian tradition, a long-standing dispute turned three East Indian devata into daevas, or demons: Indra, Sharva (sometimes called Saurva or Shiva), and Nasatyua (or Naonghaithya). Their

---

*While Saurva is a Zoroastrian archdemon, the name in Hindu means fragrant, celestial, and divine—all attributes of Shiva.

battlegrounds are the mental and physical worlds. Beings of truth wrestle with beings of lies "in the mind and in the bones."[10]

The Fravashi Angels of Protection

The *fravashi* are female warriors. Some say they perform the same protective acts as mystical guardian angels. They may appear or be invoked when one feels oneself in danger; others say the fravashi are always with us. According to the Avesta, they are one of the three soul angels of man: the breath soul [*ruwān*], the vision soul [*daēnā*], and the preexisting soul [*fravashi*], which is the most important because without the fravashi, we have no life. Made in the world of thought before the individual ever existed, the pre-soul is received in the womb, assisting in the making of the fetus and helping its birth. When we die, the breath-soul leaves the body; it and its angel soul, the fravashi, return to heaven.

The daēnā moves into the beyond to allow a person to see the true quality of their thoughts, words, and deeds on Earth.[11] The daēnā is similar to the Egyptian *ab,* or heart soul of human consciousness, which is weighed in the balance of Ma'at (Truth) on Judgment Day. The ruwān is similar to the Egyptian *ka,* or animating spirit, and the fravashi is similar to the Egyptian eternal *ba* soul. When the fravashi return to heaven and to Ahura Mazda at the end of life, they participate in the glorious renewal of all life on Earth and in the cosmos.[12] Representing the perfection toward which the soul strives, fravashi fly about as winged birds with human faces, much like the Egyptian ba souls. The winged sun disk superimposed upon them is the central Zoroastrian emblem.

The fravashi police the Earth to safeguard it against the encroachment of the Evil One, Angra Mainyu, sometimes called Ahriman. The daēnā might be thought of as the spiritual embodiment of all things, including abstract concepts, but also every human is in contact with her personal fravashi. Some texts say that under the direction of Ahura Mazda they gather the solar energy of our sun and pour it on the Earth to dispel the demonic forces of Ahriman.[13]

The Many Yazata Angels

Beneath the fravashis, the *yazatas,* or simple angels, fly about as the personified virtues of nature, working to protect us from evil. Yazatas govern everything from truth to astrological planets, to plants and humans. In yet other Zoroastrian texts, the prophet Zoroaster acquired the title of human yazata, or angel. The yazatas may be the remnant memory of an oracular tradition of communicating with spirit beings in an older Indo-Iranian cult. The Sanskrit *Rig-Veda* mentions a similar concept calling Lord Shiva a *yajata,* by which it means a celestial being worthy of worship, one to whom sacrifices may be offered. Some Zoroastrian texts say that Ahura Mazda himself is a yazata, so the term is not necessarily pejorative.[14] Mithra, the Iranian deity, also appears as one of the more well-known yazatas.

From this we can infer only that yazatas are angels because their actions are exceedingly spiritual in nature. The yazata appear both male and female. Every person has a yazata that works with them, just as everyone has a fravashi. Most importantly, all things have a yazata in the natural world and a counterpart in the world of heaven. There exist both celestial [*mainyava*] and terrestrial [*gaethya*] yazata who often work in energy pairs. The celestial yazatas preside over divine wisdom, rectitude, victory, felicity, charity, peace, spells of white magic, health, riches, and cattle. The terrestrial yazatas appear as light, wind, fire, water, and earth.[15] Because of its vision of the duality of the world and the sacredness of all things that exist, Zoroastrianism has been identified as the first religion of the parity of gender that appeared in the early Christian gnostic communities, and the first religion of ecology.[16]

Zoroastrianism is a fire religion and the yazata are fiery beings. Angelic yazatas join the amesha spentas and fravashis to pour their solar energy and light upon the Earth to heal and help mankind. In essence, the working-class legion of yazatas, or "Adorable Ones," number hundreds of thousands of angels—too many to be named individually.[17] An extant Avestan text names only about forty of them. Plutarch refers to twenty-four in his work on Isis and Osiris;[18] Herodotus, the historian, mentions a whole skyful of yazatas, primarily astrological in nature and worthy of worship. These include the sun, moon, earth, fire, water, and air.[19] These planetary angels work together each day to gather the rays of the sun.[20] Perhaps the angel who wrestled with Jacob and begged to be released before dawn belonged to the yazata tribe of angels. The Zoroastrian hymnal mentions thirty yazata who appeared as part of the sacred calendar. Each day of a lunar month Zoroastrians worshipped a different, particular yazata.[21]

Haoma, the Angel of Plant Medicine

One yazata in particular deserves mention as a great spiritual force among beings in the natural world. That is the mysterious Haoma, or in the Hindu catalog of devata, Soma. Prayers to Haoma appear in both the Avesta (Zoroastrian) and the *Rig-Veda* (Hindu). This is an example of the powerful acquisition of angelic ministry derived from plant medicines, in this case most likely the ephedra plant. In the way of all yazata, the angel spirit within this plant offers beneficent healing, and is worthy of worship. Just as one blesses and makes an offering of one's food and drink before ingesting, so prayers may be offered to haoma in sacred fire rituals. A sacred religious libation, haoma must be prepared according to definite prescriptions and imbibed in particular visionary rituals. What exactly the altering substance in the haoma might have been is not precisely known, but more than one hundred and twenty hymns are devoted to it. This is the sacred plant that will make you see the angels.[22]

In Ritual 108, Yasana 9 of the poem cycle of the Avesta we see the prophet interacting with the deity.* One morning as Zarathustra prayed and chanted before his fire, Haoma approached. He asked Zarathustra to consecrate the tawny-colored plant's juice for libations and to praise him as the sacred "death-averting" plant.[23] The first prophet to do so, Zarathustra pounded the plant for a libation, from which he derived great benefit. The prophet calls Haoma the Lord of Knowledge, possessor of good wisdom, the healing one, beautiful, and golden-eyed.[24]

---

*In this poem, Haoma attains deity status.

What haoma offers is a true vision of "intelligence, courage, victory, health, increase, prosperity, vigor of body and power to rule at will, and to smite the wicked that he may vanquish the evil done by the wicked men and demons." Haoma offered these gifts to Zarathustra and, it is said, he will give them to all humankind who honor him. "The devout worshipper, in return, dedicates his very body to him" and joy reigns.[25]

What exactly is the plant haoma? It has been linked to the Brazilian vine of the dead, but it has also been described as a *baresman,* the sacred bundle of twigs of haoma [*Haomayo gava baresmana*]. The intoxicating plant grew on the mystical Mount Mujavat, where Shiva lives, and its perfume caused the twittering birds to carry it around. The sacred texts say an eagle carried it from the top of the mountain to Earth. Unlike other drinks that can invoke evil thoughts and wrath, the haoma induces peace and joy and confers immortality.[26]

The *Rig-Veda* identifies the ephedra plant as haoma. Still others believe it could be the blue lotus or certain mushrooms of the Siberian shamans. It seems, therefore, to refer to any plant-based drink that is made with sacred purified Himalayan water. The ecclesiastical Vendidad, which contains spells for the righteous to protect themselves and their community against demons, provides an offering recipe for how to grind and prepare the twenty-three haoma reeds with milk, pomegranate juice, or sacred water.[27] Even pounding the plant into juice is equivalent to destroying demons by the thousands.[28]

The haoma ceremony offered a spiritual medicine as a way to fill the mind with angelic thoughts and wisdom that could "break the power of demons"—in other words, the power that evil and negative thoughts hold.[29] Remember that during Mohammed's heavenly visit, angels offered him two drinks—milk or wine. He chose milk because it was the drink of the righteous. Zoroastrian priests and prophets offered a haoma concoction made with milk to those who wanted to see beyond the veil of illusion. The elixir was later added to the known alchemical formulas and procedures of the magi of Iran.

Jews, Zoroastrians, and Angels

Some Zoroastrian angels find their way into the stories of other religious traditions, like Jacob possibly wrestling a yazata angel. Original Zoroastrian beliefs hold a hidden influence over Jewish culture in its beginnings. Scholars suggest that the Sermon on the Mount came from materials initially preached by Zoroastrian adherents, that is, the Sufis. Sufi orders may be surviving remnants of Zoroastrian religious traditions, all the while cloaked in Muslim garments.

When the Jewish prophet Abraham meets Nimrod, the Mesopotamian king who built the Tower of Babel, we understand that we are reading a Midrash story that pits polytheism against monotheism. After Abraham calls Nimrod an idolater, Nimrod orders Abraham to be burnt in the biggest bonfire ever, yet Abraham emerges unscathed. The Torah (Genesis Rabbah 38:11) specifically suggests that Nimrod is actually the fire-worshipping, stargazing Zoroaster. No worship of fire, or water, or humankind could influence Abraham to desert his god, so Nimrod opted to throw Abraham into the fire.

The story, in this quote from William Brinner's *The History of al-Ṭabarī,* specifically says:

> When they gathered it for him and had gotten so much that a bird passing over it would have been burned by the force of its heat, they brought Abraham and set him on top of the pyre. When Abraham raised his hand to heaven and Earth all of the angels standing on the mountains said, "Our Lord, Abraham is burning at Your sake."
>
> And He said, "I am most knowledgeable about him. If he calls on you, help him."
>
> When he raised his head to heaven, Abraham said: "O God, You are alone in heaven, and I am alone on Earth—there is no one besides me who worships You. God is sufficient for me, and how goodly is He and I trust him." When they pushed Abraham into the fire, God called out to it saying, "Fire! Be coolness and peace for Abraham," and it was Gabriel who called out. . . .

A footnote in Brinner's text identifies Gabriel as one of the divine messengers whose duty it is to bear God's orders to prophets and reveal his mysteries to them.

> . . . When the fire was extinguished, then they looked at Abraham and saw that there was another man with him, with Abraham's head in his lap. He was wiping the sweat from his face. It was mentioned that that man was the angel of shade.* For days Nimrod continued to believe that the fire had consumed Abraham and had finished him. Then one day he rode past it while it was burning all of the wood that had been gathered for it, and he looked at it and saw Abraham sitting in it with a man resembling him at his side.[30]. . .
>
> Nimrod returned from that ride and said to his people: "I have seen Abraham alive in the fire, but perhaps it was only his image that appeared to me. Build me a tall structure from which I may look down upon the fire so that I can be sure." So, they built him a tall structure from which he looked down into the fire. He saw Abraham sitting in it and saw the angel sitting by his side in a form similar to his. Nimrod called out to him, saying "Oh Abraham! Great is your God whose might and power even allowed Him to prevent what I see from harming you. Will you be able to come out of it?"
>
> Abraham answered, "Yes!"
>
> Nimrod said, "I'm afraid that if you remain in it, it will harm you?"
>
> Abraham answered, "No."
>
> Then Nimrod said, "Arise, then, and come out of it!"
>
> So, Abraham got up and walked through the fire until he had come out of it. He came out toward him. Nimrod said, "O Abraham! Who was the man whom I saw with you, like you in appearance, sitting at your side?"

---

*Brinner's footnote indicates that the word *shade* meant here a synonym for shelter and protection. In the ancient Egyptian language, the word *khaibit* similarly indicates a sunshade, a ghost, or a person's shadow or etheric form. In Arabic the word is *sahabat*.

Abraham said: "That was the angel of shade whom my Lord sent to me to be with me in the fire to comfort me. For me he made the fire coolness and peace."[31]

In the Zoroastrian tradition, as well as in the Jewish, Christian, and Islamist traditions, angels comfort and support a human being in his or her quest for a victorious life. With the Zoroastrians, one could say the angels of mind encourage us to have good sense for the purpose of securing a *future* divine life. Charles Fillmore, in the *Metaphysical Bible Dictionary,* defined the reason angels matter in any religion. "The office of the angels is to guard and guide and direct the natural focus of mind and body, which have in them the future of the whole man."[32]

YEZIDI ANGELS

Yezidi angels [*melek*] are an amalgamation of Hebrew angels [*mal'akh*] and Muslim angels [*malāk*] with similar qualities common to Zoroastrian angels of both light and darkness. This Kurdish-speaking, persecuted religious sect known as the Yezidi (sometimes called Yzaddi, Yazidi, Daasin, or Ezidi) has clustered in its community in northern Iraq in the twenty-first century. A small, obscure, diminishing religious sect, Yezidis have endured persecution and genocide for thousands of years. Their original beliefs, however, spanned the Silk Road for a millennium or more.

Although their story is hard to trace, the Yezidi bear similar attributes to the many religious traditions of peoples who traveled the Silk Road before the Christian era. Their religious ideals blend Zoroastrian, Islam, Sufi, Hindu, Buddhist, Christian, and Babylonian beliefs. When asked, they recognize Mohammed as a true prophet, and Jesus Christ as an angel in human form. Sufism offers them its mystical wisdom. Although they self-identify as Islamic, in practice they appear kin to the Mithraic mystery religion.

Their true beliefs are little understood because few written records exist. They mimic other religions to cover their own unusual beliefs.

Self-isolation protects the traditions they have. Yet they exhibit an intersection with the more obscure beliefs of early Zoroastrians, Kabbalists, and Manicheans (a now extinct and equally persecuted group). Hindus and Yezidis also share a historical link. Around 4000 BCE, when Yezidis populated the region, massive floods forced a migration to higher ground in India. Two thousand years later, some families remained in India while others migrated to Iran. At the turn of the nineteenth century, the Yezidis numbered about two hundred thousand people scattered over a region three hundred miles wide and extending from Aleppo in northern Syria to the Caucasus Mountains in southern Russia. Most of them regrouped at that time in the North Central mountains of Kurdistan and amid the Sinjar Hills of Mesopotamia.[33]

In 2014 Islamist militants spurred on by Saddam Hussein breeched the Sinjar Hills, murdering men and children, and raping Yezidi girls. Facing starvation and death, thousands left the sacred land that had been a central pillar of their beliefs. Trying to blend in within the rising tide of Middle Eastern extremists, the Yezidis claimed to also be Muslim, but the rebels of Islam branded them as "devil worshippers." This pattern of systematic persecution by Christians, Islamists, Turks, and Asian Mongols began as early as the eighth century. The remaining clans of the Yezidi banded together in the remote mountain region of Transcaucasia, near Mount Ararat. Their extreme persecution has created a xenophobic culture that does not welcome outsiders and creates a "smoke screen" around itself. Yezidis do not marry outsiders; they protect their culture by limiting it only to believers and not to converts.

Meetings with Remarkable Yezidi

One example of the Yezidis self-isolation and the power of their beliefs appears in a story told by the nineteenth-century mystic G. I. Gurdjieff in his book *Meetings with Remarkable Men*. Traveling through the region, as a young man around 1920, he came across a group of individuals taunting a young Yezidi boy. The bullies had drawn a circle about the child. He could move freely inside the circle but could not leave that circle without blacking out, suffering seizures, and falling into a coma. Gurdjieff writes, "Some strange force, much more powerful than his normal strength keeps him inside. I myself, although strong, could not pull a weak woman out of the circle; it needed another man as strong as I."[34] Dragged from the protection of his circle, a Yezidi's coma might last between thirteen and twenty-one hours before he regained consciousness. Only magical incantations from a priest might revive him more quickly.

Self-preservation became ingrained as a part of the Yezidi spiritual practice, in the past as well as today. The ancient tribe adeptly hides in the mountains from outsiders and, when confronted, masks their true beliefs by adopting the ways of interlopers. Persecuted Yezidis often offer conflicting, erroneous information to keep the sanctity of beliefs within the Yezidi community. Thus have they demonstrated a changing ethnography and religious climate for thousands of years. Illiterate by design, Yezidis primarily pass on their beliefs through a rich oral history akin to the mystery schools of the past in which priests taught initiates "mouth to ear."

Sacred Texts and Secrets

No ancient records document the beliefs of the Yezidis. They are not considered a People of the Book, such as those of Islamic, Jewish, or Christian faiths. They have no remnant texts such as the Dhammapada of the Buddhists, the Vedas of the Hindus, or the few surviving texts of the Zoroastrian Avesta. The Yezidis possess a scripture of hearsay. They refer to only two sacred books whose articles of faith are attributed to an anonymous author, Taus Melek (often Tawûsê Melek or Tawsi Melek), who is called "Peacock Angel." Sometimes he is identified as the archangel Gabriel; at other times, he is King Meleki Sadiq of Jerusalem, whom the Hebrew scriptures mention as a contemporary of Abraham.[35]

Copies of the two Yezidi sacred books rarely turn up. When they do, the translations appear to have been altered and changed. This hardly matters to most Yezidis, for their tribal leaders teach the meanings that are important to know. The most holy book, the Roj, which means "the Rays," is offered in two versions. One is called the Jalwa, or the Revelation, and the other is al-Asrar, or the Secrets. In the Jalwa, its angelic author, Taus Melek, states that "he is a supreme being, not a man who eats, drinks, and sleeps like others. He insists on blind obedience to his advice. The first chapter reminds the readers that Taus Malek [Melek] has been ever present since the beginning and that he will have no end. He exercises his rule over all creatures and 'over the affairs of all who are in my possession.'"[36]

One family alone claims to possess the sole copy of the Jalwa. This sacred text has never been shown or read to anyone. The book contains an injunction against offering any information within it to outsiders. It disallows copying for fear that non-Yezidis might alter the angel's truth. In general, one is advised not to acquire any form of learning and to memorize their scriptures lest they fall into the wrong hands. As a further injunction, Taus Melek asks the people to honor his image, the peacock, through the ritual *sanjak* (an iron peacock that is a religious icon circulated throughout the community services).[37]

Two pseudographic sacred books appear outside traditional Yezidi circles, the Meshefê Re and Ketēbā Jelwa, or the *Black Book* and the *Book of Revelations,* published in 1911 and 1913, respectively. Considered forgeries authored by manuscript traders, each book presumes to recount a credible Yezidi oral tradition, despite the injunctions against reading them. The *Black Book* retells a Genesis story that involves world creation by the Peacock Angel, Taus Melek.[38]

Clerics chant memorized core hymns known as *qawls*. Attempts now are being made to collect these oral transmissions with the consent of the community, effectively transforming Yezidism into a scriptural religion.[39] The diaspora of the Yezidis may yet prove to increase the understanding of their religion in the same way that the Tibetan diaspora introduced Buddhism to a wider audience in the last century.

Children of the Sun

As we look at the lost traditions of the Silk Road, we find tendrils of Yezidism making a foray into other religions, and vice versa. Zoroastrianism springs from Iraq and Iran along the same Silk Road route and seems to be Yezidism's closest relative. The appearance of the Divine manifested as light is a Zoroastrian principle; Yezidis likewise call themselves "Children of the Sun." They align with the sun in a prayer ritual three to five times a day.

Many Middle Eastern religions, from the ancient Egyptian to the Zoroastrian, point to the sun as the source of spiritual energy and ultimate truth. The root Farsi word *yazd* derives from a Zoroastrian word meaning "god," or "good spirit," who opposes the principle of evil, Ahriman, who appears with a ferocious leonine form, claws snatching. The Persians in Iran dedicated their ancient city of Yazd in Iran to the winged Ahura Mazda, the Zoroastrian good spirit.[40] The proximity of the remaining Yezidi tribe to the land that fostered Zoroastrianism makes it possible that most of their religious beliefs link to this connection.

Similarly, Hindus see the sun as a godly emanation. Like the Buddhists, Hindus, and pagans, the Yezidis identify themselves as one with the spirits of the natural world. The Hindu naga culture offers the same deep respect to all snakes that the Yezidis offer to their black snake. A large elongated black snake appears prominently beside the doorway of the high holy temple in Lalish (Iraq). That alone has caused other religious clerics to deem the Yezidis devil worshippers.

Judeo-Christians equate the wisdom serpent of the Hindu tradition with the sneaky snake manifesting in the Garden of Eden as Satan. The strident persecution of the snake-honoring Yezidi culture has more to do with the fact that typical Judeo-Christians have a difficult time distinguishing between a deva (a nature deity) and a devil. To the Yezidi, the serpent was wise, benevolent, and powerful. This black snake curled himself into a ball to plug the hole that sprang in Noah's Ark. Thus, the humble black snake saved all of life on the planet from the devastating flood. Mount Ararat, considered a holy mountain, may be the place where the Yezidi patriarch Noah abandoned his ark and where its relics remain to this day.[41]

The God in Me Sees the God in You

Reincarnation, a central tenet of the Hindu religion, suggests that the imperishable soul only changes *form* when the body dies. That philosophy holds a deep kinship to Yezidi beliefs. In fact, death is not really acknowledged by Yezidis; they refer to it as *kiras guhorin*, or "changing of garments."[42] Even the gods of other world cultures reincarnate to assume new forms. One's personal deity equals the power of any other person's deity. In other words, the great creative impulse of the universe simply changes clothes. This concept makes Yezidis some of the most peaceful people in the Middle East. Divine beings may even reincarnate into human form. A Yezidi, Hindu, or Buddhist may offer the blessing "Namaste" (the God in me sees the God in you).[43]

From an early age, all Yezidis understand the concept of reincarnation. The elders teach the children about the sacred *khas*, that is, "the angelic beings who became incarnated as humans in order to lead the Yezidis on the path of true religion."[44] The idea of a highly illuminated being who may manifest on Earth as an ascended master or light being also finds expression in the ancient Egyptian word *kha*. That word indicates one of the highest intelligences, a spiritual body of light and fire akin to the phoenix.

Manichaeism

From the third through the eighth centuries, a chameleon-like Christian ideology acquired theological concepts tangential to cultures that it contacted. This mass appeal spread across the Silk Road from East to West and throughout the Mediterranean region. The once great theology of Manichaeism, developed by the visionary Iranian prophet Mani, had been called a "religion of the chosen people." It included all the elements of the great Abrahamic traditions.[45] A comprehensive but partially destroyed Coptic version of Mani's supposed speech on the "ten superiorities of his religion are given in the *Kephalaia*."[46] Rather than unifying the religions as the authors had hoped, the document became a kind of arch heresy.

Some scholars claim Yezidis originally shared common ideologies with Manicheans about the combative forces of good and evil in the same way that Zoroastrians did. Early twentieth-century ethnographer Isya Joseph calls the Yezidi "illiterate Christians [whose] progressive ignorance has brought them into their present condition."[47] To Isya Joseph, that condition was a fallen one.

In the Yezidi culture, traditional holidays have been kept according to sacred calendars (possibly Sumerian) for nearly seven thousand years. The Yezidi calendar originated about 4,764 years before the arrival of Christianity, and more than five thousand years before the arrival of Islam. Many gnostic Christian traditions (such as those in Nag Hammadi, Egypt) appear heavily influenced by early Yezidi nature worship.[48]

Both Yezidis and gnostics believe that good deeds contribute to not only personal redemption, but also to the redemption of the world soul. For many Christians, Christ is a personal savior, but redemption of a world soul is a concept more familiar to Theosophists who work as light bearers for the fellowship of man.[49] The mediums H. P. Blavatsky and Alice A. Bailey channeled the metaphysical teachings of ascended masters (including Tibetan masters and Jesus Christ). As Bailey pointed out in her book *A Treatise on White Magic,* many people of traditional Christian faiths are unaccustomed to working with metaphysical laws. However, they may work with angels in groups through their churches, allowing angels to guide and protect them. The higher angels also guide and direct those who work with social reform, church leadership, and humanitarian activities. Behind those energies lie the great devas— those archangelic figures pledged to serve humanity.[50]

This is an important idea: *angels work through and with all religions, according to a person's understanding, participation, and need.*

Legends of the Sheikhs

Persecuted religious communities often carry their beliefs and rituals underground, turning them into a mystery school. The teachings become orally transmitted, the wisdom gathered only from the lips of a master teacher, and the validity of its beliefs becomes impossible to document. The Yezidis survive because of their *sir* (secret) mystery tradition.[51] After having been retold for a millennium, certain beliefs take hold and may take on another name. The religion continued in isolated pockets of the high mountains of Turkistan, Iran, and Iraq. In this way, the Yezidis acquired similar remnant belief systems.[52]

When defenders of the Christian, Zoroastrian, and Islamic faiths began to see Manicheanism as the single greatest threat to their spiritual beliefs, their crusaders crushed the infidels. Until his conversion even Saint Augustine espoused a Manichaean philosophy.[53] Abrahamists deplored the core hypocrisy of Mani's "religion of enlightenment." Whereas Mani claimed to "convince the human mind" of the proof of spiritual realities, Jews and Christians demanded faith and unquestioning acceptance.[54]

One common thread that binds Muslim and Yezidi beliefs is the arrival of religious instruction dictated by an angel. That method of spiritual instruction continues today, passing through the lips of a spiritual elder who teaches and interprets the doctrine. Even in Islam the true Qur'an requires oral delivery in just the same way that Mohammed received his message from the angel. It is possible that Mohammed acquired his visionary prowess in the same caves where Manicheans or Yezidis meditated. Nevertheless, the Yezidis have been almost wiped out by the hands of Sunni extremists, even though the principal saint of the Yezidis, a twelfth-century sheikh named Adi ibn Musafir, was recognized in his time as an orthodox Muslim.[55]

The Sufi master Musafir (died 1162) taught in Kurdistan and strongly influenced Yezidi spiritual understanding. Recognized as a great Yezidi saint, Sheikh Musafir's teachings are considered scripture. Ethnographer Eszter Spät traces the history of Yezidism to Islam through Sheikh Musafir and his Sufi brotherhood, the "al Adawiya," which originates in the valley of Lalish in the Kurdish mountains near Mosul. Spät says: "With time this Sufi order incorporated so many pre-Islamic elements from its environment that it ceased to be a part of Islam and became an independent religious entity."[56] Some Yezidis believe the Peacock Angel incarnated as Sheikh Musafir. His role as primary founding patriarch resembled that of founding father Joseph Smith of the Mormons.[57]

Despite Sunni attempts to eradicate them, Sufi and Yezidi sects demonstrate many similarities and a shared ideology. According to Sufi teacher Idries Shah, Sufi Sheikh Musafir founded the Yezidi traditions. Outwardly Musafir appears as a rather orthodox Muslim, yet as a Sufi he held "the secret doctrines of Sufism [that] have always been suspected of pantheism, and the Sufi faiths cherishing of the ancient faiths."[58]

By way of example, Shah points to the ubiquitous black snake imagery, previously mentioned, that marks the entryway of Yezidi temples. Far from being the evil symbols that fundamental Muslims and Judeo-Christians project onto it, Shah says, the black snake creates a kind of visual and linguistic pun that holds within it a connotation of the wisdom of life. A similar serpent arises as the uraeus of a pharaoh's crown in ancient Egypt. The appearance of the coiled serpent on his forehead indicates his visionary capacities. "The Yezidis were originally a community of Sufis," says Shah, "and their rituals are centered around the use of standard and familiar Sufi symbolism."[59] Legend has it that the black snake alluded to more than wisdom; it symbolized magic. According to one legend, this large black snake once lived in Lalish, apparently causing problems for its residents, so when it attempted to scale the wall, Sheikh Musafir transformed it into a solid image. Now it permanently resides in Lalish.

Another legend states that Sheikh Mend, a companion of Sheikh Adi and an earthly manifestation of one of the Seven Great Angels, turned himself into this black snake and drove back the tribe of Haweris when they tried to convert the Yezidis to Islam.[60] Magical Sufi and Yezidi stories abound, yet it is not clear whether Sufis influenced the Yezidis or vice versa.

In some ways Yezidi community members organize themselves around a religious caste system that has more to do with spiritual understanding and religious duties than with social privilege and wealth. In the same way that Jews are born into a family of Cohens or Levites,* every Yezidi is born into a clerical family or a lay family. Among clergy there are sheikhs and pirs (pronounced "peers"). Each of these has its own set of religious responsibilities. Sheikhs preside over most major holidays, while pirs preside over life cycle events like birth and marriage.[61]

Genesis and the Angel Taus Melek

Yezidi accounts of Creation are both similar to and different from narratives found in Judaism, Christianity, and Islam. The sacred *Black Book* begins its Genesis story with the arrival of the first being on Earth, the Peacock Angel Taus Melek. Taus Melek is not God, but he is the first emanation of God who created this supreme archangel from his own illumination [*ronahî*] at the beginning of time.[62] Ethnographer Eszter Spät offers a beautiful description of the Peacock Angel as the light of the world equivalent to the Christ light.

"Although called an angel, the Peacock Angel, or Tawûsê Melek, is not an angel, at least not in the sense Christianity or Islam utilizes this word. Yezidi angels are not creations or creatures of God, but are emanations or hypostases of the Godhead, who came into being, as the Yezidis say, as candles lit from another candle. The most important of all these angels is the Peacock Angel. He is simultaneously the head of the Seven Angels, the viceroy of God on Earth, and the special protector angel of the Yezidis."[63]

Upon arriving in the mountain valley of Lalish in the Kurdistan region of Iraq, he found a barren, lonely planet besieged by constant earthquakes and volcanoes. Having been sent to remedy the situation, he transformed the planet into one of the most beautiful in the universe and covered this world in rainbow peacock colors.[64] Taus Melek emerged from the light of God in the form of a seven-rayed rainbow—a form he

---

*Cohens are priests who happen to descend directly from Aaron, the brother of Moses. A Levite descends from the third son of Jacob and an ancestor to Aaron. Their prescribed responsibilities differ in the synagogue, but each is considered a holy man.

continues to manifest. From this, to assist him in the work of reimagining beauty upon the Earth, over the course of the six subsequent days God created six other meleks—sometimes called kings or archangels depending on the translation. Emanations of the Supreme God, these angels do not separate from Him. Altogether, collectively, these seven meleks (six meleks created by Taus Melek and Taus Melek himself) are the seven colors of the rainbow that encircle God, the sun.[65] The angels he created all resemble him, and yet the angels are similar in form to man.[66] Taus Melek exudes the color blue—the color of heaven and sky, which is the source of all colors. Because these seven angels share the "essence" of their Creator they are also called "the Seven Mysteries."[67]

The seven meleks of the Yezidi who appear as rainbow emanations became linked to Gurdjieff's Fourth Way philosophy and to the Theosophical philosophies of Alice Bailey, H. P. Blavatsky, Torkom Saraydarian, and others. Theosophists see this planet's custody established by God and maintained by one great presence named Sanat Kumara. From him appear the seven-ray ascended masters who, like Taus Melek and the six great angels, are also identified by color and virtue.[68]

During the sacred autumn festival Taus Melek and the other great angels visit Lalish. On the way to the nave of the sanctuary near Mount Arafat one finds several tombs belonging to the earthly incarnations of the Seven Great Angels. Different colored silks matching the seven colors of the rainbow cover the tombs. Pilgrims seeking aid from the seven angels tie a knot, or several knots, in one of the silk rags while simultaneously untying another one. The untied knot ensures that a previous pilgrim will soon find a rapid solution to his or her problem.[69]

Many stories of Taus Melek give him similar talents as the archangel Uriel. Or he is linked to Metatron, God's second, according to the mystical Jewish Kabbalah. Just as the Kabbalah listed seventy-two angels whose names are the creative breath of God, so did Taus Melek deliver to Adam and Eve a sacred book with seventy-two secret code names through which God effected Creation. God manifested Taus Melek "to give the invisible, transcendental Supreme God a vehicle with which to create and administer the universe." Thus, the Peacock Angel is a tangible, denser form of the infinite Supreme God.[70]

Seven Great Angels

Jews, Christians, Persians, and Egyptians all have seven angels who create the cosmic heptad within their tradition. Most likely these angels mirror the seven immortals of the Zoroastrians. These seven Yezidi angels may be the same ones who manifest under different forms with different names in the Sufi tradition.

Facing seven directions, including above, below, and within, they correspond to the seven heavens and the seven earths. Of the seven Sufi angels, the one with a human form protects the human race; the angel lion prays for each beast of prey; the ox angel prays for domesticated animals; and the angelic eagle oversees the winged creatures. These four angels, mentioned in Ezekiel's revelation, also appear in the corners of the modern tarot Wheel card. A fifth angel shaped like the sun offers prayers to benefit the natural world and all earthly creatures. The sixth angel in the Sufi tradition is a tree that is similar to the kabbalist's Tree of Life, whose leaves represent all God's creations. The seventh angel is a constellation who turns to God and receives His light.[71]

How did all this happen? The Meshefê Re tells a story of how the Supreme God first created a pearl containing the substance or substratum of the soon-to-be physical universe. This unseen pearly substance ostensibly refers to the molten mass that preceded the big bang postulated by modern physicists. The Yezidis maintain that this suspended substance of the universe lasted forty thousand years; all the while this "pearl" sat on the back of a primal bird.[72] The Egyptian myth describes the suspended potentiality of the cosmos as resting inside the cosmic egg of a bird known as "the Great Cackler."[73] In both cases this may be a form of Taus Melek before he divided into the Seven Great Angels. This pearl then exploded, or became dismantled by itself, to become the physical universe.[74]

Another story says that the Seven Great Angels formed the Earth out of the substratum of the original pearl. The planet remained barren for a long time, until sudden, ubiquitous, violent earthquakes and volcanic activity started to shake the planet intensely and continually. To calm the situation, the Supreme God sent the Peacock Angel to sedate the Earth by endowing it with multicolored flora and fauna. As Taus Melek descended into the physical dimension, his seven-colored rainbow-self manifested as the peacock, a magnificent bird of seven colors. Flying about and blessing every part of the Earth, he finally landed in northern Iraq, in Lalish—the most sacred part of the globe. He calmed the planet by fanning out his peacock wings and covering it with his beautiful colors.[75]

One Yezidi Genesis passage in the Meshefê Re associates the creation of the Seven Great Angels with the seven days of the week, and with seven reincarnated Sufi sheikhs who are considered demigods or prophets. Some of these founding members came from prominent Yezidi families.

> On Sunday, the first day, the Supreme God created not only the greatest angel, Taus Melek, the angel of genesis, but also his counterpart, Azazil, the angel of death.
>
> On Monday He created the Angel Darda'il, who is Sheikh Hasan and is related to the Babylonian center in Ur.
>
> On Tuesday He created the Angel Israfil, who is Sheikh Shams, the mystical Shams honored by the Sufi poet Jalal Din al Rumi.
>
> On Wednesday He created the Angel Mika'il, who is Hasan, Sheikh. Most Yezidi princes trace their lineage from the Abu Bakr family.
>
> On Thursday He created the Angel Gibra'il, who is Sagad ad-Din. Some say on this day Azra'il was created. He is identified as Melek al Mawt in the Qur'an and is the angel of death in Islamic and Jewish traditions.*

---

*Compare two slightly varying identifications in Ahmed, 154 and Joseph, 1909, 111–156. According to Joseph, angel of death Azazil and Taus Melek were created simultaneously. According to Ahmed, Gibra'il and the angel of death Azra'il were simultaneously made.

On Friday He created the Angel Shamna'il, an angel of light, who
is Nasir ad-Din of Nisroch and is an Assyrian god.

On Saturday He created the Angel Nura'il, who is Yadin, also called
Sheikh Fakhr al-Din, the ancestor of another Yezidi family.

And God made Melekê Taus the greatest of them.[76]

Note that the angel of death has two different days of origin.
Other sources suggest different names for these same seven angels,
and some identify them as Judeo-Christian angels. All are listed in the
Black Book. They are Cibrayîl, Gabriel the messenger of Abrahamic
tradition; Ezrayîl or Azrael, a benevolent psychopomp also known as
Melek al-Mawt, the angel of death in the Qur'an; Mîkayîl, the archangel Michael, defender of the Judeo-Christian faiths; the angel Şifqayîl,
found only in the *Black Book;* Derdayîl, an Islamic angel who travels
the Earth seeking communities of people who remember God; Ezafîl,
Israfil, who blows the trumpet before Armageddon; and Ezazîl, Azazil,
the same angel who was Iblis before his expulsion from heaven.[77]

Any of the seven holy angels may reincarnate into an angelic human
form called a *koasasa* at any time. Reincarnation and rebirth are common beliefs in Asian spiritual traditions. The Yezidis adhere to the idea
of soul progression, believing that one may be born again and again,
working toward perfection until that soul becomes advanced enough to
move into heaven. Similarly, Hinduism supports the idea of reincarnat-
ing to work toward release from past karma.[78]

Once evicted from heaven for not bowing to Adam, Taus Melek
descended and saw the suffering of humans in hell. The narrative continues to tell a story of compassion like that of the Buddha's awakening. For seven thousand years the Peacock Angel cried, and his tears
extinguished the purgatory fires.[79] Because this tenderhearted angel
witnessed the soul's progression through reincarnation, and because his
tears of empathy quelled the fires of hell, we are saved, and each of us is
destined for eternal life.

Taus Melek also resembles the Hindu deva Murugan, a cherubic
boy with peacock feathers growing from his tail. Both divine beings

descended from the Pleiades and taught humanity to follow the solar light that leads along the path to God. The deva Murugan appears as Sanat Kumara, an ascended master beyond the Earth plane who is known as the Regent Lord of the World. He leads seven kumaras (ascended masters) just as Taus Melek leads the Seven Great Angels.[80] As reincarnations of highly esteemed sheikhs and leaders, these seven angels are also called the seven gateways, or *babas*. Two of these "gates" are Jesus and Ali, the founder of Shi'ism.

According to the Yezidis, God entrusted care of his created world to the great Peacock Angel because of the thousand eyes revealed in its fanning tail. These thousand peacock eyes assure one that Taus Melek oversees all events occurring in the world. The peacock king may have a special relationship to the Yezidis but belongs to the entire world. Because so many other religious traditions are linked to the Taus Melek narrative, Yezidis claim that they possess the oldest religion on Earth. Taus Melek, they say, is the true creator and ruler of the universe. As a result, he plays a part in all religious traditions, even though he may not always manifest within these diverse traditions as a peacock. "Tawsi [Taus] Melek has taken on many other forms throughout time."[81]

The Creation of Man

Now that a more colorful, peaceful place existed on Earth, the Seven Great Angels moved on to their next creation: Adam. One story says that God ordered Taus Melek, his first creation, not to bow to any other beings. Then he created the other archangels and ordered them to bring him dust [*ax*] from the Earth [*Erd*] and to build the body of Adam. God gave life to Adam from his own breath, then he instructed all the archangels to bow to Adam, his great creation. The archangels obeyed—all except for Taus Melek. In answer to God, who asked why he did not bow, the Peacock Angel replied, "How can I submit to another being?! I am from your illumination while Adam is made of dust." God applauded his wisdom and thus made him leader of all the angels on the Earth.[82] God could have forced him submit to Adam, but rather he tested the perfection of Taus Melek by giving him the choice. Because he passed this test, the Yezidis respect Taus Melek and praise his majestic nature, which demonstrated the *zanista ciwaniyê*, or "knowledge of the sublime."[83]

This Creation story suggests that Yezidism is a religion of choice. While it is monotheistic there is a strong dualistic element to it. Light and dark are part of the same equation. All people have good and evil inside them, the Yezidis say, and our choices are made, free of external temptation. Given a commandment by his Maker to bow down to Adam, Taus Melek refused. Rather than being sent to hell, however, he descended to Earth. Some narratives say that Taus Melek incarnated as a human sheikh and prophet. There is no hellfire and brimstone. Through metempsychosis, or the transmigration of the soul at death, one becomes purified, thus there is no need for punishment. The idea encourages one to take the opportunity to change in a future life.

A second story tells us that each of the seven archangels endowed the first human with the physical senses to experience life. One angel gave Adam an ear; one gave him eyes. Another angel gave him a nose; another angel gave him a mouth, and so on. Yet physical sensation and form alone offer nothing more than a lifeless heap without a soul, so Taus Melek transmitted to him the breath of life.[84]

Then Adam stood, and Taus Melek quickly spun him about to face the sun, saying that this being of light exceeded the power of any angel. He told Adam to praise the sun daily as a symbol of the Supreme God. Taus Melek gave him the words to use. This beautiful prayer, called the Song of the Commoner, follows the pattern of the gnostic call to awaken daily from a slumber of the senses to the world of spiritual light. For thousands of years, Yezidi men have gathered just before sunrise to turn and sing to the sun, calling on believers to awaken.[85]

Shamsis and Angelic Singers

The Yezidi singers to the sun are sometimes called *shamsis*. That is also the name of the twelfth-century Persian poet and spiritual teacher Shams-i Tabrīzī, who taught and influenced the famous poet Jalāl al-Dīn Rūmī. Much of Rumi's poetry refers to his beloved friend simply as Shams. For the forty days that the Iranian traveling merchant captured the mind and imagination of the bookish Rumi, the illiterate spiritual master taught the snobbish poet many lessons on how to be humble. He showed Rumi how to see through the veils of illusion and to become drunk on the love of God.[86] Given the time and place of initial introduction in Konya, Iran, in 1244 CE at the height of the Silk Road's popularity as a trade route, it is possible that Shams-i Tabrīzī taught Rumi the Yezidi mysteries through the oral tradition.

Both Yezidi and Sufi prayer chants inspire one to awaken to an ecstatic love of God. The qawl known as the Song of the Commoner, as mentioned above, encourages one to rise well before dawn when, the song says, one can hear "a voice coming from high in the middle of the night; it is clearly the voice of the beyond." A cockerel, or singing bird, calls out from the High Throne. This bird accompanies "the pre-eternal Angel . . . the Greatest Angel" who is Taus Melek. The voice is that of God's revered vice-regent on Earth who brings a "gnosis in the creation myth of Adam." The word for the *commoner* who hears this song might also be translated as "soldier," just as Christian hymns metaphorically speak of the Christian soldier who fights a spiritual battle against the temptations of the unseen world as well as one's own demons.[87]

This enigmatic singing of angels at night echoes a similar American story from the Christian sect known as the Shakers. One summer night in 1837, while the children of Watervliet, New York, readied themselves for bed, they fell into trance and began to sing the most unusual songs together. Their parents asked where they had learned such beautiful singing, and the children answered that the angels had taught them the songs while they visited with them in Spirit Land.[88] Amazingly, these two similar stories, one from America and one from ancient Persia, corroborate each other, yet neither had any way of knowing about the other.

Plate 1. Isis

Often depicted as winged, Isis also appears in a spiritualized human form. Is she a goddess, angel, or *ishta devata*? In this image, Isis appears in a glade of light surrounded by other spiritual beings. In the Egyptian hieroglyphs the names of both Isis and her husband, Osiris, are written using the symbol of the throne. The artist of this painting said other spirit images began to make themselves known to her after the painting was completed. She later adapted the image to reflect the spiritual nature of the appearance of the other beings. Meaning derives from perception, and perceptions shift.

Pastel and gouache on paper; © Cosima Lukashevitz, 2008

Plate 2. The Tree of Life

Angels attend the Tree of Life. Some kabbalists assert that an angel's name appears on each leaf of that tree. Says the artist of her work, "The Kabbalah is a stunning matrix for organizing and synthesizing cosmic knowledge. The Tree of Life certainly is central to much of the imagery, and we see her in so many forms—animal, vegetable, and mineral." This image speaks to the ascending ladder of consciousness, and that of the human form ensnared—from Osiris to Odin—within the tree.

Mixed media on canvas; © Kristina Sebenick Ellis, 2016

Plate 3. Seraphim
Byzantine mosaic seraphim like this one fly about the ceiling of the Hagia Sophia
on their six wings. These red-brown angels are known as "the burning ones"
because they are the angels who fly closest to the Throne of God. Built in the
ninth century, Hagia Sophia variously has been a cathedral of the Orthodox
Christian faith, an Islamic mosque, and a UNESCO art museum—all of which
points to the interfaith nature of angels. © Bigstock

Plate 4. Thrones

In ancient Egypt the hieroglyph of the eye above the throne symbolized
the divine, watchful, and omnipresent power of Osiris over all the
universe. This solar eye in its burst of light appears over the altar
of Saint Mary's Hanging Church in Cairo. Jews, Christians, Hindus,
and Buddhists refer to the all-seeing eye as the power of their God.
The mason saw God as architect of the universe and has used the
iconography as a sign of spiritual illumination. Photo by Greg Zeman

Plate 5. Jesus Ministered to by Angels

Following his deprivations in the wilderness, Jesus received the care
of angels who restored his strength. Nineteenth-century French
painter James Tissot insisted on healing through the otherworldly
agency of indigo-hued, flame-haired angels extending their fingers to
touch the prostrate form of the exhausted Jesus.

James Tissot (French 1836–1902). *Jesus Ministered to by Angels* [*Jésus
assisté par les anges*], 1886–1894. Opaque watercolor over graphite on
gray wove paper, image: 6¹¹⁄₁₆ x 9¾ in. (17 x 24.8 cm).
Brooklyn Museum

Plate 6. Archangel Michael

The archangel Michael, who defends the weak and protects the faithful, appears in all three Abrahamic religions. In the book of Revelation he leads legions of angels onward to destroy the tribe of fallen angels led by Lucifer Morning Star. An embodiment of evil, Lucifer or Satan is depicted as the dragon of darkness. This Michael appears in the courtyard of the Coptic church, Saint Mary's Hanging Church in Cairo. Photo by Greg Zeman

Plate 7. Archangel Gabriel

The angel Jibrīl (Gabriel) was a constant companion to Mohammed; he was also the messenger who dictated the Qur'an. This particular image is from an illustrated Ethiopian book of scripture.

Art by Muhammad ibn Muhammad Shakir (ca. the thirteenth century); photo by the Walters Art Museum, Baltimore

Plate 8. Ascension of the Prophet Muhammad into Heaven

After a night ride on a spirit horse, Muhammad is greeted in heaven
by a throng of angels. Traditional Islamic art dictates that the image of
Muhammad cannot be depicted, thus an angel's wing shades his face.

Art by Nur-al-Din (Persian, ca. 1492);
photo by the Walters Art Museum, Baltimore

Plate 9. Jacob's Dream

This original painting by Jusepe de Ribera and entitled *Jacob's Dream* resides in the Museo Nacional del Prado, Spain. Originally it didn't feature the angels or their ladder, instead depicting a yellow column of light. The painting was done in 1639 and two centuries later the French lithographer L. Caracciolo added the ladder full of colorful angels to it. *Jacob's Dream* reveals angels ascending and descending this heavenly ladder of consciousness that connects the upper and lower realms. At present this image hangs in the Chapel at Camp Chesterfield, Indiana.

Courtesy of the Indiana Association of Spiritualists

Plate 10. Hindu Goddesses

Three "Shakti" devata embody the divine feminine energy that activates the cosmos. Kali, the central goddess, wearing a pyramid of animal heads, squats on a jackal and dominates the nearly obscured form of the god Shiva below her. To her left a dark blue Kali stands upon a male corpse. To the right, Durga and her lion vanquish the buffalo demon. They represent the powers of mastering negativity before the creative life force can continue.

Nepalese, 1800s, opaque watercolor on cotton; photo by the Walters Art Museum, Baltimore

Plate 11. Mount Meru

Mount Meru, also called Sumeru, is the sacred five-peaked mountain
of Hindu, Jain, and Buddhist cosmologies. Considered to be the
center of all the physical, metaphysical, and spiritual universes, it is
written that the sun, along with all the planets, circles the mountain.
Many famous Buddhist, Jain, and Hindu temples have been built as
symbolic representations of this mountain.

Thanka of Mount Meru and the Buddhist Universe, nineteenth century,
Trongsa Dzong, Trongsa, Bhutan

Plate 12. Urvashi and Pururavas

Most beautiful of all the apsaras in Indra's court, Urvashi descended to Earth and married King Pururavas. She captured his heart, and he hers. Theirs was a great love between a mortal and a celestial, but the gods became jealous of them and tricked her into returning to heaven.

Oil on canvas, by Raja Ravi Varma

Plate 13. Cherubim Tetramorph

The Cherubim Tetramorph offers an unusual synthesis of Christian iconography melded with Mesopotamian symbolism. The identifiable animals of the cherubim allude to the Gospel evangelists Matthew (man), Mark (lion), Luke (bull), and John (eagle), and to the zodiac signs Aquarius, Leo, Taurus, and Scorpio, respectively. These are not four separate angels, but one cherub as defined by John in Ezekiel 10:14: "Each of the cherubim had four faces: One face was that of a cherub, the second the face of a human being, the third the face of a lion, and the fourth the face of an eagle" (KJV). Sixteenth-century fresco, Meteora, Thessaly, Greece

Plate 14. Ahura Mazda

Initially appearing during the Achaemenid period (ca. 550 BCE) during the reign of Darius I, images of Ahura Mazda, the good being, are found at a most impressive mountain cliff monument at Behistan (present-day Iran). His name means "light and wisdom," and he often appears flying aloft in a winged disc. The image of a winged Ahura Mazda is seen as a *fravashi*. © Bigstock

Plate 15. Egyptian Ba
The eternal *ba* soul of the ancient Egyptians bore the face of the individual in life. Its hawk wings carried it in and out of heaven and anywhere on earth. Here the image adorns the wooden Coffin of Nesykhonsu (ca. 976–889 BCE). Two of Nesykhonsu's titles, "Lady of the House" and "Singer of the Choir of Mut the Great," are painted on the outside of the coffin.
Gift of the John Huntington Art and Polytechnic Trust; photo by the Cleveland Museum of Art

Plate 16.
Ethiopian Angel
In this image, an angel of the Coptic tradition appears as a winged face. This cherubim flies about the ceiling of Debre Berham Selassie, an Ethiopian Orthodox church built in the seventeenth century. In similar fashion do the winged, human-headed ba souls appear in the tombs and temples of ancient Egypt.

Photo by Willem Proos; © Travel-Pictures-Gallery.com

Plate 17. Taus Melek, the Yezidi Peacock Angel
Taus Melek is the creator angel of the Yezidis who appears
in the form of a brilliant peacock, feathers spread in a broad array of
rainbow colors. He is the progenitor of the Lalish community,
and considered God's greatest angel.
Mixed media collage; © Gina Morales, 2022

Plate 18. Yamantaka, Destroyer of the God of Death

Yamantaka is the wrathful protector of Buddhism. His awesome presence, unfurled in the
dimly lit interior of a Tibetan monastery, reminds one of the violent aspect of the
Bodhisattva Manjushri, who assumes this form to vanquish Yama, the god of death.
By defeating Yama, the cycle of rebirths (samsara) that prevents enlightenment is broken.
Yamantaka, who shares many attributes with Mahakala, is identified by his dark blue skin
and the array of attributes displayed here. He is encircled by five smaller manifestations,
each meant to depict a Yama-conqueror riding a buffalo.

Distemper on cloth, Tibetan, early eighteenth century; photo by the
Metropolitan Museum of Art. Purchase, Florance Waterbury Bequest, 1969

Plate 19. The Angels Munkar and Nakīr

Munkar and Nakīr, twin angels of death in the Islamic tradition, test the faith
of the deceased in their tombs. The angels ask the dead men to identify
Mohammed. The righteous will know him as the messenger of Allah and may
then rest in peace until Judgment Day. Infidels and sinners will find themselves
unable to reply. As a result, the two angels will beat the person every day
except Friday, for as long as Allah deems necessary.

Art by Muhammad ibn Muhammad Shakir; photo by
the Walters Art Museum, Baltimore

Plate 20. Michael/Samael

Samael is the twin of the archangel Michael, and one of the seven great
archangels of the Talmudic tradition. These angels represent the forces
of creation and destruction in the universe. Samael is both beautiful and
terrifying, both good and evil. He is his father's beloved son, an angel in the
garden, father of the Nephilim and the fallen angel Lucifer Morning Star.

Collage of found and silk-screened papers, ink, and acrylic paint;
© Cosima Lukashevitz, 2011

Plate 21. Night with her Train of Stars

Based on a poem by W. E. Henley, the painting *Night with her Train of Stars* depicts the angel of death enfolding a child in her arms and carrying her off to eternal sleep. With her finger to her lips the angel hushes the singing cherubim (the stars) who throng around her. The blue clothing, crown, and infant allude to the Virgin Mary.

Art by Edward Robert Hughes, 1912; photo by the Birmingham Museums Trust

Plate 22. Raziel, Angel of Mystery

This angel's name means "God is my mystery." Raziel knew the secrets of God—all the magic, the sacred geometry, mystical sciences, alchemy of creation and destruction, and so on. Raziel wrote it all down in a book called *Sefer Raziel HaMalakh* to cheer Adam after his dismissal from Eden.

Collage of assorted found and silk-screened papers, photocopied patterns, and acrylic and gouache paint; © Cosima Lukashevitz, 2013

Plate 23. The Gift of Compassion
The artist saw this angel as the cosmic force of compassion available to the Earth, a sacred gift to the world that transforms everyone who is open to her presence. This angel is unnamed by the artist, yet offers us a vision of a benevolent cosmic presence.
Oil on canvas; © Victoria Wilson-Jones, 2021

Plate 24. Metatron

It is thought that Metatron walked Earth as the prophet Enoch before
being raised to angel status in heaven. Metatron is said to control the
Tree of Life, but his most famous symbol is the one that bears his name—
Metatron's Cube, featured here. For those interested in sacred geometry,
this symbol acts as a metaphor for the known universe, and how
everything—no matter how seemingly small or insignificant—is connected.
Thirteen layers of laser-cut, ⅛-inch white birch plywood with wood stains;
© Gabriel Schama, 2016

Plate 25. NASA Star Angel Galaxy

The bipolar star-forming region, called Sharpless 2-106, resembles a soaring, celestial angel. It lies nearly two thousand light years from us. Twin lobes of super-hot gas, glowing blue in this image, stretch outward from the central star, creating the "wings" of our angel.

NASA Hubble Heritage Project photo, NASA Goddard Space Flight Center, February 2011; © NASA, ESA, and the Hubble Heritage Team (STScI/AURA)

A Zoroastrian tenet insists that at dawn angels are commanded to turn east, face the rising sun, and praise God. During their worship Adam and his descendants everywhere must recite the same words given to them by Taus Melek. He spoke the holy words in seventy-two languages—one language for each of the seventy-two sons destined to be born of Adam, and the seventy-two daughters born of Adam and Eve who would populate the seventy-two regions of Earth. The Peacock Angel promised Adam that, in time, if he and his children continued their righteous living, they would see and know the Supreme God personally. Meanwhile Taus Melek would protect and teach them, although he lived in another dimension.[89]

Descendants of Angels

One key idea from Genesis is the idea that because God commanded Taus Melek and the other angels to create humans from the elements, fashioning their body parts, Adam and Eve became divine creatures. They are not evolved from the natural world.[90] The Yezidis believe themselves to be the progeny of an angel. Remember that in the Zoroastrian tradition, the term *yazata* indicates an "angel being." This linguistic link underscores the angelic heritage of the Yezidis. The tribe submits only to the commands of God and their archangelic overseer Taus Melek. The Yezidi claim to be descended from Adam through his son Shehid bin Jer, rather than through the womb of Eve—a kind of paternal immaculate conception. This son married a houri (a beautiful heavenly woman) and from their union descended the race of Yezidis, which makes them more angelic than other mortals because the Peacock Angel created Adam himself.[91]

A heretical secret lies at the core of their tradition: the same angelic spirit who blew the breath of life into Adam conceived the Yezidis. For this reason, as we have mentioned previously but bears repeating here, the Yezidis prohibit marrying outside of their tribe, and to preserve their true beliefs, they limit contact with outsiders. In addition, because they are descended from Adam, their religion is the oldest original religion in the world. The Creation myth of the pearl and of Taus Melek creating a world of rainbow colors makes him the true author and ruler of the universe. Once he arrived on Earth, he created a governing board of directors and, since that time, has ruled the world from an etheric dimension.[92]

The author Manly P. Hall described the same secret Yezidi school that G. I. Gurdjieff encountered during his travels through the Caucasus Mountains, which are located at the intersection of Asia and Europe. Hall described the beliefs about the creation of creatures of light. He said: "Some secret orders have taught that the sun was inhabited by a race of creatures with bodies composed of a radiant, spiritual ether not unlike in its constituency the actual glowing ball of the sun itself. . . . These creatures resemble miniature suns, being a little larger than a dinner plate in size, although some of the more powerful are considerably larger. Their color is the golden white light of the sun, and from them emanate four streamers of [energy] often of great length and [in] constant motion."[93]

Hall proposed that the greatest, most luminous sphere of light was the archangel Michael, who was responsible for "the entire order of solar life, which resemble him and dwell upon the sun." These spirits of the light are identified by modern Christians as being archangels.[94] Still, this solar light of angels has been linked to Lucifer as a fallen angel. The name Lucifer, of course, indicates that he originated in the light.

We can see similar narratives to those of Taus Melek appear in several religious traditions from East Asia to Egypt. One native Yezidi named Salem (whom ethnographer Sami Ahmed called "the most truthful man humanity ever had") told the following story.

There appeared an angel in Yazd (a city in Iran) at a time where all the Shams (sun worshippers) were scattered in all lands . . . He laid down a formidable foundation when he said: "God is one, God is light, God is the crown of the heads." The Shamsies [sic] believed in this mission. He laid the foundation stone for Jerusalem, lived in Shechem and appeared in Egypt and Yemen. News of his might reached India, China and the West, and every citizen claimed that he appeared in his land. He is one of God's names of mercy; he appeared in Yazd . . . He is Taus Melek who appeared on Earth. At the date of this narrative, the Yezidi religion was stronger than it is now, and the Shamsies [sic] considered the religion of Mohammed as inferior.[95]

The angel incarnate of whom Salem speaks is likely Adi ibn Musafir, the twelfth-century Sufi master who attained a saintly status among the Yezidis, and the status of infidel among the Muslims. Such is the way one religion demonizes another's beliefs. Christians and pagans incorporated each other's ideas, evolving offshoot sects that were later deemed heretical. And what does this have to do with angels? More than we realize. The one thing most religions agree upon is the belief in angelic beings—messengers from God who respond to directives from the Divine Intelligence of the universe and who created them before the Earth began.

In addition to the proximity of the two cultures, the Yezidi and the Muslim, other possible connections suggest that the ancient Egyptians and the Yezidis shared a similar religious philosophy. Many Yezidi philosophies appear in gnostic and Coptic manuscripts in Nag Hammadi, but let us use only the linguistic connections here. The title of the Yezidi holy *Black Book,* Meshefê Re, which details the creation of the world through the essential light of the sun and Taus Melek, translates in the ancient Kemetic language of Egypt as "Mesh-f Re" or "Birth of the Sun." The sacred light that descends to Earth as angels or as reincarnated ascended masters are called khas.

A kha, sometimes an akh, in the Kemetic language of Egypt means a highly developed spiritual consciousness equivalent to the God spark. In ancient Egypt the predynastic rulers called Shemsu Hor, or followers of Horus, were known as the "Shining Ones of the Light," just as the followers of the rising sun in the Yezidi tradition were called "Shamsi." How old are the Shemsu Hor? The Egyptians believed their legendary predynastic rulers appeared around 30,000 BCE. In the beginning, seven sages appeared before the first Shemsu Hor to set forth the divine plan.[96]

4
Dark Angels

When the angel of death approaches, he is terrible.
When he reaches you, it is bliss.

MUSLIM SAYING

ANGELS OF DEATH

In addition to angels of light, adversarial angels fly into our lives on dark wings; they are the fallen ones and the angels of death. Many tales about the angel of death appear in the Abrahamic faiths. Only a few appear in the Eastern traditions of Buddhism and Hinduism—although they do appear. This may be because the Eastern traditions focus less on the personal story; physical life has less importance than spiritual life. Judeo-Christian stories offer stories of prophets who never died, but simply ascended into heaven.

And yet in both traditions individuals may transcend death. One such story appears in the Mahabharata. A childless couple prayed to Shiva for an offspring. Their request would be granted conditionally. Either their son would be born with a long life but limited intelligence, or he would be born with great brilliance but a short life. The couple chose the latter. Having mastered the Vedas and Shastras, their son became a great devotee of Lord Shiva. His devotion endeared him to all, but as he grew closer to his death date, his parents grew despondent. When he asked them why, they replied sadly that he would die at sixteen years. But Markandeya assured his parents that he would perform severe penances to win over death, as the following tells us.

> He then began his prayers near the Shiva Linga. When the attendants of Yama came at the ordained time to take his life, they found that they could not approach him due to the heat of his penances. Then Yama himself came and when he threw his loop over Markandeya's neck, Lord Shiva emerged from the Linga and pierced Yama with his trident. Pleased with Markandeya's devotion, he then blessed him with deathlessness and everlasting youth. At the request of all the Gods, Lord Shiva then revived Yama. Sage Markandeya is one of the Chiranjeevis (immortals) who are still said to be living in the Himalayas, guiding people towards the Godward path.[1]

Rather than trying to insert a magical spell for beating death, the story demonstrates the power of great devotion to the Deva. Because all living forms die, death is a part of the transmigration of the soul when the spirit transfers its energy to another life. Buddhists and Hindus say that occurs in one of six separate planes (three fortunate and three unfortunate). While no particular angel of death appears in the Eastern traditions, there are entities who show themselves in the three realms of samsara as heavenly beings, demigods, humans, animals, ghosts, and demons. At death the human soul may enter one of these six realms. The cycle of repeating life and death (samsara) ends when a person attains nirvana, casting off all desires and attaining true insight into impermanence and nonself reality.[2]

Eastern Devata of Death

Hindus suggest that the apsara scoop up the bodies of slain war heroes to carry them off to heaven.[3] Dying in battle, defending homeland and faith, allows the soul to bypass the samsaric cycle of death and rebirth. It jettisons these souls straight into eternity. The Lord of

Death, Yama, bears a likeness to the Egyptian Osiris, the first man-god to ever live and die. He thus entered the underworld where he reigned thereafter. A fearful figure to some, he had assimilated death to himself.[4]

Yet Yama can be propitiated. In the *Katha-Upanishad,* Yama tells a little boy named Nachiketa that "man must not fear anyone, anything, not even death, because the true essence of man, his Atman, is neither born nor dies. He is eternal, he is Brahman."[5]

Silk Road Lords of Death

The Yezidi religion maintains similar ideas to the Buddhist concept of nonpermanence and Zoroastrian ideas about dualism. As we have learned, the Yezidi view death as no more than a changing of clothes. Along the Silk Road, however, an identifiable angel of death appears. Life and death are the right and left hands of God. According to the Yezidi tradition, on Sunday, the first day of Creation, God created two beings—Taus Melek, the Peacock Angel charged with giving life to all on the planet, and Azrael, the angel of death, who appears to be Azar'il and Azazel in the Islamic and Judeo-Christian traditions.[6]

To Yezidis the angel of death waits just inside the holy Yezidi sanctuary in the mountain valley of Lalish, Iraq. On the right of the main sanctuary door, Azrael, the angel of death, stands beside a dark pool of water. In this pool of water, symbolic of his sacred lake, Azrael washes his sword after taking a soul. Others claim that this is where Azrael brings the souls of the dead to be judged.[7]

Zoroastrians deemed all life to be dually influenced, comprised of good thoughts and bad thoughts, positives and negatives, life and death. Death came into being because of the enmity of Ahura Mazda and Angra Mainyu, his counterpart, and these are states of mind, states of being. Describing them only as God and the Devil may be a little simplistic. Whether they are dueling angels or demigods is up for discussion. In the Zoroastrian belief system, we find that death and the devil (an evil being) are not the same thing. Death is simply a process.

In the Zoroastrian faith, certain angels assist the soul in transition. In the Persian tradition Yima governed the land of the dead. Yima resembles the deva Yama in the Upanishads. One legend says that Ahura Mazda gave Yima a chance to rule on Earth, but he declined. So Ahura Mazda made him a king of the underworld. A story in the Vendidad Sata tells us: "Yima did as Ahura Mazda wished; he crushed the Earth with a stamp of his heel, he kneaded it with his hands, as the potter does when he kneads the potter's clay."[8] Then the *Zend Avesta* describes what Yima did in the world he created.

> There he brought the seeds of every kind of tree, of the highest of size and sweetest of odor on this earth; there he brought the seeds of every kind of fruit, the best of savor and sweetest of odor. All those seeds he brought, two of every kind, to be kept inexhaustible there, so long as those men shall stay in the Vara.
>
> And there were no humpbacked, none bulged forward there; no impotent, no lunatic; no one malicious, no liar; no one spiteful, none jealous; no one with decayed tooth, no leprous to be pent up, nor any of the brands wherewith Angra Mainyu stamps the bodies of mortals.[9]

According to the Zoroastrian faith, the newly dead soul perceived certain beings who would help it through the confused state of death. Two of these ministering angels, Sraosha and Rashnu, appeared in the other world. The guardian angel Sraosha accompanied the soul across the bridge into the afterworld. Once in the judgment hall, Rashnu held a set of scales that weighed the soul's thoughts, words, and deeds—the good on one side, the bad on the other.[10] Rashnu's scales resemble the scales of the goddess Ma'at in the Egyptian underworld (called Restau*), where the heart, or seat of consciousness, must balance against the feather of truth.

---

*In ancient Egypt, Restau represents the astral plane between life and the realm of the dead. Sometimes it appears as the underworld, or the land of the gods.

Islamic Angels of Death

Jews, Christian Gnostics, and Muslims suggest various appearances for the angel of death—Azazel, Azazil, or Azarail.[11] Compared to the Zoroastrian angels of death, Azazel appears less abstract. In other words, the angel of death has a recognizable presence. Sometimes stories of its appearance may take surprising turns.

Several stories in the Qur'an identify an angel of death named Melek al-Mawt. On the palms of that angel's hands appear letters of light that read: "In the Name of God, Most Merciful, Most Beneficent." By showing an individual these letters of light, the angel withdraws the soul from the body "like drawing an element to a magnet."[12]

Two other Islamic angels appear—Munkar and Nakir—whose names mean "the denier" and "the denied." The hair of both angels is fine and long. They wear garments made of blue light. With their diamond eyes they shoot forth lightning bolts and their voices roar loud as thunder. These two angels resemble the Zoroastrian twin beings who attend one's death and judgment. The Qur'an (Surat al-An'am 6:111) says that God sends Munkar and Nakir to test the faith of both believers and nonbelievers when they enter the grave. In this way, we find out if the soul is destined for heaven or condemned to constriction in an eternal grave.

Sufi Ali ibn Abi Talib tells the story of how when Umar ibn al Khattab, the second caliph of Islam, died and was buried, the two angels appeared. They carried with them garments of light in which to robe the caliph, depending, of course, on the outcome of the pious man's answers to their questions.

"Who is your Lord?" they asked.

He replied: "Why are you asking me? Don't you know who is my Lord—and yours?" But because God had created them to be inquisitors at the grave, they insisted that they had to ask him the questions. So they asked again. Umar ibn al Khattab responded by punching one angel in the eye and kicking the other, shouting, "How dare you ask me? I have just come to the grave a short while ago, and you have come such a very long way. Go back to where you came from and ask yourselves!"[13]

Even great prophets do not want to take their fates lying down.

The following story from the Hadith shows an argument between Moses and an unnamed angel of death.

> The Angel of Death was sent to Moses. When he arrived, Moses punched him in the eye. The Angel returned to his Lord and said, "You have sent me to a slave who does not want to die." God said, "Return to him and tell him to put his hand on the back of an ox and for every hair that will come under it, he will be granted one year of life." Moses said, "O Lord! What will happen after that?" God replied, "then death." Moses said, "Let it come now!" Moses then requested God to let him die close to the Holy Land so that he would be at a distance of a stone's throw from it (Hadith 4:619).

In yet another poignant story, a beggar approached a proud king, who appeared sumptuously dressed and rode an equally sumptuously outfitted horse through his kingdom. The dirty beggar rushed up from the roadside to speak to the king. Grabbing the horse's bridle, he demanded an audience then and there. As much as the king tried to dismiss him, the beggar held tight and would not relinquish the bridle. "You must hear my request," he rasped.

"What is your request?" the king asked.

"Bend down and let me whisper it in your ear," said the beggar, "for it is secret."

Somewhat irritated, the king leaned down to hear the man whisper: "I am the angel of death." The king stammered and asked to go home so that he could tell his family goodbye and wrap up his affairs, but Azra'il, the angel, said: "By the one who sent me, you will never see your family and your wealth in this world again!" He took his soul there and then, and the king fell from his horse like a wooden log.[14]

The Angels of Death as Archangels

In Islam Azrael (Azra'il) attains archangel status alongside Gabriel (Jibrīl), Michael (Mikhail), and Israfil. (While not an angel seen attending one's deathbed, Israfil blows the trumpet at the end of time.) To the faithful, death shows an angelic face because it signifies a return to God. Each soul is a tiny leaf on the Tree of Life in Islam. It is believed that that leaf will wilt forty days before the intended date of a person's death. Although one may still feel vibrant and active, Azra'il choses which leaf will fall when. He also chooses a form in which to appear to that individual when the time comes, and no one else will be able to see him. Allah may claim the soul, but the angel of death and his helpers release the soul from its body.[15]

Others say Azrael is a form of Raphael, the angel of healing. Wearing a million veils, he shows four faces: one looks ahead, one looks behind, one looks above, and one looks below. Seventy-four thousand wings cover his body, which is vaster than heaven and covered with eyes—a description that is reminiscent of the thousand eyes of the Yezidi Peacock Angel. Whenever Azrael blinks one of his eyes, a creature dies.[16]

Sometimes Azra'il appears in the guise of a stranger in much the same way that the beggar appeared to the king. No matter his appearance, the angel of death is not easily distracted from his task. He cannot be refused, deterred, tricked, or cajoled to wait; yet how we choose to live our lives determines how the angel's message is delivered. When Azra'il appeared to one devout Muslim, the believer welcomed him with a loving greeting. The angel gave him a choice as to how he wished to die, "for I have been ordered to ask you." The pious man asked to pass while praying two cycles of prayer and to die in a pose of prostration. The angel granted his request.[17] The best deaths, Shaykh Kabbani says, are those when the mystic recognizes the angel and declares, "Here I am! I was waiting for you."[18]

Not all who die do so willingly. One epic Turkish tale of dissent from the tenth or eleventh century recounts the story of Dede Korkut, a brave warrior to whom God sent Azra'il. Not recognizing the stranger, Dede Korkut commanded that the brash visitor who had stalked him be caught. At that moment Azra'il flew away like a bird. Outraged, Dede Korkut sent his soldiers in hot pursuit, chasing after the strange bird.

When he tried to follow, he became lost in the forest. Suddenly the angel appeared before him. "I've got you now!" exclaimed Dede Korkut.

"No," said the angel, "I've got you!" The angel knocked him to the ground and jumped on his chest.

Feeling weak, the warrior cried out, "What did you do to me?"

Azra'il announced himself and told Dede Korkut to prepare for death. Although the warrior pleaded with the angel, the angel assured him that he could not change God's command. "I am a creature like you, and I only follow orders from the Almighty."

There and then, Dede Korkut asked God to forgive his boasting. At that point God decided to let the warrior live *if* he could find someone to take his place. Dede Korkut first asked his elderly father, then his elderly mother. Not ready for death, both declined to die in his stead. Saddened, Dede Korkut went home to bid his wife goodbye, saying that he must die because none would take his place.

His wife cried, "O my beloved husband! Why didn't you ask me? I am happy to give you what even your father and mother cannot give you. Take my life so that yours can be spared."

Hearing this, Dede Korkut wept piteously. Turning to God, he pleaded, "O my Lord! Forgive me. Take my life and spare my wife, for she is worthier and braver than me." Pleased with this prayer, God spared both Dede Korkut and his wife. Instead, God took both parents, as they had already lived long, happy lives.[19]

Not an evil entity, Azaz'il, the angel servant of God, simply performs his job. In fact, he may be one of God's most loved and respected servants. Just as the Yezidis say that God created Taus Melek and Azrael on the same day, so Azaz'il assisted God during the creation of man. At the time that God created Adam he asked his angels to gather some clay from the Earth. Yet each angel came back empty-handed saying that the Earth itself had refused to give up its clay to make any being who would one day be punished.* Finally, God sent Azra'il, who told the Earth "Obedience to God is better than obedience to you." Therefore, he took the clay from the reluctant Earth, and to this clay God added water and made Adam.[20]

Sometimes other angels besides Azaz'il arrive to attend a death. When the time came for Mohammed to transition, so legends tell us, he had just delivered his final lecture in the courtyard. Feeling faint, the prophet asked his attendants to carry him inside. When he felt death upon him, Mohammed prayed: "O Lord, I beseech Thee, assist me in the agonies of death." It was not Azaz'il who came for him, but an old friend. Almost in a whisper, gazing into the face of one whom only he could see, he repeated three times: "Gabriel, come close unto me."[21]

Deaths of the Jewish Patriarchs

The Jewish Azazel resembles Islam's Azaz'il. With as many eyes on his wings as there are people on Earth, Azazel keeps watch over every one of us, and records our deeds in his book of Records.[22] Jewish mystics count him as a fallen demonic angel, but Sufi sheikhs depict the angel's arrival in whatever form fits the individual.

Another angel of death may be Samael. He planted the Tree of Good and Evil in Eden, then slithered into the garden as the serpent that tempted Eve. At the moment she tasted the apple taken from the tree planted by Samael, Eve knew death.[23] A red-haired seducer of Adam's two wives, Lilith and Eve, Samael achieves the status of chief rogue among the angels. Called "the poison of God," Jewish lore clearly assigns to Samael the duties of *ha-satan,* "chief of the satans." In this regard, Samael is synonymous with Satan. The Zohar points to Samael as the likely wrestler with Jacob. Perhaps, some say, he suggested that Abraham sacrifice his son Isaac, although other likely candidates for the task are Michael, Uriel, and Metatron.[24]

---

*I am fascinated that the Earth itself already knew the fate of Adam before God made him. Equally fascinating, clashing motivations seem to separate heaven and earth before the first man appeared. Apparently, in this case, the angel must choose whom to obey.

Islamic and Hebrew scriptures share many of the same patriarchs. The deaths of Abraham, Moses, and King David arise in the sacred texts of both religions, although not necessarily in the same way. In Jewish legend God commanded Metatron to conduct Moses through the mansions of heaven where Moses acquired his gift of prophecy.

> In the last (seventh) heaven Moses saw two angels, each five hundred parasangs in height, forged out of chains of black fire and red fire, the angels Af, "Anger," and Hemah, "Wrath," whom God created at the beginning of the world, to execute His will. Moses was disquieted when he looked upon them, but Metatron embraced him, and said, "Moses, Moses, thou favorite of God, fear not, and be not terrified," and Moses became calm. There was another angel in the seventh heaven, different in appearance from all the others, and of frightful mien. His height was so great, it would have taken five hundred years to cover a distance equal to it, and from the crown of his head to the soles of his feet he was studded with glaring eyes. "This one," said Metatron, addressing Moses, "is Samael, who takes the soul away from man." "Whither goes he now?" asked Moses, and Metatron replied, "To fetch the soul of Job the pious." Thereupon Moses prayed to God in these words, "O may it be Thy will, my God, and the God of my fathers, not to let me fall into the hands of this angel."[25]

Exactly how Moses died is not revealed. The Hebrew scriptures and the Torah say only that he climbed to the top of Mount Nebo in the Abarim Range in Jordan, across from Jericho. He viewed Canaan, the land to be given to the Israelites, and then died at 120 years of age. Muslim author Muhammad al-Tabarí tells a different story, one of Moses preparing for death with the angels.

> The chosen one of God went out from that trellis of his one day for some need, and not one of God's creatures was aware of him. He passed by a small group of angels digging a grave. He recognized

them and approached them, until he stood beside them. He saw the angels digging a grave more beautiful than he had ever seen, nor had he seen the likeness of the greenness, lushness, and beauty that was in it. He said to them, "O angels of God! For whom are you digging this grave?" They replied, "We are digging it for a servant who is esteemed by his Lord." He said, "This servant is surely in a lodging from God that I have never seen the like of before today as a place to lie down or to enter." . . . The angel said to him, "Oh chosen one of God, would you want it to be yours?" He said, "I should like that." They said, "Go down and lie down in it, turn your face to your Lord, and breathe the lightest breath you have ever breathed." He descended, laid down in it, and turned to his Lord. Then he breathed, and God took his soul, whereupon the Angels covered him over.[26]

An old man at the time of his death, Abraham had lived a good life for many years. In al-Tabari's story, the Muslim prophet Abraham encountered on the road a reluctant angel of death, the archangel Michael, who had taken on a human disguise. Not recognizing him, Abraham engaged him in conversation. Al-Tabari writes:

When God wanted to take Abraham's soul, He sent the angel of death to him in the form of a decrepit old man. . . . One day while he was feeding the people, he saw an old man walking in the heat. So, he sent a donkey to him to bring him back so that he could feed him. Whenever the old man picked up a morsel of food and tried to put it in his mouth, he would put it in his eye or his ear and then in his mouth. When it entered his belly, it came out from his posterior. Abraham had asked his Lord not to take his soul until he himself asked Him for death. When he saw the old man's condition, he asked him, "What is the matter with you, O old man, that you do this?" He said, "O Abraham, it is old age." Abraham asked, "How old are you?" He was two years older than Abraham, so Abraham said, "There are only two years between you and me. When I have reached that age, will I become like you?" He answered, "Yes." Abraham said, "My God! Take me to you before that." Then the old man rose and took his soul, for he was the angel of death.[27]

Abraham died at the age of two hundred.

Not all angels of death are alike. Let's look at Samael, a complicated angel of death. Like Satan he tempts and frightens the living, causing them to create strife, sin, and disharmony. His actions oppose life, but he seems to appear on a spectrum of power. In the same way that a temperature may be altered from warm to cool, so at times humans may adjust and manipulate the spectrum of life and death.

For example, there are reports of deathbed contracts and conversions that result in the temporary recovery of an individual. The South is filled with such stories, and one such story that I recall takes place around 1956 in Mississippi. Five brothers, Ted, Jimmie, Charles, Darrel, and Byron Jessup knelt at the bed of their dying mother. Bargaining for the life of their mother, each promised that he would turn his life over to the Lord, if only God would heal her. Well, she lived. All five brothers went on to become gospel preachers, musicians, and religious radio personalities and televangelists. They pronounced healings and supported their ministry on the income from those who also wished to bargain with death. All five preachers ended up in prison convicted of grift, among other criminal behavior that televangelists are wont to commit. And so yes, Samael can be both a deceiver and an angel of death. Death can be coerced to delay, but he can never be fully defeated.

The Jewish legend of King David's death demonstrates an angel of death who appears only to do God's bidding. The Bible recounts that King David died at a ripe old age after declaring his son Solomon king after him. The Muslims tell a different story. Samael becomes a tricky angel of death when he created a ruckus in the garden to lure the pious King David out of his house. Deciding to investigate the noise, David descended the stairway into his garden. The stairs collapsed, killing him. In such a way does Samael use temptations and tricks to lure us away from our lives on Earth.[28]

The Sufis told yet another story about his death. King David, who never failed to lock his house and never allowed a stranger to enter, came home from an errand in town one day to find a man waiting for him. So David asked, "What are you doing here?"

The man replied: "I am the one who needs no permission to enter, who does not fear kings, and whom no one can resist." Then David recognized the stranger as the angel of death and welcomed him, saying, "I was eagerly waiting for the moment when I shall be with my Beloved." At that, the angel took his soul.[29]

Angel of the Day of Judgment

In addition to God's archangels, including Azaz'il and Gabriel, there is another important Islamic dark angel—Israfil. His name means "the burning one." Not a demon, he is the angel who appears at the final Day of Judgment. Imagine him as the ultimate angel of destruction rather than as a personal angel of death. His multiple tongues speak a thousand languages praising God. From his breath, Allah creates thousands and thousands more angels to praise him. Each day Israfil gazes into hell and weeps such copious tears that Allah must stop their flow to keep them from flooding the world. He blows a shofar (a beast's horn) that contains within it a honeycomb of dwelling places. In each cell lie the souls of the dead.[30]

The Sufi scholar Shaykh Kabbani recounts two stories of how the world will end. In one story, he describes how God first created the trumpet and hung it on his throne. Then he created Israfil, who took the trumpet and drilled in it as many holes as the angels and spirits he'd counted in the universe. The trumpet measured seventy thousand light years in length. God said, "When I tell you to blow the trumpet, you will blow it."

Now Israfil stands at the base of God's throne, awaiting his divine orders. One wing touches the edge of the cosmos in the east, and one wing touches the edge in the west. A third wing encompasses the seven earths, and a fourth wing protrudes from the top of his head to protect his eyes from the intense and blinding light of God—

even though between Israfil and God lie seven veils of light.

On Judgment Day, when God orders Israfil to blow the trumpet, at the first sound all bad things will be lifted and carried off from the Earth. All wrongdoing will dissolve and "the heavenly books will shine in every place." Angels will appear on Earth to show the places where those books have been kept in their pristine state. The memory of heavenly teachings will become fresh in people's minds. . . . "[The] angels walk upon the earth for the first time. No one will have power to do any harm in the world. Belief in God and knowledge of spiritual things will become the daily talk of everyone, young and old. Angelic light will increase upon the Earth . . ."

At the second trumpet blast all beings in heaven and earth will fall on their faces in a state of confusion. It is said: "The sound of that trumpet will be so awesome and terrifying that all beings will lose consciousness." As the Earth rolls and heaves, the stars will fall from the sky. The sun, the moon, and all light will disappear as darkness overwhelms everything. Mountains will jump up, and turn to dust clouds that cover the Earth. The oceans will dry up. "Just as wind carries away chaff, so creation will be blown away by those cataclysmic storms."

Angels will bring down garments of light to cover the good people; the wrongdoers they will smite. Upon the third sounding of the trumpet, God will adorn his human beings with angelic power and send them into the throng of His servants. In that everlasting light, they will reach paradise.[31]

The Qur'an draws heavily on Judeo-Christian traditions, so it is no surprise to find in 1 Thessalonians 4:16–17 an accounting of an angel trumpeter who appears at the rapture. "For the Lord Himself will descend from heaven with a shout, with the voice of an archangel, and with the trumpet of God. And the dead in Christ will rise first. Then we who are alive and remain shall be caught up together with them in the clouds to meet the Lord in the air. And thus, we shall always be with the Lord." However, this angel remains unnamed in the accounting. We only know that it is a high-ranking archangel, possibly Gabriel in the role of the prince of Hades.

In a second story, Shaykh Kabbani describes how after nearly all the creatures on Earth have died, God asks Israfil to take the souls of all that remain—every created being.

> Then God asks, "Who is left?"
>
> The angel of death answers, "O my exalted Lord! There is only Michael, Gabriel, and myself left."
>
> God says, "Take the soul of the angel Michael." Then he asks, "Who is left?"
>
> The angel of death says, "O my Lord, only Gabriel and myself are left."
>
> Then God says, "Die, O angel of death." Then God turns to Gabriel and asks, "Who is left, O Gabriel?"
>
> Gabriel answers, "Only Your Face remains, O my Lord, and Gabriel who is dead and extinguished."
>
> God then says to him, "You have to die." And immediately Gabriel falls in prostration, shakes his wings, and dies.
>
> Then God says, "I have created the creation and then I am the one to bring it back." Gabriel will be the second angel to be brought back to life after Israfil who blows the trumpet of resurrection. He will be responsible for the scales of the deeds of human beings on the Day of Judgment.[32]

This story of the death of the world and God's last angel reminds me of the narrative from chapter 175 of the ancient Egyptian Book of the Dead. In it, the god Osiris is told at the end of time that he must remain in the silence and emptiness of the underworld with his father, Atum. "In the end," Atum says, "I will destroy everything that I have created. Earth will become again a part of the primeval ocean like the abyss of waters in their original state. Then I will be what will remain—just I and Osiris—when I have changed myself back into the Old Serpent who knew no man and saw no god."[33]

So it is that angels and demigods play similar roles in the writings of different religions.

Death and the Healing Angels

Often unwelcomed but not unexpected, the angels of death carry healing in their wings. The healing angels Raphael, Gabriel, and Michael sometimes appear as angels of death. Often they are invoked for their healing powers in an effort to forestall what may be an inevitable outcome.

The prophet and patriarch Elijah bypassed death altogether. He ascended into heaven while still alive and became Sandalphon, the angel of life.[34] For his great work on behalf of Yahweh, prohibiting the worship of false gods, Elijah never died but arose into heaven in a chariot of fire. Some angelologists suspect that the God-fearing, raptured Elijah had been an angel all along.[35]

The chief duties of Sandalphon include overseeing the worldly affairs of God's Creation. He gathers all the prayers and petitions, then weaves them into a mystical crown for God. Sandalphon reads the words of each prayer, uttering the charm of transformation, which causes the other angels to cry out "Holy, holy, holy! Lord God of Hosts, Heaven and Earth are full of your glory." Sandalphon is the medium through which prayer gains its efficacy.[36]

He fought Azazel, and staunch angelologists invoked him to raise the dead. Sandalphon would have conquered death except that Yahweh stayed his hand because at the time he had further use of Azazel. According to the Talmudic interpretations of Rabbi Eliezer ben Hyrcanus, "Elijah is the psycho-pomp whose duty is to stand at the crossways of Paradise and guide the pious to their appointed places."[37] At the Passover seder, an empty seat and a cup of wine are left for Elijah, who one day will appear. He is "the expected guest."

Angels of death differ vastly from demons, Rabbi David Cooper says. "Demons can be overpowered by humans." Death, as we know, cannot be denied. Therefore, although some books would list Azazel as a demon, he is not; he simply has the onerous duty of taking a human life.[38] The angels are admonished if they take sides by using death to punish one person more than another. In the rabbinical commentary from the Passover Haggadah (the book of readings for the seder service), for example, the Exodus story depicts angels celebrating the escape of the Jews as the Red Sea closes over the Egyptians in pursuit. God rebukes them saying, "How can you sing when my creatures are drowning?"[39]

Angels of the Christian Scriptures

Strictly Christian angels offer us fewer stories than do Islamic or Jewish angels. Angels only appear eighteen times in the Christian scriptures— mostly to proclaim the birth of prophets, or to give advice, or to solace. None are named or extolled as they are in the Jewish or Islamic canon. In the Christian scriptures the angel of death appears twice—once to Jesus and once to Herod. The two stories, of course, are inexorably intertwined.

In the Gospel of Luke, an angel appears in the Garden of Gethsemane. Jesus asked his disciples to keep watch and pray with him, then he withdrew from them about a stone's throw away. He knelt and asked, "Father, if you are willing, remove this cup from me. Nevertheless, not my will, but yours, be done." And there appeared to him an angel from heaven, strengthening him (Luke 22:43–44 ESV).

Again, praying more earnestly, "his sweat became like great drops of blood falling down to the ground." And when he rose from prayer, he came to the disciples and found them all asleep.

The gospel does not announce this etheric being as the angel of death, and the angel apparently offers no message from God to answer Jesus's fervent prayer. The angel comes simply as a witness to the present situation. Perhaps for this reason, some biblical manuscripts omit verses 43 and 44. Perhaps they found the lack of response to a prayer of such magnitude troubling. As we have seen from authors in other traditions, the angel of death can only speak or do as God directs. While the Christian scriptures give no clues, I suspect this reticent angel is the same spirit being who led Jesus into the desert to be tempted by the devil for forty days before he began this difficult Earth walk (Matthew 4:11).

In both cases, this reticent angel appears in stark contrast to the fallen angel (devil) who talks quite a bit and tempts Jesus in the desert just before he initiates his three-year passion play. That spirit being, too, is a kind of messenger, albeit a fallen angel. Is it even the same angel in Matthew 28 who tells Mary Magdalene, Mother Mary, and Salome that Jesus has risen from the tomb?

When Jesus ascended into heaven in Acts 1:9–11, two beings robed in white accompany him, and they prophesy his return in clouds of glory. While the disciples watched, a cloud enveloped Jesus, and he rose upward out of their sight. The disciples looked steadfastly toward heaven as he disappeared. Suddenly two men stood beside them in white apparel. They inquired, "Ye men of Galilee, why stand ye gazing up into heaven? This same Jesus, which is taken up from you into heaven, shall also come in like manner as ye have seen him go into heaven."

These two white-robed figures appear to be human rather than angels. These spirits may be the only two prophets of Israel assumed wholly into heaven without ever tasting death—Elijah and Enoch. As we saw in our opening hierarchy, these two living souls, carried into heaven, became Sandalphon and Metatron.

Resurrections, assumptions, and heavens as multilayered as wedding cakes seem to abound in theological legends. Father Richard Rohr surmises that people obsess about getting into heaven because they think the universe is divided into separate levels—heaven and earth. "But it is one universe," he says, "and all within it is transmuted and transformed by the glory of God."[40]

This idea of heaven and hell as perceptions is a subject to which we will return.

Rohr exclaims that God's true world has always been here. Rather than focus our eyes ever upward, we should focus on living on Earth as spiritual beings. The angels show us that heaven and earth are the same. Both are states of consciousness created by what we choose to think about. Many of us may hope that good angels will attend us when it is time to cross from the physical into the spiritual. The deeper meaning of what the angels said—"He will come back to you the same way he left"—may be that as we live and die, God needs to be part of our consciousness, no more than a thought away. When the angel of death came for Herod, the vision was not so sweet. Acts 12:21–23 does not say whether it is the angel Samael, Azazel, or Gabriel who stands in the Roman court. Rather, "Herod, arrayed in royal apparel, sat upon his throne and made an oration unto them [the crowd]; the people gave a shout, saying, 'It is the voice of a god, and not of a man.' And immediately the angel of the Lord smote Herod, because the people gave not God the glory: and he was eaten of worms and gave up the ghost" (KJV). A similar story about Herod's death, as told by the Roman-Jewish historian Flavius Josephus, includes the fact that Herod's death occurred coincidentally with a dreaded lunar eclipse.[41]

Josephus categorized the Jews in two sects. The Sadducees, prominent temple priests, did not believe in either the afterlife or the resurrection of the dead. They believed, basically, that after death came nothing. The Pharisees ascribed to Jewish law, and believed souls in heaven resurrected. Some of them, depending upon their contact with the Manicheans and Gnostics, believed people reincarnated many times on Earth.

While the angels of death may appear frightening to us, we must not confuse them with fallen angels or demons. Author Sophy Burnham makes an eloquent distinction: "What demons (real or metaphorical) do is lie and make us think no order exists in the universe beyond our pain and doubt. . . . And if we believe it even for a fraction of a second, we are cast into hell in despair . . . But ah, the bright wings of the Angel of Death; that's another matter."[42]

The angel of death appears in many guises. At age twelve, the musician Johnny Cash witnessed the angel of death come into his room to announce the passing of his older brother Jack. A magnificent aura filled the room. Cash recalled that that same radiance came to him a second time when a faceless being Cash described simply as a brilliant, glowing light announced the death of his friend Jack Horton.[43]

In Egypt, it is the beautiful Isis who enfolds her beloved Osiris in her arms and wraps her wings around him at death. At death, then, one may gaze into the face of the Beloved.

Forty days before my mother's death, as she lay in bed, she said to me: "I don't like the look of that one standing in the corner. He's dark."

"Who?" I asked. "Who do you see?" I saw nothing.

"There's a dark figure standing in the corner of the room watching me."

Apparently, many people have deathbed visions. Kabbalists considered Samael a Jewish dark angel of death acting under the direction of God.[44] Of course, that would not be unusual as life/light and death/darkness work together as polarities of the same spectrum. No light exists without darkness, and there is no life without death. Eternity, on the other hand, is about time, and that's different. The Midrash states that God created all the angels on the first day, and thus he also created the angel of death. But according to the kabbalistic teachings of the Zohar, God created the angel of death on the second day. The telling of the Creation story in Genesis may provide us a clue about the event. The text omits the common phrase it uses to describe the making of every other day: "God saw that this was good."[45]

Do Humans Become Angels When They Die?

Since God created the angels of light and the people of Earth, most theologians concede that angels and humans differ in species. If that is the case, humans would not turn into angels after they die. Angels can assume whatever form necessary. They may adapt to earthly expectations and assume a human form at times, however, angels are not humans. Hebrews 2:7 declares that God has made human beings "a little lower than the angels." By this we are to understand that humans are not angels. When humans die, they remain human souls, albeit souls robed in spiritual light. Hebrews 12:22–23 tells us that at death thousands upon thousands of angels greet the soul, as do humans in spirit who retain their essence rather than turning into angels (NIV).

To most Muslims, angels, for the most part (Enoch and Elijah excepted), have never experienced a human form, but the reverse may not be true. In some Sufi circles, the saints (like Mary) and prophets (like Mohammad and Jesus) may attain an angelic presence. According to Shaykh Kabbani, "These human spirits are actually a part of the angelic spirits. That is why the condition of entry into Paradise for the soul of a dying person is to be accepted into the angelic realm first . . ." Human bodies are composed of different elements, while angelic bodies are composed only of light from the divine presence.[46]

The late psychic Ted Andrews did not distinguish between angels and human souls who become guides in spirit. "A loved one who has passed on," he said, "and that still watches over us is often called an angel. Another spirit being that assists us in some way is considered and often called an angel. The word angel means 'messenger' and thus any spirit being that brings us a message is technically an angel . . ."[47] He also distinguishes angels from other spirit beings or guides by defining them as a separate line of life.

Ghosts and spirit guides carry a different energy than do angels. The vibration of a disincarnate spirit, which is one who once had human life and flesh, can sometimes create in us a sense of foreboding. Perhaps because, like Marley's ghost in *A Christmas Carol* by Charles Dickens, the ghost reminds us of the fact that where they are now, we too shall be. The difference between a ghost and an angel, however, is easy to discern. "No one who has ever seen an angel mistakes it for a ghost," Sophy Burnham claims. "Angels are remarkable for their warmth and light. The mark of an angel is that it brings you peace, saying 'Do not fear. Everything is okay.' And after you have seen them, nothing is the same."[48]

The Cokeville Angels

Returning to the topic of ghosts for a moment, it should be noted that not all of them are frightening, however. Many even join the company of angels in the spirit world to accomplish the formidable task of offering peace and succor in times of trial. The stories that emerged after the Cokeville, Wyoming, bombing on May 16, 1986, confirm such a belief.

That spring day David and Doris Young entered the Cokeville Elementary School, gathered 154 students and teachers into one classroom, and prepared to detonate a bomb if they did not receive two million dollars per hostage. With duct tape, the couple drew a square around themselves and the bomb, warning everyone not to cross that line. The hostages, nearly all of them children from the small community of Latter-Day Saints, did what they could to protect themselves. They did what they knew how to do. They gathered and prayed, then a sense of calm came over them. The bomb did detonate, and in the process Doris Young set herself ablaze. Yet all of the hostages escaped the conflagration, running out of the building accompanied by teachers and strangers. It was a miracle indeed. Bomb experts agreed that if all the bombs had detonated (and only two did), the configuration of those bombs would have flattened that whole wing of the building. Instead, the bomb and most of its shrapnel appeared to have blown, not outward, but straight up.

It took a few days for the full weight of the event to reveal itself. The children and the school staff had been saved by angels. Separately the children began to tell a similar story. Inside that classroom with the students and teachers that day, strangers stood with them, all dressed in white. Some of the children told their parents, investigators, and hospital workers that they had seen them. Each child that day had an angel, filled with light, which appeared over their head. Some of the angels gave the children life-saving advice. One angel told the children to stand in a certain place and that everything would be fine; they were loved. Other children reported someone grabbing their hands and hustling them outside. Some of the children who had identified the spirit beings as angels later realized these as ancestors whom they had never met, but whom they and their parents could identify through old photographs.

The children said that just prior to detonation, the angels joined hands around the bomb and went up through the ceiling with the explosion, effectively limiting the blast to one portion of the building while shielding the children and teachers as they escaped. There is no other explanation for why the remaining bombs, configured as they were, did not detonate.[49]*

---

*A more complete version of this story appears in the book *Witness to Miracles*, which provides the collective stories of the Cokeville community members.

What the Cokeville story tells us is two things: First, while the angels and spirits of the deceased are not the same thing, they do operate on the same spiritual plane. They both work to provide comfort and protection. Second, fervent prayer, invocation, and the power of the mind to connect with Spirit can alter outcomes, calling in the angels and higher beings to attend our human lives.

FALLEN ANGELS

In Islam, all angels from the beginning of time are thought to be holy and good. Bad angels appear for our ultimate benefit as an object lesson. Most religions encourage angel appreciation, but nearly all admit that some angels are just more problematic. As the famous French poet Charles Baudelaire once said: "The devil's finest trick is to persuade you that he does not exist."[50]

As we know, followers of one faith often demonize the spirit beings of another faith, insisting that they are deceivers—neither real angels nor real gods. The Tibetan *dharmapala* named Yama and the Hindu deities Shiva and Shakti exemplify these contradictions. The supreme Egyptian god, Amon, an unseen god who created the universe, became an arch demon, Aamon, in charge of forty legions of demons, according to Judeo-Christian demonologists. He, with his dog body and serpent tail, joins Isis and Osiris in hell, along with the Babylonian deities Astarte and Ba'al. While the dog-headed Anubis joins his father, Osiris, in the underworld, the underworld is not necessarily hell, but a passage through which one must pass in order to be resurrected.

Of course, some demons are demons in any culture. The Egyptians demonized the god Set, who murdered his brother Osiris. Set emerged as the epitome of Satan, being a god of confusion, chaos, disruption, and death. Half human and half animal—or depicted as some unknown beast with long square ears, a forked tail, and a curved snout—he joined the mammoth serpent Apep in the underworld. Set ruled the desert lands, where Christ went on his vision quest for forty days. Fallen angel indeed, Set pierced through the side of his mother, the sky, and fell like a blazing meteorite from heaven in order to be born on Earth.

Other demons arise from the bad choices that we humans make but will not quite accept as our own fault. For example, the name of the well-known demon Mammon literally means "money." Beelzebub becomes the demon of gluttony; Asmodeus, lust; Leviathan, envy; and Lucifer, pride.[51] Rather than seeing Satan as a figure of temptation like the snake in the garden, the Baha'i faithful see Satan not so much as an evil demon, but as "the promptings of our own lower nature, the evil within. Likewise, demons, jinn, and fallen angels are seen as aspects of our own selves."[52]

Still, legitimate dark energies exist that must be accounted for in some way. For example, the dark angels "Iblis" (Islam), "Samael" (Judaism), and "Satan" (derived from the term *ha-satan,* meaning any evil being) command all the other lower dark forces.

The Fall of the Morning Star

By and large, Judeo-Christian faiths believe that all angels emerged from the hand of God as holy. The fall of the angels, however, complicates things. That fall happened when the beautiful angel Lucifer, also known as the "Morning Star," rebelled against God. Angry with his father for giving man dominion over all the Earth, he enticed other angels to go along with him. The Hebrew scriptures do not fully recount the rebellion and fall, but when John of Patmos wrote the Christian scriptures Revelation in 96 CE, he described the fallen angels. "[T]he great dragon was cast out, that old serpent, called the Devil, and Satan, which deceiveth the whole world: he was cast out into the earth, and his angels were cast out with him" (Revelation 12:7–9 KJV).

The rebellion spurred a war in heaven between legions of demons and the angels, led by archangel Michael. They fought a horrific war with Satan, who appeared as an enormous dragon. At this point we can see beneath the disguise of the innocent-seeming serpent in the garden. The dark angels who fell with the Morning Star angel descended like "lightning from heaven," a reference to the wicked Egyptian god Set who pierced through his mother's side like lightning in order to be born on Earth. The dark angels fell like rain from the sky.

According to legend, the crown jewel of the archangel Lucifer, "the sapphire Schethiyâ, the Lapis Exilis," fell from heaven when Lucifer did. During the conflict, Michael—archangel of the sun—and the angelic hosts swooped down upon Lucifer and his rebellious comrades. Michael's flaming sword struck the flashing sapphire. The green stone of Lucifer's crown fell through all the celestial rings into the dark and immeasurable abyss. Out of Lucifer's radiant gemstone was fashioned the Holy Grail, from which Christ drank at the Last Supper.[53]

Rebellion in Heaven

From a Persian account of Iblis, the Satan of the Qur'an, we see that pandemonium began when God asked the angels to first praise Him, then to praise the man and woman He had created. Adding insult to injury, God commanded all of the angels to serve his creatures. Iblis (Satan) insisted that because he "loved God best," he would not bow to humans. He told God, "I am not one of them. Thou createst me of fire, while him thou didst create of mud" (Qur'an 7:10–11). God rebuked Iblis angrily, saying, "Get away from me and out of my sight." Then he shunned Iblis and sent him away. As Sophy Burnham observes, "Hell is being cast aside by your beloved."[54]

Iblis becomes a *shaytan,* the Arabic word for Satan. Many shaytans provoke people and whisper wicked thoughts. Readers of the Qur'an see them as djinn rather than as fallen angels.[55] Iblis said, "I am not one of them." He meant that he was a spirit made of fire. Islamist Peter Lamborn Wilson points to the Hadith, in which the djinn Satan is also the angel Azazel, "a preacher to all the other angels before humankind was made . . . " Says Wilson: "He proclaimed the superiority of fire (psychism) over clay (flesh). For this God curses him and calls him Iblis, or Diablo."[56]

A lesser known first-century text called *The Life of Adam,* derived from both Christian and Hebrew sources, echoes this story of Satan's fall, as does the Syrian text *Cave of Treasures.* Both suggest that Satan fell due to arrogant self-aggrandizement. He tells the angels in his company to neither worship nor praise Adam "because I am fire and spirit, and not that I should worship a thing of dust." Of his own free will he separated himself from God. After losing their battle, the faces of Satan and his companions fell into horrible contortions, and their naked bodies were left naked.[57] Ephraim the Syrian says that all of this happened on the sixth day of Creation in the second hour. However, in the third hour of that same day, Satan fell, and God raised Adam to take his place in Eden. "He ascended in a chariot of fire amid much rejoicing among the angels."[58]

The angels of Islam fell after the creation of Adam and Eve. The Judeo-Christian Genesis says the angels fell before God created humans. Lucifer, the most beautiful, luminous angel of all, grew vain and jealous, wanting to be loved and adored as much as, if not more than, God. John Milton's epic poem *Paradise Lost* offers the most memorable narrative of the three-day battle between Lucifer and his angels of darkness and Michael and his angels of light. The old serpent Satan suffers a resounding loss to archangel Michael. Cursed as evil after losing their battle, about a third of the stars (angels) fell from heaven. These angels accompanied Lucifer in his fall: Beelzebub, his second in command; Moloch, the angel who reeks of the blood of human sacrifice; Mammon, greed; and Azazel, the angel of death. For nine days the renegade angels fell. Lucifer lay suffering upon the hard Earth until at last he got up and strode into Eden, stalking Adam and Eve.[59]

Where Demons Dwell

The foregoing story is one of many stories of humans bedeviled by the intrusion of dark angels. Dark angels have grown fascinated with the human world in which people inhabit bodies, make choices, and can eat, drink, and propagate. The demons received none of these opportunities. Demons use fear and projection surrounding the sensory delights that tempt humans into making wrong choices. Greedy thoughts led to such ridiculous actions as hoarding toilet paper during the COVID-19 pandemic.

The astral realm where demons live is built of thoughts and feelings as real as our material world. Beyond the human realm, unseen angels and demons dwell, but they have no superpower over humans. We are spiritual beings, too, albeit clothed in flesh. Demons exist in the same dimension with and in polarity to angels. Winged and moving as quickly as thought, they can assume any shape and divine the future—or at least propose possible future outcomes based on human activities. Their perception of time differs from human perception.

In this astral realm beyond the mental plane, humans may contact demons, angels, and ascended masters.[60] Sometimes the fallen ones leap into our dreams. For whatever pathetic reason, some are summoned. At other times these fallen ones tear through the veils that separate us. "Since they have no bodies," says religious studies professor Peter Kreeft, "they don't operate on a space-time continuum. They are quantum, making whole leaps."[61] Time and space have no hold on them.

Angelic Jealousy

If they operate on a different plane, why do the fallen ones pay any attention to humans at all? Why the perpetual conflict between spirit and matter? No matter whether the tradition is Jewish, Christian, or Islamic, the answer remains the same. "Angels are jealous of humans," Rabbi Cooper reminds us, "because we humans have free will, and they do not."[62]

Cooper expounds on a Midrash story that describes an adversarial relationship between the two realms. Before the creation of humankind, the conflict began. The angels debated among themselves and with God about whether humans should be included in Creation. During the debate God gave examples of His humans for angels to see. Naturally wishing to show His creatures in a good light, He only exhibited some of the more well-known biblical characters. The Midrash surmises that, if at the start of his plan God had revealed to the angels the true nature of human beings (rather than presenting them as model citizens), there would have been an uproar in the heavens.

Despite a preview of God's prototypes, the angels remained unconvinced. They did not want human beings made at all. Yet as CEO of heaven, God insisted that the angels help Him to create Adam. The angels declined to gather clay for their part of the dirty work. When Gabriel finally agreed and attempted to obey God's orders, "the Angel of Earth rebelled and would not give the archangel any dust for God to create humankind. The Angel of Earth protested that the physical earth would be cursed and devastated because of human thoughtlessness; it insisted that God take personal responsibility rather than send an archangel as an intermediary."[63]

Wow! The angel of Earth held God personally responsible for the outcome! God would answer to the angels for the catastrophic effect of the human life forms He created. Perhaps this thousand-year-old Midrash foresaw the environmental decay that human thoughtlessness would engender on Earth.

The angels tried to warn God, saying, "Don't do it! You will rue the day . . ." The angels told their Creator that "the days of human beings would be filled with suffering and that it would be far better if humans were never brought into existence." Yet God promised that humanity would endure. Next, He placed on the Earth the Tree of Life that offers the knowledge of good and evil.*

From this point, the Genesis 3 story becomes the one most Christians know. God told His humans not to eat from the Tree of Knowledge, but a serpent tempted Eve. She in turn then convinced Adam to eat. Later Christian narratives identify the serpent with Satan or Lucifer. Our kabbalist Rabbi Eleazar in the Middle Ages, however, correlated this serpent with Samael, the dark angel. He suggests the chief adversary of God seduced Eve, and through her became the father of Cain. The Zohar identifies Samael as the "son of the morning" who wrestled Jacob. Elsewhere he is equated with Typhon, and interchangeable with Satan—not simply as a deceiver, but also as a black magician. While he originally appears as an archangel, he simultaneously is called the greatest and the foulest of beings. His name, as we mentioned, means "poison of God."[64]

---

*Or some say, "in" the Earth, meaning inside the "clay" of man.

This suggests that he who is the poison of God performs his deeds at the behest of his Master and Maker. He is the Satan whom God sets in the garden to tempt Eve, and the Satan whom God sends into the desert to tempt Jesus in a battle between magic and prayer. He is also the Satan with whom God bargains over the soul of Job, sending him trial after trial to prove a theological point, even if a bet in heaven makes no sense to Job on Earth.[65] God's decisions are His alone.

So exactly what happened in the garden that day? In his inimitable way of merging myth and poetry, the late social philosopher William Irwin Thompson describes the moment of Creation and its outflow, saying: "With the creation of Adam, history itself becomes a mystery school for the elect of God." He suggests that the creation of man destroyed the angelic stasis of heaven; thus, the angels rebelled, and war broke out. Samael falls, taking with him nearly half the heavenly host. "Unity is lost," writes Thompson, "and existence becomes more intensely polarized. Now separations become important, and one must choose sides. The whole universe shifts, and everything is on the move . . . The Fall of the Angels is," he says, "the prelude to the fall of man."[66]

The Devil's Son

We see God's poisonous adversary at work in a lesser-known Jewish legend that offers a disturbing view of Samael's scripted deceit in paradise. In this tale the dark angel and a boy approached Eve in the garden. The angel asked Eve to watch his son until he returned, and she agreed. When Adam returned from his walk, he found a howling, screaming child; Eve told him the boy belonged to Samael. Annoyed and vexed at the violently screaming boy, Adam decided to quell the tantrum. So he hit the boy and killed him. Yet the corpse continued to emit ceaseless wails and screams. Desperate, Adam hacked him into bits; then, trying to hide the body, he cooked the remains and served them to Eve. They both ate.

Scarcely had they finished their repast than Samael reappeared, looking for his boy.

"What boy?"

The two denied everything, pretending not to know about Samael's son. While they lied to Samael, suddenly the boy's voice could be heard speaking from the chests of Adam and Eve. The boy told Samael: "I have penetrated the hearts of Adam and Eve, and never again will I quit them, nor the hearts of their children, nor their children's children, unto the ends of all generations."*

Samael departed but Adam grieved pitifully, putting on sackcloth and ashes. He fasted for one hundred and thirty years until God appeared, saying: "My son, have no fear of Samael. I will give you a remedy against him, for it was at my instance that he went to you in the first place." Apparently the revelation of divine deception does not quite shock Adam; instead, Adam asked, "And what is this remedy?"

God answered, "The Torah."[67]

The Book of Raziel

God then gave Adam the book of Records, written for humankind by the angel Raziel (sometimes called Radweriel). It contained all the mysteries of God's cosmos, and reading it would make Adam wise, so he studied it day and night. After a while the angels became curious and visited Adam. Envious of the wisdom he had gained from the book, they tried to destroy him with cunning. They called him a god and prostrated themselves before him.

"Stop it!" Adam said. "We should magnify the name of the Lord together."

The angels grew so jealous that they stole the book and threw it in the sea. Adam searched for it in vain, and the loss distressed him. He grieved so much that God finally stepped in and asked the angel of the sea, Rehab, to retrieve the book for Adam.[68]

The Sufi tradition suggests that God made Adam recite, just as the angel Jibrīl later commanded Mohammed to recite. Genesis 2 reveals Adam naming the creatures—"everything inner and outer"—in a recitation taught to him by God. Then God elevated Adam so that he could

---

*Now there is a story that returns a kind of innocence to Eve's apple!

teach the angels. "The Qur'an teaches that humans can reach a point where they command angelic power."[69]

The book that the angel left with Adam has two names: the book of Adam and the book of Raziel, written by the angel whose name means "the secrets of God." "This book contained sacred knowledge, [that is] 72 branches of wisdom that revealed the formation of 670 inscriptions of higher mysteries. In the middle of the book appeared a secret writing that explained 1,500 keys to the universe, which were not revealed even to the holy angels."* The book contained the names of all the generations that would follow Adam, the secrets of astrology, of astronomy, and numerology. Inscribed upon sapphire, this book offered a complete guide to how to prosper in life and make decisions to satisfy every need. To preserve the sanctity of these divine secrets, God covertly sent the angel Hadarniel (his name means "Greatness of God") to warn Adam not to reveal the glory of the Master. "For you alone and not to the angels is the privilege given to know these things," he said.[70]

Once the book arrived, however, the angels grew curious. They gathered around to ask Adam and Eve to read it to them. For a great while, the Midrash tells us, Adam kept the book to himself. After a round of angelic kowtowing, however, a reading commenced. That reading in turn confused the angels about the divinity of man. Adam broke his promise to God to keep the book to himself; as if it were an angel itself, the book magically flew away from him. Adam's shame and regret so deeply wounded him that he immersed himself in the river Gihon and stayed submerged up to his neck until he became wrinkled and haggard.

Then God sent Raphael to return the book, which Adam studied for the rest of his life. Rabbi Cooper tells us, "He left it to his son Seth, and it went through the generations to Abraham. It is still hidden today, somewhere in the world, for those who know how to read it."[71] Other legends say that when Adam died, the book of Secrets disappeared. Later, God revealed to Enoch in a dream the cave in which the book had been hidden.

---

*No wonder the angels were upset!

The Zoroastrian Angra Mainyu and the Druj

God's duality rules Zoroastrian thought. In that tradition, the two prominent deities Ahura Mazda and Angra Mainyu (sometimes called Ahriman), or the Lord of Goodness and the Evil Spirit, reflect God's created world; both exist together from the beginning of time. Angra Mainyu, the evilest angel of the Zoroastrian tradition, created death.

Zoroastrian messengers appear as either white-light angels or dark-of-night devils. Deeply embedded in this story is the idea that both streams of energy emerge from one fountain that is sourced in the divine mind.

In Persian lore, the druj represents a class of mostly female evildoers, sorcerers, monsters, fiends, and hell-raisers. The druj are the minions of Ahriman, the principal evil being. Some specific druj and their attributes are as follows:

Druj Nasu, also known as the corpse fiend, would beat its wings in such a way that it created the droning sound of millions of buzzing flies, accompanied by the smell of decaying flesh. This creature represented corruption, decomposition, decay, contagion, and impurity. It can be expelled from a living person by a bathing and purification ritual that lasts nine days;

The Azhi Dahaka cut a frightening figure as a half-man and half-monster, with three heads, six eyes, three jaws, and two serpents emerging from his shoulders. Ahriman created Azhi Dahaka to destroy the world. This demon committed incest with his mother, Autuk, who was also a demon;

Sej personified pestilence, bringing about annihilation and misfortune;

Jahi was a debauched female druj, associated with wizards and sorcerers. Her name meant "harlot." Through her and the kiss of Ahriman, menstruation came into the world;[72]

The grand dame of wickedness, a female demon known simply as Druj epitomized falsehood and deceit. In the final confrontation between good and evil, Asha will destroy Druj.

Along the Silk Road the Iranian evil spirit Ahriman becomes the Christian and Muslim devil who first appears in the book of Job as *ha-satan*, "the accuser." The numerology of seven archangels, seven heavens, seven archdemons, and seven hells in Jewish, Christian, Muslim, and even in Hindu mythology and Greek philosophy relates to the seven vices and virtues of the earlier Zoroastrian religion.[73]

The Yezidi Angel and Devil

Christians, Jews, and Muslims consider themselves People of the Book. The Yezidi have no such God-given book. As a result, the People of the Book equate the Yezidi angel Taus Melek with Shaitan (Satan), the source of wickedness in the world. In contrast, the Yezidis consider him to be chief among archangels and not fallen at all. They forbid speaking the name Shaitan, which, they believe, is a thought that puts Satan on an equal footing with God. As the ultimate progenitor and the most powerful force known, God knows no evil equal. Good and evil exist in the minds and spirits of humans. The appearance of good or evil depends on one's choices. Yezidis honor the example of Taus Melek himself, since the angel was given the same choice between good and evil, and he chose God.[74]

Yezidis argue that God's command for the angel to bow to Adam was only a test. If God commands a thing, it must be done. Monotheistic religions since the late sixteenth and early seventeenth centuries have depicted the rebellious angel as Satan whom God cast out of heaven for being too proud to bow to Adam. Because Taus Melek refused God's order, fundamental Islamists depict him as the angel who rebelled. To them, the recalcitrant Peacock Angel equals the rebellious angel Satan.[75]

Unfortunately, by making it taboo to mention the name Shaitan, the Yezidis may have accidentally fostered the idea that the Peacock Angel and the dark, fallen tempter are identical. One gnostic (Mandaean) holy book portrayed the Peacock Angel as a spirit and a prince of light originally concerned with the destinies of this world. Because of a divine appointment with destiny, he plunged into the darkness of matter. Thus he became a savior, a son of the Divine sent for the benefit of humankind.

Lady Ethel Stefana Drower, a British anthropologist studying the Mandeans, also interviewed the Yezidis and became among the first to connect Yezidi and Mandean beliefs. She writes:

> I talked of this with the head of the *qawwâls* (also qwals/sun singers) in Baashika who, honest man, was not very clear himself about the point, for one of the charms of the Yazidis (sp) is that they are never positive about theology. It seemed probable to me, after this talk, that the Peacock Angel is, in a manner, a symbol of Man himself, a divine principle of light experiencing an avatar of darkness, which is matter and the material world. The evil comes from man himself, or rather from his errors, stumblings and obstinate turnings down blind alleys upon the steep path of being. In repeated incarnations he sheds his earthliness, his evil, or else, if hopelessly linked to the material, he perishes like the dross and illusion that he is.[76]

Theosophical writer Charles W. Leadbeater compares Lucifer/Satan and the master teacher Sanat Kumara. In the predawn of our civilization, the Kumara arrived on Earth from Venus. Both Sanat Kumara and Lucifer are associated with the morning star (Venus).[77] That connection has become a messaging problem for Theosophists for decades, even though Theosophists view Jesus as a man manifested on Earth as the Son of God and overshadowed by the Christ consciousness.

More recent theosophical thinker Mark Amaru Pinkham takes that a step further. He explicitly links the Yezidi Peacock Angel, a fallen angel, to the Kumaras and the resurrected Christ. "The Peacock Angel's higher self was represented by Christ, the historical Jesus being Ananda Kumara, Sanat Kumara's brother." While admitting the Peacock Angel's rebellious, fallen state, Pinkham believes that the angel eventually succeeded in redeeming himself. The redemption of the Peacock Angel, he says, serves as the redemption of the entire world and the ushering in of the eternal kingdom of God. For this reason, Pinkham claims, the Yezidis refuse to refer to Taus Melek as Satan because his higher self is the Christ. He further connects the angel Raphael, whose wings contain the thousand eyes of the peacock, with Taus Melek as an emblem of divine love, and the sacred union of the masculine and feminine.[78]

Having a renegade like Taus Melek as archangel becomes a problem for the Yezidis. Yasmine Hafiz, writing for the *Huffington Post* about the persecution of the Yezidis, tells the story of the angel's fall this way: "They believe that once God created Adam and Eve, he ordered the angels to bow to his creations. While the other angels did so, Taus Melek was the only one to refuse, because he believed that he should submit to (only) the Supreme God." This part of the story sounds quite familiar to readers of the Abrahamic faiths, but then Hafiz's story diverges. "He was then thrown into Hell, until his tears of remorse quenched the fires, and he became reconciled to God. He now serves as an intermediary between God and humanity."[79]

Hindu Ahura/Asura and Deva and Daeva

The rather black-and-white, good-versus-evil ideology that dominates Abrahamic religions becomes more convoluted in the Eastern traditions. To strike an analogy, what begins as two pairs of socks—one white and one black—becomes a wad of socks twisted together and in need of sorting. Somehow, along the Silk Road trade route, that theology begets a conflict between two similar ancient Indo-European religious sects vying for supremacy.

The celestial conflict between heaven and earth has multiple meanings, and esoteric application. As above, so below, says the dictum. The struggle is "astronomical, theogonical and human struggles," Blavatsky says. Every conflict relates to

> . . . the adjustment of orbs, and the supremacy among nations and tribes. The "Struggle for Existence" and the "Survival of the Fittest" reigned supreme from the moment that Kosmos manifested into being. . . . Hence the incessant fights of Indra, the god of the Firmament, with the Asuras—degraded from high gods into Cosmic demons . . . the battles fought between stars and constella-

tions, between Moon and planets—later on incarnated as kings and mortals. Hence also the War in Heaven of Michael and his Host against the Dragon (Jupiter and Venus*), when a third of the stars of the rebellious host was hurled down into Space, and "its place was found no more in Heaven."[80]

Just as the natural and spiritual worlds become divided, so do the Zoroastrians of Iran and Iraq separate themselves from the Zoroastrians who influenced India and the development of Hinduism and later Buddhism. As the two groups vied for regional dominance, the Persian *ahuras* became the Indian Asuras, and the Persian daevas became the Indian devata. Over time these pairings are recognized as two distinct groups of angelic beings. The first group, ahuras/asuras, terrorized the second group, daevas/devata, with their warlike fiery demonstrations of power. The destructive energy of the asuras and ahuras ran rampant.

Changes in the Creation myths followed, making devils of the daevas and devata. As Zoroastrianism met Hinduism, devata became demigods and Asuras became demons. The confusion between good and evil is exacerbated by the fact that etymologically we no longer know the difference between a *deva* and a *devil*—two terms that derive from the same root word.[81]

An Asura in southern Asia resembles a dark entity in Hinduism. The Vedas (1500 BCE) interchangeably used the words *asura* and *deva* to refer to a god or goddess. But in the period in which the Ramayana (500 BCE) and Mahabharata (400 BCE–200 CE) appeared, Asuras had become the demonic, and the devas had become the divine. Throughout the Puranas, however, the devas and Asuras engage in perpetual combat. Unlike the Christian archangel Michael who will propel Satan to hell once and for all, the rebellious Asuras often storm out of the underworld, taking over heaven and driving out the devas, who then appeal to Vishnu or Shiva to set things right.[82]

Asuras assimilated the energies of deities worshipped by non-Vedic

---

*Venus, the morning star, is code for Lucifer, "the shining one."

tribes and the ancestral spirits of aboriginal tribes. Asuras got lumped together with genii, the giant evil spirits known as *daityas,* and the dark-skinned, superhuman sorcerers known as *danavas.*[83] These wily and cunning Asuras knew the art of deception and kept magical secrets. Through illusion, they assumed shapes and forms that appeared to be "people," but could turn themselves into frightening, rampaging elephants, ferocious lions, and ravaging tigers. They might twist their forms into snakes; they might seem to be semidivine nagas, or they might simply vanish into invisibility. Their offspring possessed the magic arts, too.[84] The Asuras live in mountainous caves, in oceanic depths, in the bowels of the Earth; they dwell in cities of light built by their magician Maya. These night wanderers, cannibals, giants, barbarians, demons of time, and stellar spirits all worship Shiva the destroyer, who is one of the triumvirate aspects of God.[85]

Dharmapalas of the Buddhists

In the same way that the archangel Michael defended the Christian faith, the *dharmapalas,* eight wrathful temple guardians of the Tibetan Buddhist tradition, appear as defenders of the faith. They guard the temple and the traditions. Some of these eight dharmapalas derive from the more shamanic Bon ancestral tradition. Their many arms lash out with flashing knives, swords, and pikes. Their eyes stare and bulge. From their screaming mouths, tongues of fire spew—even their eyebrows are flames.[86] Wrathful, indeed! They must be as terrifying as the angels of old that filled the early desert-dwelling Hebrew people with dread. Perhaps only terrifying guardians could frighten away evil influences. And yet many of these spirit deities have a beatific and benefic side to them.

The eight "Terrible Ones," stand in the cardinal and quarter point directions. They are often drawn or sculpted around the perimeter of the Buddhist temple. The bodhisattva, or enlightened being of compassion (think "succoring angel"), Avalokiteshvara of Buddhism appears in his dark, wrathful form as Mahakala, wearing a crown of six skulls. He destroys confusion and ignorance, taking particular interest in those nomadic tent-dwellers who tend their yaks outside the temple confines. Hayagriva, another form of Mahakala, cures diseases and protects herds of horses. Yama, an equivalent Tibetan angel of death, rules the bowels of hell. At one time, Yama, a human and holy man, sat peacefully meditating in his cave. Robbers entered and slaughtered a bull before they noticed that the cave-dwelling mystic had been watching them. The robbers cut off his head, too. At that moment, the gentle mystic assumed the terrible form of Yama by putting the bull's head in place of his own. He killed the robbers, drank their blood, and, upon leaving the cave, threatened all of Tibet. Only one divine being could calm his wrath—Yamantaka, the wrathful, bullheaded demonic form of the bodhisattva of wisdom, Manjushri.

Joseph Campbell once surmised that the angel with the flaming sword sent to guard the Garden of Eden and to protect its wisdom might be none other than the Buddhist bodhisattva, Manjushri.[87] Manjushri's sword untangles ego, ignorance, and mistaken views from true wisdom. With his flaming sword he offers transformative light and cuts away obstacles to whatever wrong thinking separates us from the ineffable divinity. In the *Rig-Veda,* Yama reigns as Lord of Death and the Underworld, but the most wrathful deity, Yamantaka, the black bull, emerges exceedingly strong, purposeful, and persistent. This great bodhisattva of compassion stands upon Yama, indicating that he himself is stronger than death. Yamantaka contains the essential male life-force energy. By defeating death and the cycle of rebirth (samsara), he shows himself to be a deity of enlightenment. Brahma, the Hindu creator, manifests as a wrathful Tibetan deva called Tshangspa Dkarpo. Mounted on a white steed, waving his sword, his murderous, lustful rampage covers the whole globe, until at one point he tries to assault a sleeping goddess. When he wakes her, she strikes him a blow that cripples him, eventually turning him into a protector of the dharma.

The only female dharmapala, Palden Lhamo, is a wrathful version of Saraswati. She secures the lineage of the Dalai Lamas and protects the Buddhist government in exile in Lhasa, India. Before becoming a consort of the dharmapala Mahakala, she had married a ruthless and evil king in Lanka. Her husband spent all of his time training their son to betray and destroy Buddhism. While the king was away one day, Palden Lhamo took matters into her own hands in rather dramatic fashion. She killed her son, drank his blood from his skull, cannibalized his flesh, then rode away on her horse, sitting on a saddle made from her son's flayed skin. The king tried shooting her with a poisoned arrow, missed, and struck her horse. Palden Lhamo healed the horse, and its wound became a magical eye. She used this eye "to watch the 24 regions and [prayed] may I be the one to end the lineage of the malignant kings of Lanka."[88]

Palden Lhamo descended into Tibetan hell for her deeds but was reborn and appeared to the Buddha, who asked her to become a dharmapala, a guardianship role that she accepted. According to legend, she lived around the "oracle lake" near Lhasa, where pilgrims went to seek visions. There she appeared to the first Dalai Lama of Tibet, and vowed that she would protect and defend every subsequent Dalai Lama and all the tenets of Buddhism.

The avenging dharmapala Begtse of the sixteenth century is the youngest celestial guardian. Dressed in Mongolian boots, this avenging spirit wears full armor, wields a sword in one hand, and carries the heart of his enemy in his other hand. According to legends, Begtse appeared to the third Dalai Lama as he traveled along the road to meet the great Mongolian warlord Altan Khan. The Dalai Lama had been called to convert him. Begtse confronted the Dalai Lama, trying to stop him. The Dalai Lama in turn transformed himself into the bodhisattva Avalokiteshvara. Overcome with compassion at the sight of this gentle man standing courageously before him, Begtse, the Mongolian, became Buddhist himself, and a protector of the dharma.[89] As you can see, the dharmapalas—these Tibetan guardian angels—can show either an angry or a benevolent face, depending upon the spiritual nature of the one he encounters.

The Eastern tradition suggests an antidote to the rather all-or-nothing thought of the Western traditions. Angels and demons *do* transmute. While the Western tradition limits the idea of free will to humans, believing that angels serve God and demons do not, it does not account for the fact that a rebellious angel must *choose* to be rebellious. There are legends of angels who have their own opinions about many things, including whether to make humans at all. The suggestion is that angels do have a certain amount of free will, as well as a clearer understanding of what that free will entails.

The Enigma of Free Will

If certain angels disobey and are in a fallen state, the question becomes: Do they, like their human counterparts, have an opportunity for reformation? If all things return to God, what about demons? The second-century Alexandrian theologian Origen appears to have believed that all souls—whether human, demonic, or angelic—were created equal. Some fell because of their choices, but they could eventually repent and be saved—even Satan. "The power of choosing between good and evil is within the reach of all," Origen wrote.[90]

The church, however, condemned that opinion and denounced Origen. They insisted that while human beings immersed in matter can repent, angels, for some reason, cannot. Three centuries after his death, the Council of Constantinople (553 CE) resoundingly stamped Origen as a heretic: "Whoever says or thinks that the punishment of demons and the wicked will not be eternal . . . let him be anathema."[91] Not part of the organized religion of Christianity, Origen had nothing to gain for believing that good could conquer evil, except the belief in the power of men to behave in ways that were Christian. On the other hand, the Christian Church had everything to lose. If they accepted the fact that evil could be conquered through good intentions, willpower, mindful thinking, and righteous behavior, then the church leaders might be out of a job.

In the Eastern tradition we have seen the possibility of redemptive behavior among Asuras in order to become devata. There are essentially two ways in which an Asura can become a deva, or a demon become an angel—and the avenues are the same for humans: one either practices through *tapas* (practicing austerities) or attains *siddhi* (acquiring metaphysical or magical abilities). Tapas basically means practicing asceticism to raise the individual consciousness, controlling one's desires and acting in good conscience and faith. It does not include sacrifice or battle. The Eastern mystics say that one must do the work—"the work" being fasting, practicing yoga, donating wealth, making pilgrimages, and so on. Through these practices the Asura could become a deva, acquire new strength, and even exhibit miraculous abilities.

Humans, gods, animals, demons—all could attain these powers. The problem with demons following the practice to attain these magical powers was that once acquired, they might quit fasting, worshipping, and meditating in order to pursue immortality and invincibility.[92] Even in human terms, the pursuit of heaven often holds less attraction for the metaphysician who is more fascinated with wielding magic, acquiring power, and accruing wealth. Because demons are accustomed to acting demonically, as are those with worldly ambitions, change is difficult.

The Puranas tell us the story of Bala, an Asura, who knew and taught his tribe ninety-six kinds of magic to inflict chaos and control over the deva. Whenever he yawned, three seductive women emerged who could entice whomever they pleased. In a battle with Indra, king of the devas, Bala, king of the Asuras, won. Indra then heaped praises upon Bala. In return, Bala wanted to thank Indra, saying he would do anything Indra wished. Indra then asked for Bala's body, which Bala gave because, after all, an oath is an oath. Indra then cut the body into pieces and scattered them. Where they fell, gold mines could be found—proof that Bala was an Asura of merit and honor for keeping his promise to Indra.[93]

Philosopher and mystic William Irwin Thompson postulates an interesting outcome of the angelic dissent. If angels have no free will and never die, they do not have the opportunity to experience the glorious possibility of resurrection—a kind of annunciation that Buddhists call "samadhi." After attaining enlightenment, the Buddhist initiate returns to the city and is put to work "with bliss-bestowing hands." Thompson compares this idea with the return of the prodigal son.

One returns to where one started, but not at the same level of the spiral, for the resurrection of the body means that one is able to carry to the heavenly realm the wisdom of the fall into time. In the return of the prodigal son to the father, the wisdom is taken back and honored almost above the loyal son who never fell. The angels remain with God the father and do not fall into an animal body in physical time and space, but when a human being is able to liberate his consciousness from that physical entrapment and re-ascend to the heavenly realms, he is honored almost above the angels.[94]

Nephilim, Children of Fallen Angels

Before departing from the discussion on fallen angels and demons, it seems important to address the mystery of the Nephilim, those legendary giants, half-angel and half-human, conceived by the union of fallen angels and the daughters of man. Rabbi David Cooper translates *Nefilim* as "lizards, or giants," but the root word for these creatures, *n-f-l,* means "to fall."

While in the first chapter of Genesis God made humans and saw their divine nature and deemed it good, by the sixth chapter of Genesis, God demonstrates deep regret. The book of Enoch suggests that God sent two hundred angels to Earth. They descended onto Mount Hermon, took human form, and became the appointed guardians of Eden. Some texts call them "the Watchers." Perhaps God created these beings to already be in a "fallen" (or less noble) state. Rabbi David Cooper relates one story in which "their original purpose was to offer mankind the teachings of law and justice; but the daughters of men seduced these angels, and thus they fell."[95]

Both the apocryphal books of Enoch and Jubilees tell the stories of these fallen angels. They demonstrate mixed motives for mingling with humankind. In one instance, they came to satisfy their lusty appetites. In other legends, they descended to teach humankind heavenly secrets. The book of Enoch (revered in Ethiopia as Holy Scripture) makes clear that the fallen ones lusted for the young women of Earth, and descended to the physical plane in order to seduce them. They vowed if one fell, all two hundred angels would fall together. Their leaders were Semyaza, Liba, Ramiel, Kokabiel, Tamiel, Daniel, Ezeqiel, Baraqiel, Asael, Armaros, Ananel, Zaqiel, Samsiel, Satael, Turiel, Yomiel, and Araziel. "And it came to pass when the children of men had multiplied that in those days were born unto them beautiful and comely daughters. And the angels, the children of the heaven, saw and lusted after them, and said to one another 'Come! Let us choose us wives from among the children of men and beget us children.'"[96]

And so they produced a race of giants.

Enoch continues to describe the children of the fallen Watchers as being filled with avarice and greed. These warlike giants, bent on destruction and human corruption, took all the fruits of the Earth and consumed all the game they could find. When the supply ran out, they began to cannibalize humans. God condemned their wicked ways and ended their reign of terror with the Great Flood (Genesis 6:9–9:17).

The apocryphal book of Jubilees, sometimes called "the Lesser Genesis" (ca. 200–100 BCE), declares that the Watchers intentionally sent angels to earth to instruct humankind in spiritual knowledge. Once they left heaven and descended to earth, however, many fallen angels, as we've noted above, began to sin with human women. Perhaps not all; some fulfilled their purpose. Enoch himself "acquired his supernatural knowledge from the instruction of angels." The book of Jubilees mentions that this teaching came to him in dreams.[97]

Semyaza, the most lustful of the fallen angels, incited the rebellion and gained the allegiance of the other fallen angels, who passed along divine secrets and taught black magic to humans. They acquired their knowledge from the scattered leaves of the Tree of Knowledge in the Garden of Eden, but their knowledge was incomplete and distorted.[98]

Enoch also had a vision of the falling star, the cleverest of heaven's angels. Winged, gloriously beautiful, and arrogant, the angel Azazel corrupted two hundred other angels, all of whom appeared as falling stars. After his fall, Azazel taught humans sorcery and alchemy, including how to forge metals into weapons and use makeup as part of the art of seduction (1 Enoch 86:1–6). Such corruption changed Azazel's appearance into a that of a demon with a forked tail, eighteen wings sprouting from his back and both sides, yellow eyes, and the head of a goat.[99]

Enoch ascended through the seven heavens to report these offenses against God. The prophet felt sorry for the angels who carried him through the seven heavens to the Throne of God, where he learned the secrets of the universe and the ineffable mysteries of generations to come.[100] In the original telling, nine-tenths of the Watchers fell, but later theologians reversed the proportions because otherwise the reported number of fallen influencers gave satanic legions the upper hand. By the fourth century, the church considered the ten leaders of the Watchers to be fallen.[101]

To correct the error of the fallen angels and preserve Earth, God sent his four archangels. God told Gabriel to enflame and incite the Nephilim to wage battles and slaughter each other. Gabriel then imprisoned the giants in the earth until Judgment Day. The archangel Raphael bound Azazel hand and foot, then threw him in a hole in the desert and covered him with rocks. God sent Michael to battle Semyaza, and to bind him and his legion of sinners underground for seventy generations. In biblical time, seventy generations of five hundred years each would mean that he was bound for thirty-five hundred years. God dispatched the archangel Uriel to Lamech to warn Noah of the coming flood.[102]

Biblical scholar Peter Kreeft matter-of-factly said that he does not believe that the parentage of the Nephilim are angels. He assures us, too, that angels are not extraterrestrials. They are extracosmic—that is, from some universe beyond the one we occupy.[103]

I find myself weighing these biblical legends of Watchers, fallen angels, and the Nephilim against what I can find of archaeological histories, and I cannot say that I disbelieve any of it. How can the Great Flood that ended the Nephilim be mere myth when the story appears in every culture? When it happened and why it happened, and what results it had, of course, are matters of speculation. That the flood happened is not much disputed. There is an archaeological record of it in the Earth itself. Deuteronomy 1:28 refers to the legendary giants the

Anakites* who appeared in Canaan in the time of Moses. The Anakites are mentioned again in Numbers 13:32 as living near Mount Hebron, the origin site of the Yezidi ancestor Noah, who built the boat that survived the Great Flood that wiped out the Nephilim. Of course, the Yezidi call themselves descendants of angels.

There is some great mystery here. There are legends and there are stories, but were there angels? Even if one believes those who proclaim the Anunnaki as aliens and not angels, still they descended from the heavens, perhaps like stars falling from the sky. If they tried to insemi-nate Earth women, creating a race that drowned in the Great Flood . . . I still say that they were sons of God—that is, God's creatures. I do not believe, however, that they came from the same spiritual plane that angels do.

---

*Nephilim, perhaps.

5

Human and Angelic Interactions

The man form is higher than the angel form; of all forms it is the highest.

Man is the highest being in creation because he aspires to freedom.

PARAMAHANSA YOGANANDA,
AUTOBIOGRAPHY OF A YOGI

Human beings have free will; do angels? Is adherence to divine will a choice that angels make or an imperative that they must follow? What caused the fallen angels to fall if not free will? The Sufi scholar Shaykh Kabbani looks toward the angels as immutable creatures. "They have a mind and a heart, but no will and no desire other than to serve and obey God."[1] He believes that angels have the highest of intentions; they appear in order to aid mankind in their spiritual climb. Furthermore, human interaction with angels is vitally important. Kabbani asserts that God made Adam so that he could learn and utter truth in order to teach the angels. The Qur'an, he said, teaches spiritual dedication and soul progression so that humankind may reach a point where we command angelic power. Kabbani believes that "angels can take the form of human beings, and human beings can purify themselves to the point of possessing angelic attributes."[2]

Soul progression through the manifestation of various forms appears to be an idea that originated in the East rather than in the West—although more and more Westerners attach their consciousness to it. Rabbi David Cooper postulated that only humans have free will, and angels had no will except to obey God. The exercise of human free will created jealousy in the divine world that led to the fallen state of angels. Even Thomas Aquinas said that angels are incorporeal, made of the substance of God. Yet if angels are God's messengers and represent God's goodness, why do some angels rebel and fall? Are they then representatives of God's innate distemper? Can and do angels ever separate from their Creator?

Aquinas believed the incorporeal angels have choice and free will, just as the Creator does. An angel's will is linked to its intellect, he said, but the two faculties are not the same. For an angel, "Will is an intellectual longing, [a choice about] what is proposed by the intellect as good." Man has free will but lacks the perspective of an angel. But Aquinas said, "an angel exercises free will more perfectly than man does," because human will is subject to outside influences arising from sensual appetites. "Angels choose with a will uninfluenced by such nonspiritual tendencies."[3]

Angels originated in the mind of God and certain angels fell through disobedience, Aquinas said. Yet if the mind of God begat all thoughts and energies, does the mind of God contain potentially dissenting thoughts? Suppose angels have no free will and are solely messengers? Who then is the adversary suggesting the temptation? Rabbi David Cooper states his objection unequivocally, saying "We need to be clear . . . that even the idea of angels falling away from the God-field and becoming separate entities in conflict with the will of God is completely unacceptable in monotheistic theology." He suggests that in Hasidism every aspect of Creation begins with the naturally good, naturally perfect, divine spark. "Even so-called evil," he says, "could not exist without being sustained by God. If this is so, we must conclude that there is a necessary place for some degree of 'evil' in the divine cosmology."[4]

Whatever would tempt an angel to fall anyway? Stories about just such temptations fill Jewish legends. It might be useful to look at a few of these.

God asked the angels to help him to make humans, which they did not especially want to do. "The objections of the angels would have been much stronger, had they known the whole truth about man. God had told them only about the pious and had concealed from them that there would be reprobates among mankind, too. And yet, they knew but half the truth . . ."[5] Then God asked the angels to bow down to the foolish mortals. Reluctantly, at least two-thirds of the angels obeyed. The angels grew unhappy with their new heavenly neighbors, but God insisted that they do his bidding. Having no free will, if they wished to remain in heaven, the angels did as God commanded.

Prior to the appearance of mortals, angels existed in a kind of heavenly stasis. Their angelic perfection became complicated when humans entered the scene. The appearance of humankind introduced a creative disequilibrium that shifted everything, and created a whole new universe with different operating instructions. Not even the angels could tell what might happen next because those humans had free will. As William Irwin Thompson comments: "Small wonder the angels are said not to like us, for when man was created, all hell broke loose in heaven."[6]

Satan (previously Lucifer) adamantly opposed the idea and was unwilling to go along with God's plan. Why should an earth creature be so admired? Brilliant, filled with white light, and with twelve wings instead of six like the other angels, Lucifer knew that certainly he was more impressive than Adam—even greater than the other angels. Perhaps, he surmised, his glory and power even equaled that of his Creator.[7] Satan followed his own tempting, arrogant logic. Not only would he not bow down to Adam, but he would take himself far beyond the reach of God—a thought that so angered God that He cast Satan out of heaven. Lucifer's desire for recognition grew into a willful choice to defy God. Thus, he fell.

Like a star from the crown of God, he fell. He fell out of the mind of God, which is the archetype of heaven and the universe itself. Yet how can God's thoughts be in conflict, and can a divine thought be negated altogether?

Natural Laws and the Angels

We can look at this on a cosmic rather than a human scale in order to attain a larger perspective. *The Kybalion* affirms the hermetic dictum As above, so below, meaning that these hierarchies of beings—according to the Law of Correspondence—operate in their realms as we operate here on Earth. Theosophist Richard Smoley says that it is through understanding just this one principle that man is able to solve many "a dark paradox and hidden secret of nature."[8]

The conundrum of what is and what is not in the universe moves according to the natural laws of mind, vibration, rhythm, polarity, and cause and effect. The greatest of these, the Law of Mind, combines with many of the other natural laws. The Law of Polarity, for example, demonstrates that the spiritual power of thought can manifest in either an angelic (positive) or demonic (negative) way. We and all sentient beings participate in this cosmic operation. Our cosmos is a masterpiece of paired oppositions. Angels and devils occupy a polarity of spiritual dimension. There must be emptiness for there to be fullness. There must be destruction for there to be creation. The big bang that created all planets, creatures, and extant things seen and unseen exists in a continuum with the concept of the black hole that sucks up the universal life force in the cosmos. This life force then rolls back into itself, and makes it appear that something that is or was has never existed. It does all this in order to spew out, creating, yet again, the dual nature of life itself: positive and negative, and light and dark. In short, we are led to believe that most angels appear along the light spectrum while most devils hang out in the dark. Zoroastrian and Hindu traditions see good and evil as having been created all at once from a single source.

Mystic Jakob Böhme agrees, saying that angels good and bad dwell near each other, although it feels there is a great distance between them. Heaven and hell, he contends, exist within each of us, and occupy the same space. The difference is simply perception. "[A]lthough the Devil should go many millions of miles, desiring to enter into heaven and to see it, yet he would still be in hell and not see it."[9]

Rabbi Cooper suggests that a spiritual magnetism pulls us toward positive or negative polarities. The most obvious symbol of this polarity is the Tree of the Knowledge of Good and Evil that God placed in the Garden of Eden. Choice and free will have existed from the beginning, it seems, but he acknowledges that an "attraction to good pulls consciousness to increasingly higher levels of understanding," while attraction to evil casts more veils over one's eyes.[10] We call those errors in thinking "seductions"—potent forces that may propel us toward greed, lust, and a desire for power. Dark angels and wrong thinking may exist to test us, to trip us up, to tug on our sleeves and pull us off track. These glaring evils appear after we have followed seemingly innocent yet impulsive tugs in the wrong direction. The invocation of angels to attain mastery over an earthly situation sometimes thrusts one even further beyond the reach of more pious interoperation with divine forces.

The angels who appear in the Genesis story of Lot have come to deliver a dire message. It is not a warning. The humans have already made their choices and sealed their fate. The angels deliver a verdict based on the willful actions of community members—and the consequences affect them all. The angels agree (intellectual will) to spare Lot and his family the fate that will befall the entire cities of Sodom and Gomorrah, but these mortals must make their choice to follow God's command. Do not look back, they are told; in other words, do not regret your choice. The angels physically grab the hands of Lot, his wife, and his daughters and run with them (Genesis 19:16 KJV).

As we know, Lot's wife looks back and turns into a pillar of salt. Angels, apparently, can do more than deliver messages. They can offer us choices, but they cannot save us from the consequences of our own decisions.

In the thirteenth century the Bishop of Paris surmised that Lucifer fell from heaven along with one-third of the angels. He suggested that nine orders of angels remained, but a separate tenth order included the fallen angels and Lucifer. After he fell, Lucifer's name changed to Satan. As we learned in the last chapter, far from being sexless and sinless, those angels in the tenth heaven—known as "the Watchers"—lusted after the human Earth women, at least according to the book of Enoch. *The Legends of the Jews* by Louis Ginzberg (a compilation of Jewish interpretation and narratives from the Midrash, Mishnah, and Talmud) suggests that the Earth women used their sensual charms to tempt the angels from the path of virtue.[11] Scripture itself showed damning evidence of the giant offspring produced by human and angelic intercourse. Having a tenth heaven as the place where renegade angels lived and from which they fell solved a sticky theoretical problem about the nature of good and evil angels.[12]

Invoking Angels

Apparently our biblical forefathers never invoked the power of angels. No such event occurred in the King James Bible. Angels simply appeared, and humans had to figure out their intended message, whether it was an omen for good or ill. They certainly prayed, but they did not necessarily invoke or call down an angel.

At the time that the Roman Catholic Church had a grip on the Western world, from the British Isles to the Mediterranean at the beginning of the last millennia, the legendary book of Raziel and other grimoires grabbed the attention of learned, pious men who wished to know the secret of everything in God's universe. Many versions and translations of the book appeared, written in Latin, Hebrew, and Aramaic, detailing magic rituals and spells for invoking the aid of angels. "A number of these works survive in the British Library," observes dream shaman Robert Moss. "They seem heavily tainted by the Faustian desire to wield secret power for its own sake."[13]

By the thirteenth century, just after the era of the kabbalist Eleazar ben Judah of Worms, the idea of esoteric angelology had taken hold, especially in the Jewish community. More and more Jewish communities felt the need for angelic protection and assistance amid the chaos of the plagues, the marauders of Genghis Khan, and the Crusaders who were tearing through Jewish homes, killing men and raping Jewish women. Just such an atrocity happened to the daughter and wife of the Jewish prophet and kabbalist Eleazar ben Judah.[14] By the thirteenth century God seemed to have retreated to an even higher heaven while the angels looked on and wept. Esoteric angelology, as it took hold, offered a kind of hope. Occult manuscripts recorded which angels ruled which heavenly planets, which ruled the months and days of the week and even the hours of the day. Spells and incantations abounded. By the fourteenth century the angelic hosts who dwelled at the borders of our temporal universe numbered 301,655,722. Of these, 133,306,668 were fallen angels. Other calculations offered nine choirs with 6,666 legions of angels, and each legion had 6,666 angels. These bedeviling numbers perhaps figured into the idea of the clerical Inquisitors that witches and Jews who had invoked fallen angels caused the plagues at that time.[15]

Invoking angels became a common practice in the fourteenth century—most notably through the work of Edmund Kelly and John Dee, consultants to Queen Elizabeth I. They traveled as practicing alchemists and diviners throughout Europe. For what reason might a devout Christian such as John Dee become interested in invoking and conversing with angels? In her thesis for the English and Philosophy Department at Barrett, The Honors College at Arizona State University, Lindsey Rae Bosak asked just that question. After investigating five hypotheses, she concluded that Dee had been trying to converse with angels for many different reasons. "The main reason," she writes, "was somewhat selfish. He was a scholar with the chance to learn the secrets and knowledge of the divine, there was no other motivation needed."[16] What was good enough for Adam and the angels was good enough for John Dee.

The practice of invoking angels for magical work has continued into the new age study of angelology. A number of books offer methods to attain divine intervention via angelic contact, and thus to influence the outcome of a situation. Not all provide the same names, intonations, and rituals, however. In addition to developing the concept of angelology, our medieval, metaphysical rabbi Eleazar ben Judah of Worms spent a lifetime parsing out the divine names, attributes, and appearances of angels and demons. In the same manner John Dee set forth his ideas on the art of compelling, or persuading, an angelic being to do one's bidding. Such a metaphysical and human need to command angels suggests that there is still much to learn about the subjects of invocation, prayer, and free will among both men and angels. Is the burning of frankincense in High Mass Catholic rituals a bit of magical action designed to make the prayer more palatable to God? What began as devout theurgy, prayer enhanced with white magic, ran amok and became *goetia,* a strict, ritualistic summoning of primarily fallen angels for usually personal and less than godly motivations.

Problems arise with trying to gain control of one's life through invoking angels or trying to manipulate the cosmos so that whatever we wish to gain comes out in our favor. Is that necessarily a good thing? The angels of light work for good, but not all spirit beings are of the light. Human desires can be cloudy. Theologian Richard Rohr makes an interesting point about calling on angels to alter outcomes or fix the broken things of our lives. Most of us imagine that the unexpected situation creates the most life stress, yet psychologists say that planned change is even more disruptive. "Somehow things that just happen are seen as 'acts of God.' We can fight them, ignore them or accept them," Richard Rohr reminds us, "but we know we can't fix them or change them." After the initial shock of the unexpected wears off, humans usually find the wherewithal to deal with their situation.[17]

Even though Eleazar ben Judah knew a great deal about the qualities and powers of angels, he forbade his students to invoke their divine names. The rabbi once warned his students not to attend a wedding because they had to travel a dangerous road. He forbade them to go or to call on angelic protectors, believing that would have been dabbling in magic. The students went anyway and relied on the protection of magically invoked angelic names. Indeed, they met the robbers, but met no harm. When the rabbi found out, he insisted that the students return to the same spot in the road and refrain from invoking any divine names for protection. They may have saved their lives, he reasoned, but they had "lost the world to come." So the students returned, and all were killed.[18]

On the other hand, Meister Eckhart believes it is possible to commune with angels on a regular basis. By design, angels existed to assist human beings in their spiritual mission. "The angel remains unencumbered in his soul," he says. "Therefore, he surrenders himself to every soul completely."[19]

Nowhere does the Bible say people must not pray or invoke angels. Most religions make a distinction between the two. Prayer is reserved for the worship of God. The angels respond to our needs as God sees fit to send them. Apparently, in the absence of Jesus, his followers began to seek the advice of angels. In Colossians 2:18 Paul admonished the church members to turn away from false teachers who claimed special mystical connections to angels. This is because angels, even though they dwell in Spirit, are creatures made by God—and creatures are not to be worshipped in the same way that God is worshipped. That would be idolatry.

In Revelation 22:9 when God sent an angel to reveal the future to John, John fell down in adulation. The angel stopped him, saying, "I am a fellow servant with you and with your brothers, the prophets—Worship God!" (NIV). Yet believers continued to petition angels as compassionate beings who want to help us. Perhaps if we are familiar with them on a daily basis they will not seem so far away when we need them the most.

When Angels Become Human

Humans are curious about angels, and perhaps angels are equally curious about humans. In one Sufi story, God created the angels Harut and Marut whom he sent to Earth to experience the human condition. The angels lived as humans by day and reported their doings to God at night. Alas, they succumbed to the wiles of a beautiful woman named Zahara who wanted to know their secret. When they revealed to her their angelic identities, they doomed themselves to live as humans without being able to return to God. They repented, seeing the error of their ways, but God commanded them to continue living on Earth as a test for human beings. Students of magic flocked to them, wanting to know the sacred name of God by which the angels performed such magical acts. The angels warned them: "We are only a temptation! So, beware! And remember God."

In any event, the angels did teach them the mysteries of astrology, alchemy, numerology, magic, and the healing arts. They warned their proteges to remain pure of heart, or else they would be in danger of losing themselves to the djinn. Music, poetry, and the like contained the magical euphoria of good spell-making and constructive magic. However, God did not accept the kind of language that separated husband and wife or cast maleficent events into the lives of others. Says Kabbani, "The duality of magic is reflected in the story of the two who are both men and angels, whose human dimension is to forget and whose angelic dimension is to remind and teach. People who deal in psychic forces nowadays are similarly divided into two groups."[20] Perhaps it is not so terrible that the angels taught us astrology and the like, if we can use it to heighten our spiritual work. It is a detriment to use such magical knowledge in harmful ways.

Calling All Angels

In the Middle East, in the predawn and evening hours, one hears the evocative voice of the muezzin calling the faithful to prayer. After the first vocalization fades, one can feel the awed silence that seems to rise into the ethers, as if waiting for Allah to answer. The invocation of angels relies upon a similar breathy vocalization of sacred names and mantras. The Christian Church intones the *Hoc est Corpus Meu* ("This Is My Body") as part of the Holy Communion rite. When a priest invokes angelic hosts into a religious service through canticles, Leadbeater commented, "Angels of a special type take those words as a call, and at once attend to play their part in the service which is to be held."[21]

From where do the angels appear when we summon them? Does one have to know from which heaven, or wait for the request to move up, then allow the angel's response to filter down? No. Remember that space and time are irrelevant to light-force energies. The angels have not come from any faraway distant heaven. The lines of force and energy are always present, always ready, "but they turn themselves outward in response to the call."[22]

In his book *The Secret Teachings of All Ages*, Manly Palmer Hall provides an angelic invocation gleaned from an unpublished manuscript by eighteenth-century occultist Francis Barrett. Hall recreates an invocation ritual for contacting and verifying the identity of the angel Zadkiel, who is known as "the Righteousness of God," for the purpose of banishing demons. In addition to Zadkiel, the invocation summons the dark spirits "by whatever names they are known" to appear, in order for them to be banished.[23] The imprecision of the invocation is worrisome. It is unlikely that any good can come of such mispronounced angelic petitions. Manly Hall goes on to say that "if the pact is signed in blood between a man and a demon, the demon will eventually gain control of the individual. If the human fails to fulfill his end of the bargain, then the soul belongs to the Lucifer." Manly Hall did not approve of such pacts any more than Eleazar ben Judah approved of invoking angels. Of this bond, Hall says: "Black magic is not a fundamental art; it is the misuse of an art. It merely takes the emblematic figures of white magic and inverting and reversing that signifies that it is left-handed."[24]

Working with angelic energy must be for the highest intention of manifesting spiritual energy in a terrestrial situation. Angels and their power are not sent down to satisfy egos. They intend to inspire God's servants, to execute his decrees, and to help people resolve problems in their daily lives, said Shaykh Kabbani. "Angels and their angelic powers do not help tyrants and oppressors dominate this world. . . . They disconnect their energies from anyone who tries to harm nature, animals, or human beings, or exploit them for selfish purposes."[25]

Angels of Protection

Powerful Zoroastrian angels are said to assist humankind with "the most mighty, most glorious, and most victorious of the spells. To utter their names is synonymous with efficacy and power."[26] While one cannot influence the will, the truth, and the thoughts of God, nor alter His essence, the petitioner may find that the use of Zoroastrian angelic names—which are divine attributes—positively influences human affairs. To invoke Rashnu is to invoke the justice that the sacred name personifies.

In the Eastern tradition, people may petition spiritual forces for personal and community protection. Fearsome dharmapalas guarded Chögyam Trungpa Rinpoche, the Tibetan Buddhist who enacted a harrowing yearlong escape through the Himalayas after the Chinese destroyed his monastery. Eventually landing in Boulder, Colorado, he established Naropa Institute, but retained his spirit guardians. While he taught Vajrayana Buddhism in the West—an esoteric meditative practice that demanded a strict adherence to silence and compliance—the Vajrayana guardians acted as protective personal angels for him and his teachings.[27] Any challengers to the so-called "Crazy Wisdom" of the Rinpoche met resistance, often tangling in the ethers with his Vajrayana guardians.[28]

When faced with a choice about whether or not to invoke an angel, Rabbi David Cooper disagrees with Eleazar ben Judah. When he feels entirely helpless, he finds himself drawn to the "mysterious force of healing" by angels, which offers him comfort and a release from fear. Angelic energy that is healing can indeed can be palpable. Rabbi Cooper reports a Christian friend who consistently sang a prayer to the archangel Michael for the several days after her son suffered a tragic accident and fell into a coma. When the boy awoke, he not only remembered the words to the prayer, he also told his mother that while he lay unconscious he had been surrounded by beings filled with a white light.[29]

The story is similar to a message delivered in 1981 by Our Lady of Medjugorje (Yugoslavia), in trance, to six children. Certainly Mother Mary, whose divine conception was announced by an angel, would know a thing or two about angelic prayer. Our lady told the children "to pray for others because when you pray for someone, an angel goes and sits on the shoulder of that person."[30]

Our understanding of the spirit world often appears childlike, filled with wonder and wild imaginings; sometimes it appears like the bemused ramblings of a fevered mind. The idea of angels intervening in our lives is often dismissed, even at times by those who invoke them! Still, when our life circumstances become unbearably tangled or difficult, the human heart and mind try to leap out of the pain body to attain a wider, larger, more insightful and healing perspective. That is the time we begin casting about for the aid of angels. The desire for divine help and guidance seems hardwired into human beings, as if the trials of life force us to try to remember the larger spiritual home from which we came.

Legends speak of Mary Magdalene, the companion of Jesus, whose faith was tried again and again, and whose reputation has been battered for centuries by traditional church fathers. The legends say that after the death of Jesus, she departed her homeland for the south of France. There she taught compassion, healing, and faith. For the last thirty years of her life she lived in a cave. Seven times a day "angels gathered her up and transported her to the peaks of the mountain range, to the rarified air where their messages could be heard more clearly."[31]

Angelic Books of Secret Knowledge

In the book of Revelation, the second-century mystic John of Patmos described seeing the seven seals, seven angels, and seven flames before the throne. He also saw an angel clothed in a cloud, his face as radiant as the sun, and his legs like pillars of fire. Straddling the earth and sea, this angel gave to him "a little book, bidding him eat it, which the seer did. The book is representative of the secret doctrine—that spiritual food which is the nourishment of the spirit. And St. John, being 'in the spirit,' ate his fill of the wisdom of God and the hunger of his soul was appeased." What medicine did that angelic book contain? John of Patmos tells us "the secret doctrine of the ancients had been given to men who had profaned it . . . "[32]

Could this profaned doctrine be the aforementioned book of Raziel, the book scribed of brilliant white fire by the angel known as the Angel of the Secret Regions of the Supreme Mysteries of God? As we learned earlier, this magical text contained the 72 most holy names of God, the 670 mysteries, and the 1,500 keys in the book that Adam received. Even the angels didn't know everything contained there.[33] Raziel's book was written to console Adam and Eve after their expulsion from the garden. According to one tradition, Raziel stood behind the curtain in heaven, listening and recording all of God's decrees.[34]

God took pity on Adam and sent Raziel with the book "so that he might look into the mirror of existence and so see the Divine Face and himself so illuminated as an image of God." Within the pages of this magic book, Adam learned the secrets of the angels and of Deity, the magical names, and all the celestial and earthly knowledge. Even to this day the angel holds the key to heavenly mystery. "Raziel stands upon the peak of Mount Horeb and proclaims the secrets of men to all mankind."[35] The book of Enoch tells us that from every word going out of the divine mouth, an angel is created. Raziel stands in the service of the ministering angels and sings before the Thrice Holy One. Each time a name of God is spoken, which are the names of his angels, sparks of lightning shoot forth. "Lights shine from each of them, and each one is surrounded by tents of brilliance so that not even the Seraphim, who are greater than all the children of heaven, are able to look at them."[36]

Call it the book of Raziel, the book of Adam, or the Torah, the mysteries inside these pages are so important to humankind that they are delivered in three different versions to three different prophets—Adam, Noah, and Moses—and by three different angels: Raziel, Hadraniel, and Raphael.[37]

In the book of Adam and Eve, Adam is called "the bright angel"; in Enoch II, he is called a "second angel." God originally made Adam androgynous like Himself—an exact image of his Maker, according to the Talmud. At death, says the ancient Greek text known as the Apocalypse of Moses (330–140 BCE), the archangel Michael whisked Adam to heaven in a fiery chariot. A Christian legend states that Jesus fetched Adam from hell and transported him into heaven along with the other "saints in chains." Yet a third pseudographic legend from the Revelation of Moses (200 BCE–100 CE) informs us that the four archangels—Uriel, Gabriel, Raphael, and Michael—buried Adam.[38]

After Adam's death, this revered book became his son Seth's inheritance and moved through ancestral hands until received by Enoch, who incorporated much of it into his tome: the book of Enoch. Then the angels Raphael and Metatron kept it hidden until Raphael offered the book to Noah to help him build an ark in which to survive the coming flood. Noah's son Shem inherited the book from his father. It then passed to Abraham, then to Isaac, and down the line of Jewish patriarchs.[39] The book passed down among them until after the death of Solomon, when it disappeared.

One legend suggests that the book reappeared during the time of Moses. During the vision quest when Moses climbed Mount Sinai to receive the Torah and the Commandments, he followed God's instructions, continuing to climb up and up. As he approached the highest heaven, seven angels tried to stop him. The whole idea of giving a human the holy book of power that contained the secret names of the creation of everything threatened both angels and demons. According to Rabbi Eleazar, when Moses entered the cloud on Mount Sinai, the great angel Kamuel, in charge of twelve thousand angels, tried to overpower him. However, Moses spoke the twelve names of God that he had learned at the burning bush. The utterance blasted the angel twelve thousand leagues away.

Other angels, each mightier than the last, tried to stop Moses. At last the voice of Hadraniel, the gatekeeper of God, stopped Moses in his tracks. No wonder Hadraniel hesitated to give Moses any books of Holy Scripture—he knew how poorly it had turned out when the angels delivered the book of Adam. Hadraniel so overpowered Moses that the quaking prophet could not pronounce the names of God. After God himself encouraged Moses to speak, Hadraniel took Moses to see the angel Sandalphon, who stood behind the curtain of his master while weaving a crown of glory for God. Hadraniel advised Moses to go no further for fear of being burned in the fire of Sandalphon. Trembling, Moses ran past Sandalphon and crossed a stream of purifying fire before he reached the Throne of Glory. There he met Raziel, the angel who dwells beyond the veil and who sees, hears, and knows everything. Moses quaked with terror, but God told him to hold tight to the throne and no harm would come to him. Then, for the next forty days, the angel Raziel taught Moses the Torah.[40]

The book of Raziel, as we know it now, did not appear in any real form until early in the medieval era. Many scholars believe Rabbi Eleazar ben Judah of Worms authored it. The book's contents include Eleazar ben Judah's favorite topics—angelology, the names of God, magical uses of astrology, gematria, protective spells, and a method of writing magical healing amulets. The book explains how the creative life energy starts with a thought from the spiritual realms, transcends into speech, and moves into action in this physical world. The book insists that the eternal divine creative life energy of this Earth is love. The spiritual laws of birth, death, reincarnation, and many laws of "change" are among the first metaphysical texts to speak of the natural laws. These laws are defined later in *The Kybalion,* a seminal text written in 1901, which we will discuss later. While its reputed author was a saintly rabbi who abhorred the dark arts and the invoking of angels, because of its extensive contents the book became notorious in German Renaissance magic.[41]

The book *Sefer Raziel HaMalakh* first came into print in Amsterdam in 1701. Many people who could neither read nor understand it bought it simply for the spiritual protection it offered. Simply owning a copy was said to protect the individual, his home, and its occupants from fire and robbery. Knowing its contents and using them metaphysically could "drive away evil spirits and help parents to raise wise and intelligent sons."[42]

Today fragments of the aforementioned book of Enoch actually exist in papyrus and parchment. Currently, copies of the book are said to be hidden in the back rooms of the Vatican. We know that the book of Enoch holds the mysteries of the angels who fell, the Nephilim, and the demons, but it also holds another mystery about the connection between humans and angels. Is it possible that there is another mystery here, the mystery of how consciousness, honed over many human lifetimes, can ascend into the sprit realm to bear the title of angel?

In certain kabbalistic circles the identities of Enoch, the prophet, and Metatron, the archangel, merge. Metatron is known as the angel (mal'akh) of the presence. "Tradition states that this fiery creature at the head of Creation was once Enoch the man . . . who walked with the Elohim (Genesis 5:22). The name Enoch, or *hanokh* in Hebrew, means 'initiated' or 'dedicated.' Because of this commitment, Enoch did not taste death, we are told, but was taken directly up into Heaven."[43]

In book three Enoch describes being assumed into heaven to become Metatron. "The Holy One blessed me. He put his Hand upon me and blessed me with 5360 blessings. And I was raised and enlarged to the size of the length of the world. And he causes 72 wings to grow on me, 36 on each side and each wing was the whole world. And he fixed on me 365 eyes: each eye was as the great luminary. He left no kind of splendor, brilliance, radiance, beauty of all the lights of the universe that He did not affix to me."[44]

This merger of Enoch with Metatron depicts the feathered wings covered in eyes, and seems to mimic the description of the angel as a peacock, an angelic image that finds its resonance in Hindu and Yezidi traditions. Enoch/Metatron is transformed into a galactic consciousness and the other angels tremble in his presence.

The assertion of the unity of Metatron and Enoch refutes the idea that angels differ in species from human beings. It negates the idea that angels have never touched Earth nor engaged in an earthly, physical form. One solution to this problem of a saintly man who became an angel is to envision the transformation the other way around. What if Metatron, the angel, took on human form in the guise of Enoch? In this way Enoch was never born mortal but only appeared to be so.

As previously discussed, the book of Raziel, it is said, passed into the hands of Enoch, who drew upon its contents while writing the book of Enoch. In this way, Enoch, the prophet in a human form, could subsequently foretell what would be written on the tablets later given to Moses when he ascended Mount Sinai. Enoch possessed the miraculous rod that Moses later used to confront pharaoh. He knew the astronomical secrets of the heavens and sacred calendar days long before Moses received his wisdom.[45] In the pages of Enoch's book, Noah found the information and gematria he used to craft the ark.

QBL and Angelic Wisdom

The Kabbalah (Qabalah or QBL), as we know it today, probably owes much to the Middle Ages and the centuries of angelologists, theologists, and copyists who tried to preserve the divine knowledge well before the age of the printing press. Traces of oral versions of the book of Raziel, the books of Enoch, and many other spiritual traditions may still exist within the teachings of the Kabbalah.[46] People often have been persecuted for their religious beliefs. Not surprisingly, much mystery even today surrounds the origins of the Kabbalah.

Three separate versions of its dissemination to man are offered. The first legend indicates that God created a wisdom school for angels. In this school he taught the Kabbalah and its mysteries; the angels then taught its secrets to Adam.[47] God and the angels intended the wisdom book to be used for the transformation of humans—specifically so that "fallen humanity might regain its lost estate." However, the humans found the material pleasures of the world more interesting, so God took the book away from them. When the book returned to man, various patriarchs handed it down to their sons, and different angels taught its sciences. The angel Tophiel taught Shem, Noah's son; Raphael taught Isaac; Metatron taught Moses; and Michael taught David.[48]

The second legend suggests that Melchizedek taught Abraham the mystical knowledge as part of the covenant with God that Abraham and his descendants received.[49] He carried the wisdom with him to Egypt (ca. 1700 BCE), where he allowed a bit of its magic to ooze out and influence the Egyptians.[50] This story does not exactly match up with the time line of the Egyptian wisdom school traditions and the Kabbalah, but it does provide a glimmer of assurance that there is a link there. It does in some way explain why the ark of the covenant bears two angelic images on its golden lid that duplicate the winged goddesses Isis and Nephthys, who are said to watch over the coffin of Osiris. The Egyptian Isis and Nephthys bear striking resemblance to the Jewish cherubim.

Moses carried with him the mystical teachings of Egypt and became most proficient in his study of the Kabbalah during his wanderings in the wilderness. He not only devoted the leisure hours of his whole four years to it, but he received lessons in it from the angels. On Mount Sinai Moses received the outer teachings (the Ten Commandments) and the inner teachings of the great mystery. During his second visit, Moses ascended into heaven, where the whole book of kabbalistic teachings unfolded before him. "When Torah was transmitted to Moses, myriads of celestial angels came to scorch him with flames from their mouths, but the blessed Holy One sheltered him."[51] He carried the wisdom down the mountain, and then he initiated the seventy elders into the secrets of this doctrine. They, in turn, transmitted them from hand to hand. Of all who formed the unbroken line of tradition, David and Solomon became the most initiated into the Kabbalah. No one, however, dared to write down any of it until Simon ben Jochai, who lived at the time of the destruction of the second temple.[52]

The Sepher Yetzirah, or the book of Formation, is the earliest documented copy of one of the books of Kabbalah. Written by Abraham and hidden in a cave, it was rediscovered in the second century BCE. Some say the Sepher Yetzirah owes its origin to Moses De Leon who, in the fourteenth century, also wrote the Zohar. Others believe it to be the work of Rabbi Akiba ben Yosef, the rabbi most noted for developing the biblical interpretation known as the Midrash (ca. 120 CE).[53]

A Transfer of Wisdom from the Angel Metatron

How is the knowledge of this mystical and sometimes confusing text intended to aid humankind? Its magical wisdom must become internalized through study, of course, and through the intervention of angels.

Through the divine light that created angels, the transformation of the prophet Enoch was accomplished. His body turned into celestial fire, his flesh became as flame, his veins flared like flames, and his bones glimmered like coals. A heavenly brightness filled his eyes, and his eyeballs became torches of fire. His hair flared as a burning pyre, and all his limbs and organs transformed into burning sparks. His whole frame was consumed in the fire. This description resonates with the image of the phoenix on its pyre.[54]

In the third book of Enoch the angel Metatron appears as a separate entity before Enoch. He actually places these particular spiritual gifts inside him: Brilliance, Understanding, Subtlety, Life, Loving-Kindness, the Torah, Wisdom, Knowledge, Beauty, Splendor—essentially all of the sephira that are a traditional part of the kabbalistic Tree of Life.[55] After the angel places these gifts inside the body of the human Enoch, he merges into Enoch, thus making him a human angel. Enoch then is not just a lesser angel, but the embodiment of the greatest angel of all, Metatron himself. This image suggests the mystical knowledge that the Tree of Good and Evil, or the Tree of Life, has to offer. This divine tree is rooted within the self, and through it each individual has the capacity to ascend to heaven to become a companion of God.

> Each of the tree's branches (called "sephirot") symbolize a particular type of creative force that a different Archangel oversees . . . As the angel of life, Metatron is at the top of the [Tree of Life], directing God's living energy throughout the universe . . . As the angel of mysteries, Raziel reveals divine mysteries to people that help them become wiser . . . As the angel of compassionate understanding, Tzaphkiel [Zaphkiel] leads the angels who send the spiritual energy of understanding to people . . . As the angel of mercy, Zadkiel and the angels he supervises send the energy of God's mercy throughout the universe . . . As the angel of peaceful relationships, Chamuel excercises tough love to strengthen relationships . . . As the angel of joy, Haniel expresses God's eternal energy by helping people rely on God . . . Michael and Raphael join forces to express God's glory . . . As the angel of revelation, Gabriel is a master communicator . . . As the angel of music and prayer . . . Sandalphon's efforts are designed to keep the divine energy flowing freely.[56]

Communion with the Angels and Devata

Paramahansa Yogananda tells us that God has personified himself in every human, and every human personifies one of his many divine forms. Angels, humans, and deities alike join in the creative work of uplifting ever-evolving souls. But he cautions, "Communion with these devata or 'shining ones' is not to be misunderstood as the spirit communion of Spiritualists. Truly divine ones cannot be contacted by this means.* Only by lifting one's own consciousness, through the right method of meditation, to the higher spiritual realms of the astral home of the divine forces that uphold the material world can such attunement with the deities be realized."[57]

The prophet Abraham dined with angels; he erred in thinking, and then learned the error of his ways as taught by the angels. He made his pact with God for future generations, studied, and wrote for posterity. In all this, he understood the importance of human and angelic interaction. Abraham attained a greatness that bridged human and angelic realms. The prophet accomplished the greatest task, one that angels, we are told, are unable to attain.

Rabbi Simhah Zissel Ziv, a nineteenth-century Lithuanian Jew, surmised that angels can recognize the dignity of the physical world, but they cannot "put their wisdom into action. Human beings are able to reach this level, as angels are not, and it would be the height of folly for humans to fail to put their wisdom into action." While other scholars counted angels and humans as two different species, Simhah Zissel believed humans could attain the status of angels and that human prophets could attain a level of excellence that even angels cannot.[58] Abraham joined together the physical and spiritual worlds, a capacity that is open to all of us. Even ordinary human beings who are not partially angelic, Rabbi Zissel suggested, can inherit and implement Abraham's teachings on how to bring loving-kindness into the world.[59]

Studying the Kabbalah brings one back around to thinking about the angels of the sephira and whether or not those angels have form,

---

*Meaning clairvoyance and channeling.

and, if so, are those forms more or less palpable? If they have forms, how do they acquire their forms, and can anyone see them?

Theologians surmise that angels differ in species from human beings, even though at times they may appear to take a human form. Meister Eckhart believed that angels descended to Earth, acquiring human form to inspire us to interact with our essential goodness. Eckhart tells the story of a student who asked his teacher about the essence of angels. The teacher replied:

"Go away and think deeply into yourself until you understand the angel and give yourself up to that with all of your being and realize that you consist of nothing else than what you find in that angel. Then you will realize that you are one with the angels. And when you give yourself to this realization with all your being, it will dawn on you that you are all angel and with all the angels." The student went away and lived deeply and inwardly in himself until he found the truth of all of this.

A second time he returned to thank his teacher, saying: "Everything happened just as you said. As I gave myself over to the essence of the angel and soared into its being, I realized that I was all angel with all the angels."

The teacher then advised him to continue meditations with the angels if he wished to advance further, and "miracle upon miracle will be performed in your soul."[60]

Jacob's Ladder and the Tree of Life

In his book *God Is a Verb* Rabbi David Cooper suggests that Jacob's Ladder "is not a ladder at all, but a sign of higher consciousness."[61] The rungs of the ladder mark the Kabbalah's four planes of existence on the Tree of Life—the physical, emotional, mental, and spiritual planes. Jacob standing in the middle of the three pillars on this ladder observes the angels on either side coming and going. In so doing, he sees the potential for the totality of consciousness. Each rung of the ladder of the Tree of Life represents a climb further up into a plane of existence or into another level of consciousness.

In John 1:50–51 Jesus refers to this same ladder of consciousness when, after Nathaniel testifies to the powerful spiritual truth of Jesus having seen him clairvoyantly, Jesus says, "You will see greater things than that . . . Truly I tell you, you will see heaven open, and the angels of God ascending and descending on the Son of Man" (ESV). Jacob's Ladder is available to all. It is the Tree of Life, which is the spiritualized human, and the angels contained within are many. I'm repeating: *It is the spiritualized human and the angels contained within are many.*

On the Tree of Life, the archangel Gabriel stands at the gateway that is the sephiroth Yesod. Kabbalists perceive Yesod as the doorway between heaven and earth. Overall, Gabriel functions as the most frequent go-between in the heavenly and earthly realms. This angel often shows his human form. He visited Abraham, Joseph, Daniel, Zacharias, Mary, Mohammad, and others, showing them his humanity. All Abrahamic religions recognize this mal'akh for his "special role as a mediator between human consciousness and the higher realms from which spirit descends into the body."[62] His sacred angel name combines two Hebrew words: *Man* and *God*. Gabriel carries an angelic vibration that infuses spiritual energy into human form. Conversely, he moves the human vibration upward to humanize God.[63]

No single archangel named Gabriel serves all of mankind. There are many Gabriel energies, a network of vibrations that are likened to his angelic code. His messages are available to every one of us, supplying the communication from above that we need.

Angelic States of Consciousness

Rabbi David Cooper tells us that every atom of the universe has an angel. Every thought, he says, has its angel.[64] We speak of the angels of our higher nature, by which we mean the inspired realizations, the lightheartedness, the loving feelings toward humankind. Yet the darker emotions—anger, criticism, egotism, cruelty—beget darker beings; what we envision as the fallen angels that bedevil us. These are not imaginary beings. They are realities that our minds create.

Reiteration: *The realities that our minds create,* Rabbi Cooper said, *are the bedeviling creations derived from thought.*

In 1901, Theosophist William Walker Atkinson wrote *The Kybalion,* which claims to be a translation of the work of Hermes Trismegistus. He used a pseudonym, "The Three Initiates." In the book, Hermes Trismegistus alluded to the Egyptian master teacher, Thoth the Atlantean. In this way Atkinson created a classic book of new thought and the science of mind. The pen name and occult authorship cast a mystical patina on the book. In no way does it invalidate Atkinson's points about the power of the mind to create reality. One could say that the Torah, the Bible, and the Qur'an contain equally inspired narratives that attempt to explain the truth about God, angels, and human interactions.

The Kybalion hits upon the main point—that all is mind. Belief becomes reality. *The Kybalion* synthesizes many esoteric traditions that say similar things. It explains overlapping religious traditions as a way that angels attempted to validate each tradition. *The Kybalion* describes the hierarchy of spiritual beings throughout the cosmos.

The book tells us that on seven minor planes of the great spiritual plane reside the beings we call "angels," "archangels," and "demigods." This is the plane that we have been examining. On the lower minor planes dwell "those great souls whom we call masters and adepts. Above them come the Great Hierarchies of the Angelic Hosts, unthinkable to man; and (in the plane above that) come those who may without irreverence be called 'the Gods.'" These "Gods" are so great in intelligence, power, and essence that all races of men conceive of them as Deity. An excerpt from *The Kybalion* expands on this.

> Many of these Beings, as well as the Angelic Host, take the greatest interest in the affairs of the Universe and play an important part of its affairs. These Unseen Divinities and Angelic Helpers extend their influence freely and powerfully, in the process of evolution, and Cosmic Progress. Their occasional intervention and assistance in human affairs have led to the many legends, beliefs, religions and

traditions of the race, past and present. They have super-imposed their knowledge and power upon the world, again and again, all under the law of THE ALL, of course. But, yet even the highest of these advanced Beings exist merely as creations of, and in, the Mind of THE ALL, and are subject to the Cosmic Processes and Universal Laws.[65]

CONCLUSION

I Am That I Am

That's all an angel is, an idea of God.

MEISTER ECKHART, AS QUOTED IN
BREAKTHROUGH BY MATTHEW FOX

It all comes back to the Mind of the All, the "All" being the universal life force of God. We are both mortal and divine, and only a few enlightened masters have ever been able to stay with their mountaintop experience. One cannot live on the mystical level all the time. Kabbalist Joseph Gelberman suggests that his students meditate upon the Tree of Life using the image of Jacob's Ladder. "The angels are always going up and down, not remaining in one place."[1] And there are many paths up the mountain, many paths on the Tree of Life. There are many means by which to approach God and byways on which we may meet angels of many kinds. One path may be mystical and another scientific. Our minds contain multiple intelligences and ways of knowing.

The brain perceives varying vibrations of color, heat, light, and sound. Their degrees of intensity stretch beyond what human eyes and ears can know. More than any other thing, an angel is created by whirling electrons and light. It may be that the appearance of angels establishes itself on a continuum, much as light waves appear on a continuum of color, extending beyond the visible spectrum into the X-ray,

182

the infrared, and ultraviolet. In his far-reaching metaphysical description of all universal divine beings, C. W. Leadbeater said:

> Try to imagine the whole universe filled with and consisting of an immense torrent of living light, the whole moving onward, without relativity, a resistless onward sweep of a vast sea of light, light with a purpose (if that is comprehensible), tremendously concentrated, but absolutely without strain or effort—words fail. At first, we feel nothing but the bliss of it, and see nothing but the intensity of the light; but gradually we begin to realize that even in this dazzling brightness there are brighter spots . . . Then by degrees we begin to comprehend that these subsidiary suns are the Great Ones, the Planetary Spirits, great Angels, karmic deities, dhyan chohans, Buddhas, Christs, and Masters, and many others who are to us not even names, and to see that through them the light and the life are flowing down to the lower planes.[2]

Thoughts and Things

But the mind also transmits thoughts, which are vibrations themselves. Thought vibration is the essence of consciousness and of manifestation. We become what we think about, and we create what is in our thoughts constantly. Psychologist James Hillman in *Re-Visioning Psychology* reminds us that our words create our realities, seen and unseen. "We need to recall the angel aspect of (any) word, recognizing words as independent carriers of soul between people. We need to recall that we do not just make up words or learn them in school, or ever have them fully under control. Words, like angels, are powers which have invisible power over us."[3]

Or as the Sufi teacher Idries Shah has said, "The angels are the higher developments of the mind." He reminds us that some angels are of the nature of beauty [*jamal*], and some are of the nature of grandeur [*jalal*].[4] Asian studies scholar Barbara O'Brien suggested that in order for religion to take back the power it once had, we must pry it away from literalism.[5] The battle ground between the angels in heaven or hell, between the devata and the Asura, is neither myth, fantasy, nor historical fiction. The battle takes place every day within the self. We win the world for Ahura Mazda by working within our own good and noble mental capacities. The battle ground lies within our thoughts, which precede our words and deeds. Angels indeed ride in on the alphabet and the breath. The mind is a human being's most divine defense and its greatest weapon.

Those things that exist, from the densest rock to the most gossamer angel and things still unseen, all exhibit energy patterns that vibrate at varying rates. The higher rates occupy higher planes of existence, but by *plane* one does not mean a place or a condition per se, although it may have the qualities of both. Everything that exists in the cosmos emanates from the energy (vibration) of God. All angels are energy forces, says Rabbi Philip Berg, paraphrasing the sixteenth-century kabbalist Rav Isaac Luria, author of *The Etz Chaim*. All energy forces, Berg says, are both good and bad, formed by people's words and deeds. He continues to elucidate how thought and intention create the reality of angels in our lives. "When a person occupies himself or herself with spirituality, prayer, meditation, and acts of sharing, the breath of air that leaves the mouth becomes a chariot, a vehicle for these angels—they are informants of our own creation. Although these positive and negative entities have existed since long before we came into this world, they remain dormant, in a state of suspension, until such time as we create the suitable garment or vehicle through which they reveal themselves or make themselves manifest."[6]

Good fortune or tragedy are not events suddenly thrust upon us by our Creator. Quite simply, we are solely responsible for what happens to us and for which angels appear in our lives. While angels have no free will of their own, Berg believes, "their essential energy is drawn to us by our words and our deeds."[7] It is not bad karma that draws negative events and influences into our lives. Most often it is human error—bad choices, ignored instincts, or egoic responses to circumstances and people. All that is covered under the admonishment: "What were you thinking!?"

Rather than labeling it bad karma, as if karma had nothing to do with one's actions in this lifetime, Rabbi Cooper emphasizes cause and effect and calls it cosmic justice. "Cosmic justice," he says, "is the spiritual law that every action, word, or thought reverberates throughout the universe." Angels, he goes on to say, are concentrations of cosmic influence without dimension. They represent forces that raise consciousness. As humans we find ourselves pulled and swayed between the positive or negative poles of existence, but nothing pulls the angels in either direction. That is because, as Rabbi Cooper notes, angels are fully immersed in God; again, they have no free will. This is true as well for demons. "This is one of the most important teachings of the Torah. Once we recognize the part within us that is connected with God, we can never be defeated."[8]

These rabbinical writings suggest that, although God created angels for the express purpose of maintaining balance within the cosmos, they have essentially evolved into entities that man alone creates. Whether they support or work against an individual depends on the purity and the level of consciousness of the individual. This is an important point, worth underscoring through repetition here: *God uses the available energies of the universe he has created, and these repetitive energies have evolved into entities or angels that man alone summons (or creates). Their appearance depends upon our own consciousness.*

Physics and Angels

Allow me to digress into physics for a moment, for perception, physics, and angels have everything to do with each other. Recent scientific papers have refocused on a physics experiment that took place in the early 1800s called the "double slit experiment" in which particles of light projected through a barrier with two slits resulted in varied results. The variance only happened in the presence of a human scientist, one Dr. Thomas Young. When the experiment ran without being observed, it created a randomly scattered array pattern, but when the projection of the light beam was observed, it resulted in a wave pattern. The difference depended upon whether or not a human consciousness observed the light stream.

Thomas Young's experiment cracked modern science open to quantum mechanics. He demonstrated that mere observation of an energy source could alter light patterns—not just metaphysically, but concretely: "Thoughts are things." In other words, the way we see the world becomes the world we live in. This quality of mind and the mind have everything to do with the observation of angels, and their purposes.[9]

German physicist Max Planck examined quantum physics more thoroughly in 1931. He became curious about how our thoughts create and influence reality through the phenomenon known as the "observer effect." Most people believe the physical world is solid. Actually 99.99999 percent of it is empty space held together by a mysterious web of energy.[10] This fabric of the universe, and reality as we know it, is influenced by, and reacts to our thoughts. Consciousness creates reality, not the other way around.

In quantum physics the observer becomes part of his observed world and can no longer be sure that so-called objective phenomena are not just a thought cast into emptiness, or at best, a shifting stream of thought fields of imagined, possible worlds. The universe is no longer the solid substantive place as understood by the Victorians only a century ago. Dr. Amit Goswami, physics professor and author of *The Self-Aware Universe* provided several key ideas that might be applied to our study of angels. He demonstrated that a quantum object such as an electron can exist in two places simultaneously, and that it can move between two places at once, a principle known as bilocation or teleportation. It appears without ever having traveled the space intervening. Also, one observed quantum object simultaneously influences a correlated object; no matter the space between them, whatever happens to one will happen to the other. Sometimes the exact opposite happens, but the two are correlated.[11]

The many legends and stories of angels tell us that they may exist simultaneously in two places. Often these stories appear to collapse heaven and earth into a single place in which an angel appears. An angel appears, and then it disappears—there is not really any distance covered from one place to another. One angel may appear to a number of people at the same time. Anyone who witnessed the angel's appearance most likely received the angel's message by mental impression rather than by an actual voice speaking. This last point implies that if God created angels and humans from the same divine substance, there is not any distance between us.

The appearance of angels in one's life has more to do with perceptions of holiness in the world all around than with any random appearance. Certainly, angels appear, summoned by our thoughts, but sometimes they are not immediately recognized because, for whatever reason, we are not aligned with their energies. Disappointment, sorrow, or worry can prevent us from experiencing angels. The more we become aware, and the more we immerse ourselves in their inspired and holy world, the more we converse with them. And the more we meditate regularly, the more likely we are to have an angelic encounter, regardless of the religion we adhere to. One's chosen faith will color the angel's appearance and our understanding of it. That said, angels/devata appear in all religions.

They may arrive with wings (less likely), or veiled in light (possible), or perhaps in a human form. They may arrive in the nick of time, summoned by need or purposeful invocation. In his article "New Age Angels" in *Crisis Magazine,* Christian author Leon Podles notes that intuition often plays a part in the angelic transaction. "My own feeling is that angels are at work in the preternatural events that defy rational explanation: sudden feelings that something is happening to someone you love; brief glimpses that seem to overcome space and time. These happen too often to be dismissed as coincidence . . . "[12] It may be that this precognitive connection is not such an unusual a phenomenon if one considers the fact that we are all part of the God force energy of the cosmos. We are, and angels are—just as the little toe of my left foot is a part of me. If a bee stung it, the rest of me would know. I imagine that if God created the angels out of his own substance and then similarly created mankind, then mankind, the angels, and God are intertwined eternally. The spiritual dimension of all matter originates in the creative God principle.

Making Contact with Angels

Rather than waiting for an angel to appear to impart a glad tiding or drag us out of harm's way, Rabbi Cooper suggests that daily contact with angels offers more empowering ways to help ourselves and others through difficult situations.[13] That daily practice may be the recognition that we are engaged in spiritual contact all the time. The more we are drawn into leading a daily mystical life, Rabbi Cooper believes, the more likely angels will appear in an awareness that can only be described as a kind of poetic sensibility. "The puff of a breeze, the dance of a shadow, all shapes, movements, energies—each has a special quality. Moreover, when angels are invoked, there is a fascinating experience of never feeling alone. There is a sense of being in the midst of a constantly unfolding creation that is rich, awesome, brilliant, and complete; each and every moment is stunning."[14]

While angels, or demons for that matter, appear drawn to us through our own thoughts, that does not mean that they originate in our minds. They originate from within the Mind of God. Rabbi Halevi, the kabbalist, describes the coming and going of angels up and down the Tree of Life, which the Torah described in the vision of Jacob's ladder. Angels descend to Earth from the mind of God. Because they come from the highest spiritual planes located in the highest of the seven heavens, they see beyond our temporal time and space. Their messages are prophetic. "Are they not like a man on a high mountain who can see over a whole landscape?" Z'ev Ben Shimon Halevi asks. "They observe events and see them unfold on a cosmic scale. While humans have free will, the angels have prophetic vision."[15]

Armed with a foreknowledge of the future, they may step in to guide and make adjustments to the holy narrative when necessary. This may account for the many angelic prognostications that appear in the Torah, the Bible, and the Qur'an, but he notes, "It is important to observe that each angelic being only carries out one particular order and no other; another spirit has to be sent if a second operation is to be done."[16] Some angels are creative, some protective, some healing; others perform duties related to the end of life.

Angels seem to be summoned or sent instantaneously at the speed of thought—perhaps even whether or not that thought is conscious. As easily as they fall, angels also appear to rise. "Since they have no bodies," Peter Kreeft suggested to his religious studies students, "angels do not operate on a space-time continuum . . . They are quantum, making whole leaps."[17] They can appear anywhere at any moment in as many places as they desire or as they are needed. Angels do not stay on their designated planes, as their movement along Jacob's Ladder attests. Again, they appear to move up or down the spectrum of existence, if you will, increasing in visible density as necessary. Kreeft describes the movement of angels as resembling an electron, which "can move from one orbit around the nucleus in the atom onto another orbit without ever passing through the space between and without taking up any time at all."[18]

THE QUANTA QUESTION

Here we enter the strange territory of angel and human interactions that have very few boundaries at all. Let's call it "the quanta question." *Quanta,* a word that gets bandied about these days, essentially means "a whole chunk of energies." Everything consists of quanta "too small to be seen, too swift to be captured, too numerous to even imagine." All those angels that we used to say could fit on the head of a pin pale in comparison to the astronomical number of quanta inside a single cell underneath the tip of a finger. "Quanta give form and substance to the reality that we are."[19] This approaches the edge of physical sciences—the absolute edge of what we can tangibly see, know, and understand. It is the basis of concepts like quantum physics, quantum mechanics, and quantum entanglement. All of these relate to our study of angels.

"Energy is a form of angelic power," Shaykh Kabbani reminds us. "Human beings have been granted permission to use it." This power is the light energy of each cell of our bodies and minds—synapses firing, making connections, sending out vibrations. As we develop our capacities to hold more compassion and attain a greater vision in tune with a divine vision, we can develop greater sophistication in the use of our own light bodies. Increasingly, we can achieve more visible powers in the material world. Similarly, angelic energy changes from one stage to another. The source of our mutual energy, however, is the same. Kabbani goes on to say, "When human beings elevate themselves to higher states of purity, they can use this energy to be more powerful and visible to others as servants of God, and they themselves become messengers of this angelic power.[20]

As mentioned earlier, the late neuroscientist Paul MacLean identified the prefrontal cortex as responsible for visionary experiences of love, empathy, compassion, and altruism as "the angel lobes." It is the seat of creative possibility. We might call it "higher mind." The Zoroastrians might say it is the access to Ahura Mazda. When we experience situations that call us to be more loving, more empathic, to think of the higher plan for our lives, this is the part of the brain that is activated. This is where our connection to angels and the divine mind resides.[21]

But is it possible (setting aside "likely") for one to train oneself to become more attuned and receptive to angelic intervention? We can examine that possibility by examining states of consciousness. Recent studies in the biology of consciousness ask whether consciousness originates beyond the brain. One might ask, are we something greater than simply a brain in a meat suit? Recent studies indicate that consciousness is directly linked to light, which is the biophotons in our brains. Whereas a rat's brain emits one biophoton per second, the average human brain emits around one hundred thousand biophotons. That is enough to appear in a visible light spectrum from near infrared through violet light. It's enough to demonstrate that the brain might have optical communication channels that may link our consciousness with what many religions or cultures name as Spirit. It is further possible to raise the rate of biophotons conveyed into more than a billion per second. That suggests the possibility that raising one's biophotons increases one's consciousness.[22]

Meditating with Angels

It's also true that enlightenment can be an observable phenomenon. Those Spiritualist mediums who speak of the gathering of ectoplasm and the perception of orbs of light in darkened, enclosed rooms may be tapping into the increased expression of biophotons at one time. In a situation in which a group of like-minded people sit meditating in a darkened room with the express intention of increasing their capacities for enlightenment and higher consciousness, the more likely it is for visible phenomena to appear. Parapsychologist June Beltzer explains the phenomena through metaphysical eyes. "Angels and spirit beings appear by attunement when one blends one's mental activity and ectoplasm with an etheric world intelligence during a trance state of consciousness."[23]

The emission of visible light, or a visible auric field, may account for the appearance of halos about the heads of saints, and it may speak to the light bodies of angels and ascended beings. In my opinion, this biophotonic production occurs regularly during meditation.[24] The practice of varying meditation techniques has been highly regarded among modern mystics, the Yezidis, and the Essene community to which Mary and Joseph reputedly belonged. Mohammed practiced meditation to gain enlightenment, as have Buddhists and Hindus. This deep meditative practice accounts for the appearance of the angels to these prophets. The prophet attuned his frequency to an angelic frequency, which made communication between human and angels, or higher consciousness, that much easier.

Interestingly as well, there may be more light and more biophotons in the universe than we currently acknowledge. That light communicates with us, reaching toward us from the vast dense regions of the universe with as much energy as we expend reaching back to attain it. It is through even the light (or darkness) of our thoughts that we can communicate our intentions and meaning to our bodies. In this way we carry on the cosmic imperative to be fruitful and multiply. God said in the beginning "Let there be light." And there was light. And there was consciousness. Of course when Elohim said, "Let there be light," there was on that first day, according to the mystical traditions, the appearance of angels.

Sufi masters like Shaykh Kabbani believe that the angels and other "prophetic spirits" have increased their consciousness capacity to the point where not only do they shine, but "they acquire all manners of gnosis and spiritual states. These in turn enable them to become beacons of light . . . carrying God's message to his creation."[25]

In deep meditation we contact that God essence in which we live and move and have our being. The lesser light within us becomes magnified in contact with the Divine. Mary, the Essene, said it best in Luke 1:46: "My soul doth magnify the Lord" (KJV).

Angels and Humans Entangled

That enlightened contact leads us to ponder the idea of quantum entanglement, which is what the scientists call the phenomena, with far-reaching implications. Physicist John Bell discovered that the elements of nature do not have to be in the same locale in order to connect. Nonlocality in physics says that two subatomic elements that once had interacted and are now separated by a distance can reconnect again. The reconnection is not only instantaneous, but also faster than light and occurs no matter how far apart the two elements are.

The idea is that two entangled photons can react to one another *no matter where the other photon exists in the universe.* A photon out there somewhere in the universe resonates to a biophoton within us. Quantum entanglement tells us that these two interact without delay; they interact as quickly as a thought. Boom! Angelic contact. Boom! Enlightenment. Perhaps consciousness and Spirit are not necessarily contained within the physical body as we have assumed. There truly may be somewhere out there in the midst of the galaxies a conversation of angels that can connect with us.

Quantum entanglement can be defined by an interaction and an intermingling of energies between two systems or between two species: human and angel. Once the system separates, something of each remains in the other, leaving the two connected within the quantum realm.[26] As an article on the Decode website states, "Maybe there is a world that exists within light, and no matter where you are in the Universe photons can act as portals that enable communication between these two worlds."[27] The angels that we see, which are sent by the Deity at a speed faster than a thought, may be reflections of the angels who, from the beginning of swirling cosmic stardust, are already a part of us.

The more we awaken to the available light within us, as the angels have guided, the more we can raise the level of our spiritual development. It is my belief that angels do not *have* beautiful thoughts; rather, angels *are* divinely beautiful thoughts. They are consciousness itself. Angels are the way in which our consciousness can communicate with the living mind of God. The prophet Jeremiah said, "I will put my law in their minds and write it on their hearts" (Jeremiah 31:33 NIV).

Few enough of us have spoken face-to-face with angels, but Edgar Cayce and Emanuel Swedenborg did. Swedenborg said: "[An] angel is a heaven in the smallest form. For heaven is not outside of the angel but is within him." In such similar words did he describe the essence of man.[28] Edgar Cayce reminded us that heaven and hell are within us; they reside in our thoughts.

Clearly there is more to consciousness than we can know through our normal channels of understanding. Mystics and poets tell us so. Shaman and monk alike allude to the same levels of consciousness that neuroscientist John C. Lilly described. After years of atheism, he at last approached what he called "Essence," remarking that that radiant center of light that was Essence existed within each of us, and that same radiant Essence in each individual connected us to each other. "The miracle," he concluded, "is that the universe created a part of itself, to study itself, and that this part in studying itself finds the rest of the universe in its own natural inner realities."[29]

In examining those conscious and unconscious planes, Lilly explored the edges of the mental realms and declared that what we know of consciousness, that part of life of which we are aware, is only the tip of the iceberg. His lifelong studies, detailed in his autobiography, describe a superconsciousness unfolding above us that is nine times more expansive as consciousness, while still beyond that blossoms a cosmic consciousness ninefold greater than superconsciousness. And in the unconscious realms below us, the mystics and shaman say, there dwell things of which we normally are unaware. Below us lies a realm nine times vaster than our consciousness, and below that exists a ninefold collective unconscious.[30]

If we want to know more precisely the creatures who are populating heaven and hell, we must examine our own minds, the containers of that Essence to which John Lilly alluded. Certainly those are the realms to which the ancient Egyptian and Mahayana Tibetan Book of the Dead alludes. Angels and devils dance upon the rungs of a ladder so vast and so high that we cannot see its furthest reaches. To follow the interaction of angels and humans is to pursue only the barest truth of the universal reality.

The Law of Attraction

Besides the idea of quantum entanglement, Rabbi David Cooper offers an additional reason for the congress of certain angels and humans— the Law of Attraction. Metaphysically, we attract that which is likened to us. Rabbi Cooper describes angels as electromagnetic vibrations that are similar to the invisible energetic force that a magnet emits as it attracts to it visible metal filings. Rather than seeing angels as entities with personalities, he believes the angels "represent lines of force, packets of energy like light photons . . . and they cannot be distinguished except through results." This explains the more positive (angelic) and negative (demonic) attractions that humankind is heir to. He goes on to say that "Every move we make is supported by an angel or demon; moreover, everything we do creates new angels and demons."[31] I suggest that the personalities and the stories that we give angels actually reflect our own psyches, foibles, and desires for higher spiritual awareness. For the most part they reflect our longed-for connection to the Divine, and the ways in which we approach it or may have missed the mark.

Manly P. Hall said that Lucifer's fallen crown "represents the intellectual mind without the illumination of the spiritual mind; therefore, it is 'the false light.' The false light is finally overcome and redeemed by the true light of the soul, called the Second Logos or *Christ*. The secret processes by which the Luciferian intellect is transmuted into the Christly intellect constitute one of the great secrets of alchemy that is symbolized by the process of transmuting base metals into gold."[32] The task is not easily accomplished. The secret to mastering a bedeviling power is to invoke the light within us to take charge of our lives. As we transform negative surroundings, events, and feelings, we move closer to the angels and the divine spark within, and to our goal of heavenly illumination—the golden light of Christ/Buddhic consciousness.

Sri Aurobindo expounds upon the Hindu essential philosophy of divining the difference between good and evil that runs through all Hindu literature as learning to distinguish between devata and Asuras, or the gods and the Titans. "The fundamental idea of the Rig Veda," he says, "is a struggle between the gods and their dark opponents, between the Masters of light, signs of destiny, and the children of division and night." In human terms, the dichotomy between the qualities of the deva and the Asura seems like a description of the angel on one shoulder and the devil on the other. The devic nature exhibits self-control, sacrifice, cleanliness, candor, truthfulness, calmness, and self-denial. It expresses compassion toward all beings, gentleness, modesty, forgiveness, patience, and a "deep sweet and serious freedom from all restlessness." The asuric nature exhibits wrath, greed, cunning, treachery, malice, pride, arrogance, and excessive self-esteem.[33]

The central story of the Bhagavad Gita depicts the hero Arjuna riding along in the chariot of his life, while learning from Krishna, his Divine Teacher disguised as the charioteer. He must learn to curb the warrior (Asura) nature that he has been taught will bring him acclaim, and to nurture instead his own deva nature. "He has to see only the work that must be done, to hear only the divine command breathed through his warrior nature . . ."[34] In this way Krishna becomes the angel on Arjuna's shoulder. Krishna does not command; he instructs. The lesson for our modern culture is to battle the ego (Asura) nature and its attendant fallen angels. The once shiny vision of success against all odds tempts the soul into losing its way amid the glitter of worldly possessions and acclaim.

Being of Two Minds

In his conversation with Bill Moyers, American mythologist and lecturer Joseph Campbell spoke of the disparate polarity of spiritual beings and angels, saying, "[T]he meditation Buddhas appear in two aspects, one peaceful and the other wrathful. If you are clinging fiercely to your ego and its little temporal world of sorrows and joys, hanging on for dear life, it will be the wrathful aspect of the deity that appears. It will seem terrifying. But the moment your ego yields and gives up, that same meditation Buddha is experienced as a bestower of bliss."[35]

Another way to approach this idea is to remember Edgar Cayce's admonition that we must protect ourselves from darker universal forces by vigilantly patrolling our own negative thinking and dark emotions. He underscored the power of the mantra and the power of the mind against dissolution. Spoken like an ancient Zoroastrian philosopher, Cayce implored his community to "stay close to the good, the light," and to keep constructive thoughts and feelings uppermost.[36]

We are all of two minds, and that becomes the problem—a divinely ordained problem that the human soul must work out. The divided self, our agathokakological mind, was created when Adam and Eve ate the apple from the tree. When the angel sat on one shoulder and the devil on the other, so to speak, Adam and Eve came to possess the knowledge of good and evil. Dichotomy began when the mind created paired oppositions, but before that human action only God's time existed. Only God's mind created the universe, and so all of the angels in heaven resonated as one with the thoughts of God. Until, that is, Adam and Eve asserted their willful independence, and the one truth cleaved. Then a chasm opened with heaven and hell, good and evil, and angels and demons lining up on opposite sides.

Choice—free will—becomes the salvation, the deciding factor that God envisioned when He created humankind. Of course, the angels knew the outcome. Those humans would create hell on Earth if allowed to have their way. But if humans learned to control their egoic functions, their animal desires, and their mental capacities, the quality of their life experiences would alter them. They would attain the alchemical gold, the illumination of the soul.

Whether or not you or I have directly experienced angelic contact or even believe that angels exist, the subject still matters. The reality we live in, by whatever tradition, has been directly crafted by the multi-millennial stories of angels told by our ancestors and passed on to us. Whether the details of Jacob wrestling with his angel actually happened the way it has been told, the retelling of the *story* of Jacob wrestling with his angel certainly happened. It is, after all, the story that has entered our psyches and has affected how we see the world. Angels have entered our thoughts.

In conclusion, our question "What is the purpose of angels?" has led me to consider at the end of this exercise a new question: What is the purpose of man? The angels may be on the right track to ask God: Why do you care about them? An angel does not die, nor does it evolve. It obeys God and follows divine directions, therefore, it might not understand God's reason. So while we ask: What is the purpose of angels? the angels ask again: What is the purpose of man? I like Edgar Cayce's answer. "For a man is a little lower than the angels yet was made that he might become the companion of the Creative Forces; and thus, was given—in the breath of life—the individual soul, the stamp of approval as it were of the Creator; with the ability to know itself, to be itself, and to make itself as one with the Creative Forces—irrespective of other influences."[37]

It has not been my intention to prove that angels exist, only to prove that whether we learn about angels from personal experience, from the pulpit, or from stories told by travelers along the way, the messages and interventions of angels have shaped the cultures in which we exist. And through whichever door those angels have arrived, they have become a part of us. The true message of the angels lies within.

An Invocation of Archangels

As a ceremonialist, I love to invoke the archangels. Sometimes I add to this ceremony the invocation of Egyptian goddesses, which is also a part of my training as a priestess of Isis. Reverend A. Win Srogi taught me this way to invoke the energies to participate in the cocreation of a sacred becoming.

Before any ceremony, I use my index finger to imagine a blue flame emerging from my fingertip. Keeping constant mental focus, I walk around the perimeter of the room, drawing a sacred fire about me and the place where I will do my work. Everything begins in the east, where the sun rises. Moving counterclockwise to the south, to the west, to the north, and back to the east, I visualize the sacred protection of divine light. The circle always concludes in the east.

Now the invocation can begin.

If you will, visualize the east, or face east. Visualize sunlight at the break of day, and the green, healing energy of a forest. As the sun rises, the yellow sunlight moves between the trees, over and across the horizon, flowing toward your feet. Standing before a yellow door, you knock or ring a bell, calling the archangel Raphael. "Ra-phi-a-El!" you call.

"Oh, mighty Raphael, archangel and light of the east, bringer of springtime, guardian of the air and clouds, the blue sky, the winged ones, we welcome your new beginning. You bring the healing sunlight with you. You awaken us from death and sleep. Bless our endeavors this day and every day of our lives. Help us to see the new day possibilities as we begin a new chapter in our lives.

"We thank you for your presence in our lives."

Now turn to the south and visualize the risen sun high in the sky at noon. Feel its heat upon your forehead, as if you were a tall sunflower reaching up to the light. You offer your fullness to the world. This is the blessed place of summer, the busy-ness of our spiritual lives. A red door appears. You knock or ring the bell, calling for the archangel Michael. "Mi-ki-a-El!" you call.

"Oh, mighty Michael, archangel of fire, dragons, and creatures of heat, guardian of the south, you bring us strength and courage to do the mighty work of the Creator. You fortify our will to do good and to give service. Bless us as we go about your sacred business. Protect and shield us with your wings. Bring up our passion to cocreate a world we shall live in with joy and vigor. We will ourselves to do the will of the Great One.

"We thank you for your presence in our lives."

Now turn toward or visualize the west. See the close of day. See the brilliant orange, purple, and rose colors of sunset. You can hear ocean waves lapping on a nearby shore. The blue door of heaven appears on the horizon. Knock or ring the bell, calling for the archangel Gabriel. "Ga-bra-a-El!" you call.

"Oh, mighty archangel Gabriel, protector of the western gate, champion of the finned creatures, the fish, the dolphins, the whales, and all things of the sea, we welcome you into our lives. You are the mighty messenger of transformation. Wash away our recalcitrance and stubbornness, our clinging to the past and to that which no longer serves us. Cleanse and heal us so that in drawing closer to the source of life eternal, we are blessed and made whole. Awaken in us the possibility of the renewal of our sacred purpose.

"We thank you for your presence in our lives."

Now turn to face the north and visualize a brilliant night sky. As if you had climbed to the top of a mountain to stand beneath the vault of heaven, you are enveloped in innumerable stars. This is the place of crystals and the solid Earth that sustains us. Visualize a door opening in the sky and a ladder descending from the height of heaven to touch the earth at your feet. A brilliant star appears. Knock on the door or ring a bell, calling for the archangel Uriel. "OO-rye-a-El!" you call.

"Almighty and most high archangel Uriel, guardian of the north and leader of all the angels of heaven more numerous than the stars, we invite the mystery of your presence into our lives as we speak and work as spiritual lights in concert with the prophets, the ascended masters, the devata, and the angels. We invoke the holiness of your being to enlighten us, to guide us, to inspire us, and to draw us in closer to an eternal relationship with the Creative Power of the Universe and its manifestation on Earth and in all things of Earth.

"Thank you for being a powerful presence and witness to this sacred moment of our lives."

After you have invoked the four archangels of the directions, return to face the east, then bow.

When the time comes to release the archangels, simply return to the east again. Say the name of each archangel one at a time, in their direction, and thank them for attending your ceremony. After calling their name, repeat this ending sentence: "Go in love and peace, blessing all along the way." Turn to the next archangel and continue until you wind up back in the east.

You may now open the circle by pointing down to the Earth, drawing the energy up, and then opening your hands over your head.

Notes

INTRODUCTION. ANSWERING THE CALL

1. Emerson, *Complete Works,* 437.
2. Moss, *Conscious Dreaming,* 246.
3. Hopler, "Can People become Angels?"
4. Leadbeater, *Masters and Path,* 215.
5. Rohr, *Hope against Darkness,* 69.
6. Burnham, *Reflections on Angels,* 55.
7. Kreeft, *Angels (and Demons),* 50.
8. Berg, *Angels.*
9. Saraydarian, *Symphony of the Zodiac,* 100–101.

1. WESTERN TRADITIONS

1. Eckhart and Fox, eds., *Breakthrough,* 384.
2. Singer, "Eleazer ben Judah," 100.
3. Kohler and Broydé, eds., "Eleazar ben Judah," 101.
4. Freeman, *Touched by Angels,* 64.
5. Lamsa, *Holy Bible.*
6. Aquinas, *Summa Theologica,* Q50.
7. Gemsforliving.net, "How Many Angels Can Dance on the Head of a Pin?"
8. Piankoff, *Pyramid Text,* Utterance, 306.
9. Angel, Klenicki, and Wigoder, eds., *Jewish-Christian Dialogue,* 40.
10. Cooper, *God Is a Verb,* 137.
11. Godwin, *Endangered Species,* 8.
12. Ginzberg, *Legends of the Jews,* 1:52.

13. Ginzberg, *Legends of the Jews,* 1:48.

14. Geisler, *Thomas Aquinas,* 99.

15. Damascene and Böer, eds.; Salmond, trans., *An Exact Exposition,* 46–48.

16. Halevi, *Kabbalistic Universe,* 45.

17. Michael, *Alchemy of Sacred Living,* 70.

18. Pseudo-Dionysus the Aeropagite, *Celestial Hierarchy,* 161.

19. Fox and Sheldrake, *Physics of Angels,* 144.

20. Halevi, *Kabbalistic Universe,* 58.

21. Cooper, *Invoking Angels,* 58.

22. Burnham, *Reflections on Angels,* 182.

23. Paz, "Metatron Is Not Enoch," 50:15.

24. Cooper, *Invoking Angels,* 64.

25. Cooper, *Invoking Angels,* 65.

26. Ginzberg, *Legends of the Jews,* 1:14.

27. Cooper, *Invoking Angels,* xi.

28. Aquinas, *Summa Theologica,* Q50.1.1.

29. Aquinas, *Summa Theologica,* Q50:2.

30. Matt, *Zohar,* 1:43.

31. Kabbani, *Angels Unveiled,* 25.

32. Butterworth, "Antecedents of New Thought."

33. Hall, *Secret Teachings,* 252.

34. Vanden Eynden, *Metatron,* 16–18.

35. Kabbani, *Angels Unveiled,* 42–43.

36. Paz, "Metatron Is Not Enoch," 21–22.

37. Cooper, *Invoking Angels,* 135.

38. Kabbani, *Angels Unveiled,* 38.

39. Podles, "New Age Angels."

40. Rees, *Gabriel to Lucifer,* 11.

41. Kabbani, *Angels Unveiled,* 24.

42. Kabbani, *Angels Unveiled,* 36.

43. Eckhart and Fox, eds., *Breakthrough,* 268.

44. Grant, *Edgar Cayce,* 49–59.

45. Grant, *Edgar Cayce,* 80–83.

46. Steiner, *Angels,* 111.

47. Steiner, *Angels,* 118.

48. Lachman, *Rudolf Steiner,* 19.

49. Kabbani, *Angels Unveiled,* 68–70.

50. Kabbani, *Angels Unveiled,* 26.
51. Kabbani, *Angels Unveiled,* 29.
52. Kabbani, *Angels Unveiled,* 39.
53. Kabbani, *Angels Unveiled,* 64–65.
54. Brinner, *History of al-Tabari,* 2:86–87.
55. Hall, *Secret Teachings,* 559.
56. Lings, *Muhammad,* 44.
57. Hall, *Secret Teachings,* 559–560.
58. Kabbani, *Angels Unveiled,* 37–38.
59. Kabbani, *Angels Unveiled,* 38–39.
60. Kabbani, *Angels Unveiled,* 38.
61. Lings, *Muhammad,* 44–45.
62. Brinner, *History of al-Tabari,* 3:199–200.
63. Lings, *Muhammad,* 46.
64 Lings, *Muhammad,* 50.
65. Hall, *Secret Teachings,* 56.
66. Hall, *Secret Teachings,* 189.
67. Lings, *Muhammad,* 103.
68. Lings, *Muhammad,* 104–105.
69. Kabbani, *Angels Unveiled,* 102.
70. Kabbani, *Angels Unveiled,* 103.
71. Kabbani, *Angels Unveiled,* 113.
72. Al-Jabouri, *Tragedy of Fatima,* 48.
73. Kabbani, *Angels Unveiled,* 115.
74. Kabbani, *Angels Unveiled,* 37.
75. Kabbani, *Angels Unveiled,* 120–125.
76. Hall, *Secret Teachings,* 190.
77. Muir, *Life of Mohammad,* 494.
78. National Association of Spiritualist Churches, "Declaration of Principles," Principle 8.
79. Mitchell, *Genesis,* 54–75.
80. Hopler, "Who Was the Angel?"
81. Davidson, *Dictionary of Angels,* 222.
82. Davidson, *Dictionary of Angels,* 255.
83. Davidson, *Dictionary of Angels,* 192.
84. Bloom and Rosenberg, *Book of J,* 218.
85. Bloom and Rosenberg, *Book of J,* 218.

2. EASTERN TRADITIONS

1. Wilson, *Rig Veda,* 33.

2. Campbell, *Masks of God,* 284.

3. Parrinder, *World Religions,* 200.

4. Altman, *Deva Handbook,* 3.

5. Doniger, *Hindus,* passim.

6. Blavatsky, *Secret Doctrine,* 1:326–328.

7. Blavatsky, *Secret Doctrine,* 1:213.

8. Yogananda, *God Talks with Arjuna,* 718.

9. Temple Purohit website, "Untold Story."

10. Temple Purohit website, "Untold Story."

11. Daniélou, *Myths and Gods,* 141.

12. Hudson, "How Angels Are Viewed."

13. Ganguli, *Mahabharata,* III:210.

14. Klostermaier, *Survey of Hinduism,* 101–102.

15. Coomaraswamy, *Angel and Titan,* 373–374.

16. Yogananda, *God Talks,* 718.

17. Bloom, *Devas, Fairies, and Angels,* 3.

18. Enthoven and Jackson, *Folklore,* passim.

19. Frawley, *Inner Tantric Yoga,* 14.

20. Enthoven and Jackson, *Folklore,* 22.

21. Yogananda, *God Talks,* 866.

22. Yogananda, *God Talks,* 788.

23. Yogananda, *God Talks,* 866–867.

24. Yogananda, *God Talks,* 352.

25. Yogananda, *God Talks,* 353.

26. Kabbani, *Angels Unveiled,* 29.

27. Yogananda, *God Talks,* 356.

28. Daniélou, *Myths and Gods,* 144.

29. Daniélou, *Myths and Gods,* 144–145.

30. Oliver and Lewis, *Angels A to Z,* 115.

31. Findhorn Community, *The Findhorn Garden,* 58.

32. Chisholm, ed., "Apsaras" in *Encyclopedia Brittanica,* 231.

33. Ganguli, *Mahabharata,* III:43, 97–98.

34. George, *Modern Indian Literature,* 481–483.

35. Doniger, *Hindus,* 152.

36. Pickthall, "The Meaning of the Glorious Qur'an." Qur'an, Sura 56:35–38.

37. Rathod, *Into Buddhahood.*

38. Gimian, "Mahasattva Avalokiteshvara," 431–451.

39. Gunaratana, *Path of Serenity,* 223–224.

40. Daniélou, *Myths and Gods,* 224.

41. Yogananda, *Taittiritya Upanishad,* 2.6.1.

42. Gunaratana, *Path of Serenity,* 139–142.

43. Gimian, "Mahasattva Avalokiteshvara," 436.

44. Hua, *Shurangama Sutra,*177–191.

45. Dallapiccola, *Hindu Lore and Legend,* passim.

46. *King of Glorious Sutras.*

47. Sangharakshita, *Transforming Self and World,* 134.

48. Charles, trans., *Book of Jubilees,* 21.

49. Chaudhuri, *Hindu Gods and Goddesses,* passim.

50. Aurobindo, *Essays on the Gita,* 82.

51. Kamenetz, *The Jew in the Lotus,* 76–80.

3. SILK ROAD TRADITIONS

1. Mark, "Zarathustra," in *World History Encyclopedia* online.

2. Skjærvø, *Spirit of Zoroastrianism,* 13.

3. Dhalla, *History of Zoroastrianism,* 41.

4. Dhalla, *History of Zoroastrianism,* 158.

5. Bhagavan Das, *Essential Unity,* 23.

6. Dhalla, *History of Zoroastrianism,* 162.

7. Dhalla, *History of Zoroastrianism,* 163.

8. Bhagavan Das, *Essential Unity,* 23.

9. Stevenson, *Complete Idiot's Guide,* 222.

10. Rose, *Zoroastrianism,* 37.

11. Skjærvø, *Spirit of Zoroastrianism,* 31.

12. Skjærvø, *Spirit of Zoroastrianism,* 19.

13. Dhalla, *History of Zoroastrianism,* 232–243.

14. Dhalla, *History of Zoroastrianism,* 173.

15. Dhalla, *History of Zoroastrianism,* 173–174.

16. Foltz, *Religions of Iran,* 152.

17. Dhalla, *History of Zoroastrianism,* 232–243.

18. Dhalla, *History of Zoroastrianism,* 173.

19. Rose, *Zoroastrianism,* 33.

20. Stevenson, *Complete Idiot's Guide,* 223.

21. Rose, *Zoroastrianism,* 185.

22. Dhalla, *History of Zoroastrianism,* 204.

23. Skjærvø, *Spirit of Zoroastrianism,* 217.

24. Dhalla, *History of Zoroastrianism,* 205.

25. Dhalla, *History of Zoroastrianism,* 206.

26. Dhalla, *History of Zoroastrianism,* 165.

27. Rose, *Zoroastrianism,* 142.

28. Dhalla, *History of Zoroastrianism,* 165.

29. Dhalla, *History of Zoroastrianism,* 164.

30. Brinner, *History of al-Tabari,* 2:59–60.

31. Brinner, *History of al-Tabari,* 2:59–60.

32. Fillmore, *Metaphysical Bible Dictionary,* 52.

33. Joseph, "Yezidi texts," 25:2, 113.

34. Gurdjieff, *Meetings,* 66.

35. Ahmed, *Yazidis: Life and Beliefs,* 11.

36. Ahmed, *Yazidis: Life and Beliefs,* 148.

37. Ahmed, *Yazidis: Life and Beliefs,* 150–151.

38. Joseph, "Yezidi texts," AJSLL 25:2, 112.

39. Asatrian and Arakelova, *Religion of the Peacock,* 16.

40. Joseph, *Devil Worship,* 18.

41. Spät, *Yezidis,* 56.

42. Magazine Monitor (blog), "Who, What, Why" by Darke and Leutheuser.

43. Yezidi International website, "Reincarnation."

44. Spät, "Peacock Sanjak," 108.

45. Andreas and Henning, *Mitteliranische Manichaica,* 295–296.

46. Iranica Online website, "Kephalaia," 370–375.

47. Joseph, *Devil Worship,* 115.

48. Yezidi International website, "Ser Sal or Charshma Sere Nissana."

49. Johnson, *Initiates of Theosophical Masters,* passim.

50. Bailey, *Treatise on White Magic,* 354.

51. Spät, "Peacock Sanjak," 106.

52. Andreas and Henning, *Mitteliranische Manichaica,* 295–296.

53. Foltz, *Religions,* 6.

54. Andreas and Henning, *Mitteliranische Manichaica,* 295–296.

55. Drower, *Peacock Angel,* 6.

56. Spät, "Peacock Sanjak," 106.

57. Hamblin and Peterson, "Who and What?"

58. Shah, *Sufis,* 466.

59. Shah, *Sufis,* 465.

60. Spät, "Peacock Sanjak," 107.

61. Spät, "Peacock Sanjak," 106.

62. Yazidis Info website, "Religion: God and Tawûsê Melek."

63. Spät, "Peacock Sanjak," 106.

64. Yezidi International website, "Lalish."

65. Joseph, *Devil Worship,* 116.

66. Ahmed, *Yazidis: Life and Beliefs,* 154.

67. Spät, "Late Antique Motifs," 71.

68. Bailey, *Seven Rays,* 34–59.

69. Yezidi International website, "Lalish."

70. YezidiTruth.org, "What is the Peacock Angel?"

71. Kabbani, *Angels Unveiled,* 43–44.

72. Asatrian and Arakelova, *Religion of Peacock Angel,* 14.

73. Budge, *Fetish to God,* 134.

74. Finney, "Peacock Angel and Templars."

75. Saldaňa, "Reflections on Lalish."

76. Ahmed, *Yazidis: Life and Beliefs,* 154; Joseph, *Devil Worship,* 111–156.

77. Avdoev, *Historical-Theosophical Aspect,* 314.

78. Yezidi International website, "Reincarnation."

79. Joseph, *Devil Worship,* 55.

80. YezidiTruth.org, "What is the Peacock Angel?"

81. YezidiTruth.org, "What is the Peacock Angel?"

82. YezidiTruth.org, "Yezidi reformer: Sheikh Adi."

83. Cultural Center of Caucasian Yezidis website, "God and Tawuse Melek."

84. Yezidi International website, "Tausi Melek."

85. Spät, "Song of the Commoner," 664.

86. Franklin, *Rumi, Past and Present,* 154–161.

87. Spät, "Song of the Commoner," 672.

88. Blinn, *Manifestation of Spiritualism,* 15–16.

89. Yezidi International website, "Tausi Melek."

90. Joseph, *Devil Worship,* 112.

91. Asatrian and Arakelova, *Religion of Peacock Angel,* 33.

92. YezidiTruth.org, "What is the Peacock Angel?"

93. Hall, *Secret Teachings*, 52.

94. Hall, *Secret Teachings*, 52.

95. Ahmed, *Yazidis: Life and Beliefs*, 239.

96. West, *Serpent in the Sky*, 217.

4. DARK ANGELS

1. Shah, "Markandeya and Yama."

2. Buswell and Gimello, *Paths to Liberation*, 7–8, 83–84.

3. Chisholm, ed., "Apsaras," in *Encyclopedia Britannica*, 231.

4. Boyce, *History of Zoroastrianism*, 92.

5. Nasr, *Knowledge and the Sacred*, 99.

6. Ahmed, *Yazidis: Life and Beliefs*, 154.

7. Yezidi International website, "Lalish."

8. Darmesteter, *Zend Avesta*, 18.

9. Darmesteter, *Zend Avesta*, 19.

10. Boyce, *Zoroastrians*, 27.

11. Davidson, *Dictionary of Angels*, 64.

12. Kabbani, *Angels Unveiled*, 223.

13. Kabbani, *Angels Unveiled*, 226.

14. Kabbani, *Angels Unveiled*, 220.

15. Rees, *Gabriel to Lucifer*, 209.

16. Burnham, *Reflections on Angels*, 208.

17. Kabbani, *Angels Unveiled*, 224.

18. Kabbani, *Angels Unveiled*, 147.

19. Kabbani, *Angels Unveiled*, 222–223.

20. Kabbani, *Angels Unveiled*, 218.

21. Muir, *Life of Mohammad*, 494.

22. Hastings, ed., *Religion and Ethics*, 617.

23. Patai, *Jewish Folklore and Traditions*, 463.

24. Davidson, *Dictionary of Angels*, 255.

25. Ginzburg, *Legends of the Jews*, 2:308–309.

26. Brinner, *History of al-Tabari*, 3:87.

27. Brinner, *History of al-Tabari*, 3:129-130.

28. Ginzberg, *Legends of the Jews*, 4:113–114.

29. Kabbani, *Angels Unveiled*, 224.

30. Burnham, *Reflections on Angels*, 107.

31. Kabbani, *Angels Unveiled*, 201–202.

32. Kabbani, *Angels Unveiled*, 210–211.

33. Clark, *Myth and Symbol*, 139.

34. Cooper, *Invoking Angels*, 65.

35. Davidson, *Dictionary of Angels*, 106.

36. Cooper, *Invoking Angels*, 63–64.

37. Davidson, *Dictionary of Angels*, 104.

38. Cooper, *God Is a Verb*, 139.

39. Rees, *Gabriel to Lucifer*, 13.

40. Rohr, "Christ, Cosmology, and Consciousness."

41. Josephus and Whiston, trans., *Complete Works of Josephus*, 987.

42. Burnham, *Reflections on Angels*, 151–152.

43. Burnham, *Reflections on Angels*, 150.

44. Cooper, *God Is a Verb*, 281.

45. Cooper, *God Is a Verb*, 137.

46. Kabbani, *Angels Unveiled*, 33.

47. Andrews, *The Intercession of Spirits*, 27.

48. Burnham, *Reflections on Angels*, 37.

49. Armstrong, "The Astonishing True Stories."

50. D'Monte, *Discerning of Spirits*, 17.

51. Guiley, *Demons and Demonology*, 231–232.

52. Rees, *Gabriel to Lucifer*, 200.

53. Hall, *Secret Teachings*, 54, 263.

54. Burnham, *Reflections on Angels*, 135.

55. Rees, *Gabriel to Lucifer*, 189.

56. Wilson, *Sacred Drift*, 87.

57. Budge, *Cave of the Treasures*, Folio 5.

58. Rees, *Gabriel to Lucifer*, 199.

59. Burnham, *Reflections on Angels*, 142.

60. Cooper, *God Is a Verb*, 139.

61. Kreeft, *Angels and Demons*, 69–70.

62. Cooper, *Invoking Angels*, 10.

63. Cooper, *God Is a Verb*, 135–136.

64. Davidson, *Dictionary of Angels*, 55.

65. Rees, *Gabriel to Lucifer*, 197.

66. Thompson, *Time Falling Bodies*, 15–16.

67. Ginzberg, *Legends of the Jews,* 1:89.

68. Ginzberg, *Legends of the Jews,* 1:21–22.

69. Kabbani, *Angels Unveiled,* 60.

70. Cooper, *God Is a Verb,* 135–136.

71. Cooper, *God Is a Verb,* 136.

72. Guiley, *Encyclopedia of Demons,* 70.

73. Foltz, *Religions of the Silk Road,* 31–32.

74. Yezidi International website, "Myths Buster."

75. YezidiTruth.org, "What is the Peacock Angel?"

76. Drower, *Peacock Angel,* 7.

77. Leadbeater, *Masters and Path,* 296–299.

78. Pinkham, *Christ Myth,* 58.

79. Hafiz, "Yazidi Religious Beliefs."

80. Blavatsky, *Secret Doctrine,* 202.

81. Oliver and Lewis, *Angels A to Z,* 198.

82. Oliver and Lewis, *Angels A to Z,* 55.

83. Daniélou, *Myths and Gods,* 141–142.

84. Koltypin, "Adityas, Daityas, and Danavas."

85. Daniélou, *Myths and Gods,* 143.

86. O'Brien, "Eight Dharmapalas."

87. O'Brien, *Rethinking Religion,* 155.

88. Laird, *Story of Tibet,* 139, 264–265.

89. O'Brien, "Eight Dharmapalas."

90. Packer, *131 Christians,* 333.

91. Packer, *131 Christians,* 334.

92. Williams, *Hindu Mythology,* 30.

93. Williams, *Hindu Mythology,* 71.

94. Thompson, *Time Falling Bodies,* 243.

95. Cooper, *Invoking Angels,* 73.

96. Book of Enoch 6:1–2; Genesis 6:1–4.

97. Charles, trans., Book of Jubilees, 54–55.

98. Stevenson, *Complete Idiot's Guide,* 130.

99. Mythology.net, "Azazel."

100.Stevenson, *Complete Idiot's Guide,* 132.

101.Godwin, *Endangered Species,* 72.

102.Lumpkin, *Books of Enoch,* 34.

103.Kreeft, *Angels (and Demons),* 81.

5. HUMAN AND ANGELIC INTERACTIONS

1. Kabbani, *Angels Unveiled,* 25.
2. Kabbani, *Angels Unveiled,* 59.
3. Aquinas, *Summa Theologica,* 59:1–4.
4. Cooper, *Invoking Angels,* 71.
5. Ginzburg, *Legends of the Jews,* 1:28.
6. Thompson, *Time Falling Bodies,* 25.
7. Ginzburg, *Legends of the Jews,*1:32.
8. Smoley, ed., *Kybalion,* 17.
9. Böhme, *Confessions of Jacob Boehme,* 126–127.
10. Cooper, *Invoking Angels,* 72.
11. Ginzburg, *Legends of the Jews,* 4:67.
12. Godwin, *Endangered Species,* 70.
13. Moss, "The Book of Raziel."
14. Singer, "Eleazer ben Judah" in *Jewish Encyclopedia,* 100.
15. Godwin, *Endangered Species,* 73.
16. Bosak, "Conversing with Angels."
17. Rohr, *Hope against Darkness,* 67.
18. Marcus, *Sefer Hasidim,* 52.
19. Eckhart and Fox, eds., *Breakthrough,* 384.
20. Kabbani, *Angels Unveiled,* 173.
21. Leadbeater, *Masters and Path,* 140–141.
22. Leadbeater, *Masters and Path,* 152.
23. Hall, *Secret Teachings,* 274–275.
24. Hall, *Secret Teachings,* 277.
25. Kabbani, *Angels Unveiled,* 214–215.
26. Dhalla, *History of Zoroastrianism,* 162.
27. Midal, *Chögyam Trungpa,* 53–251.
28. Clark, *Great Naropa Poetry Wars,* 15–26, 51.
29. Cooper, *Invoking Angels,* 6.
30. Burnham, *Reflections on Angels,* 61.
31. Watterson, *Mary Magdalene Revealed,* 19.
32. Hall, *Secret Teachings,* 187.
33. Biale, ed., *Cultures of the Jews,* 674.
34. Rees, *Gabriel to Lucifer,* 82.
35. Godwin, *Endangered Species,* 56.

36. Lumpkin, *Books of Enoch*, 252–254.

37. Ginzberg, *Legends of the Jews*, 1:21.

38. Davidson, *Dictionary of Angels*, 6.

39. Learn Religions website, "Sefer Raziel."

40. Ginzberg, *Legends of the Jews*, 3:111–114.

41. Roth et al., *Encyclopedia Judaica*, 11:612.

42. Biale, *Cultures of the Jews*, 674.

43. Halevi, *Kabbalistic Universe*, 60.

44. Lumpkin, *Books of Enoch*, 229.

45. Cooper, *Invoking Angels*, 59–60.

46. Godwin, *Endangered Species*, 67.

47. Moss, Book of Raziel.

48. Hall, *Secret Teachings*, 307.

49. Slick, *Origins and History*.

50. Hall, *Secret Teachings*, 307.

51. Matt, trans., *Zohar*, 27.

52. Hall, *Secret Teachings*, 308.

53. Ginsburg, *The Kabbalah*, 84–85.

54. Ginzburg, *Legends of the Jews*, 1:82.

55. Lumpkin, *Books of Enoch*, 228.

56. Learn Religions website, "Kabbalah Tree of Life."

57. Yogananda, *God Talks with Arjuna*, 357.

58. Claussen, "Struggle for Moral Excellence," 33.

59. Claussen, "Struggle for Moral Excellence," 9.

60. Eckhart and Fox, eds., *Breakthrough*, 94.

61. Cooper, *God Is a Verb*, 148.

62. Moss, *Conscious Dreaming*, 259.

63. Moss, *Conscious Dreaming*, 262.

64. Cooper, *God Is a Verb*, 141.

65. Smoley, ed., *Kybalion*, 82.

CONCLUSION. I AM THAT I AM

1. Gelberman, *Physician of the Soul*, 105.

2. Leadbeater, *Masters and Path*, 214.

3. Hillman, *Re-Visioning Psychology*, 9.

4. Shah, *Sufis*, 335.

5. O'Brien, *Rethinking Religion,* 5.

6. Berg, "Angels."

7. Berg, "Angels."

8. Cooper, *God Is a Verb,* 148–149.

9. Trussel and Malatt, "Double Slit Experiment."

10. *Healers Journal,* "Quantum Physics Explains."

11. Goswami, *Everything Answer Book,* 128–143.

12. Podles, "New Age Angels."

13. Cooper, *Invoking Angels,* xviii.

14. Cooper, *Invoking Angels,* 4.

15. Halevi, *Kabbalistic Universe,* 59.

16. Halevi, *Kabbalistic Universe,* 59.

17. Kreeft, *Angels (and Demons),* 70.

18. Kreeft, *Angels (and Demons),* 54.

19. Winter, *Paradoxology,* 29.

20. Kabbani, *Angels Unveiled,* 214.

21. Larsen, "Angel Lobes and EFT."

22. Lifecoachcode website, "Scientists Discover Biophotons."

23. Beltzer, *Encyclopedic Psychic Dictionary,* 50.

24. Clapp, *Essenes,* 4.

25. Kabbani, *Angels Unveiled,* 33.

26. Winter, *Paradoxology,* 144–145.

27. Lifecoachcode website, "Scientists Discover Biophotons."

28. Swedenborg, *Heaven and Its Wonders,* 41.

29. Lilly, *Center of the Cyclone,* 1.

30. Lilly, *Deep Self,* passim.

31. Cooper, *God Is a Verb,* 134.

32. Hall, *Secret Teachings,* 119.

33. Aurobindo, *Essays on the Gita,* 470–472.

34. Aurobindo, *Essays on the Gita,* 60.

35. Campbell, *Power of Myth,* 279.

36. Van Auken, *Angels, Fairies, Demons,* 136.

37. Cayce, *Complete Readings,* Reading 1456–1.

Bibliography

Ahmed, Sami Said. *The Yazidis: Their Life and Beliefs*. Miami, Fla.: Field Research Projects, 1975.

Al-Jabouri, Yasin T. *The Tragedy of Fatima, Daughter of Muhammad*. Bloomington, Ind.: AuthorHouse, 2013.

Altman, Nathaniel. *The Deva Handbook: How to Work with Nature's Subtle Energies*. Rochester, Vt.: Inner Traditions, 1995.

Andreas, Friedrich Carl, and Walter Bruno Henning. *Mitteliranische Manichaica aus Chinesisch-Turkistan II*, SPAW xxvii, 1993.

Andrews, Ted. *The Intercession of Spirits: Working with Animals, Angels, and Ancestors*. Jackson, Tenn.: Dragonhawk Publishing, 2008.

Angel, Marc D., Leon Klenicki, and Geoffrey Wigoder, eds. *A Dictionary of the Jewish-Christian Dialogue*. Mahwah, N.J.: Paulist Press, 1995.

Aquinas, St. Thomas. *The Summa Theologica*. Translated by the English Dominican Province. Documentacatholicaomnia.eu (website).

Armstrong, Jamie. "The Astonishing True Stories behind the Cokeville Miracle Movie." LDS Living (website).

Asatrian, Garnik S., and Victoria Arakelova. *The Religion of the Peacock Angel: The Yezidis and Their Spirit World*. London: Taylor & Francis, 2014.

Aurobindo, Sri. *Essays on the Gita*. New York: The Sri Aurobindo Library, 1950.

Avdoev, Teimuraz. *The Historical-Theosophical Aspect of Yazidiism*. Athens, Greece: Kastalia Editions, 2018.

Bailey, Alice A. *The Seven Rays of Life*. New York: Lucis Publishing, 2003.

———. *A Treatise on White Magic: The Way of the Disciple*. New York: Lucis Trust, 1979.

Bauscher, David, trans. *The Peshitta Holy Bible Translated*. Research Triangle, N.C.: Lulu.com, 2019.

Beltzer, June. *The Encyclopedic Psychic Dictionary*. Lithia Springs, Ga.: New Leaf Distributing, 1986.

Berg, Rav. "Angels." Kabbalah.com (website). November 1996.

Biale, David, ed. *Cultures of the Jews: A New History*. New York: Random House, 2002.

Blavatsky, Helen. *The Secret Doctrine: Cosmology (v. 1)*. Wheaton, Ill.: Theosophical University Press, 2014.

Blinn, Henry Clay. *The Manifestation of Spiritualism Among the Shakers 1837–1847*. East Canterbury, N.H. Iapsop (website).

Bloom, Harold, and David Rosenberg. *The Book of J*. New York: Grove Press, 1990.

Bloom, William. *Devas, Fairies, and Angels: A Modern Approach*. Glastonbury, UK: Gothic Image Publications, 1986.

Böhme, Jakob. *The Confessions of Jacob Boehme, "Mysterium Magnum."* London: Methuen and Company, 1920.

Bosak, Lindsey Rae. "Conversing with Angels: John Dee and His Quest for Divine Knowledge." Abstract/Honors Thesis. Barrett, the Honors College. December, 2014.

Boyce, Mary. *A History of Zoroastrianism: The Early Period*. Leiden, Netherlands: E. J. Brill, 1989.

———. *Zoroastrians: Their Religious Beliefs and Practices*. Oxfordshire, UK: Routledge, 2001.

Brinner, William M., trans. *The History of al-Tabari: General Introduction and From Creation to the Flood*. Vol. 1; *Prophets and Patriarchs*. Vol. 2; *The Children of Israel*. Vol. 3. Albany, N.Y.: State University of New York Press, 1987.

Budge, Sir E. A. Wallis. *Cave of the Treasures, Tract by Ephraim the Syrian*. Folio 5. London: Religious Tract Society, 1927.

———. *From Fetish to God in Ancient Egypt*. New York: Dover Publications, 1988.

Burnham, Sophy. *Reflections on Angels Past and Present, and True Stories of How They Touch Our Lives*. New York: Random House, 1990.

Buswell, Robert E., and Robert M. Gimello. *Paths to Liberation: The Mārga and Its Transformations in Buddhist Thought*. Honolulu, Hawaii: University of Hawaii Press, 1992.

Butterworth, Eric. Antecedents of New Thought: Lecture 8 (podcast). "Emmet Fox and Ernest Holmes, the Five M's of Religion—Man Message Movement

Machine Monument." TruthUnity Ministries. Truthunity.net (website). 2019.

Campbell, Joseph. *The Masks of God: Oriental Mythology (v. 2) and Creative Mythology (v. 4)*. New York: Viking Press, 1969.

———. *The Power of Myth*, New York: Anchor Books, 1991.

Cayce, Edgar. *The Complete Edgar Cayce Readings*. Virginia Beach, Va: A.R.E., 1995.

CBS News (website). "Nearly 8 in 10 Americans Believe in Angels." December 23, 2011.

Charles, R. H., trans. *The Book of Jubilees*. New York: Macmillan, 1917.

Chaudhuri, Saroj Kumar. *Hindu Gods and Goddesses in Japan*. New Delhi, India: Vedams eBooks (P) Ltd., 2003.

Chisholm, Hugh, ed. "Apsaras" in *Encyclopædia Britannica*. 11th ed. Cambridge: Cambridge University Press, 1911.

Clapp, Ann Lee. Essenes commentary in *The Essenes: A Compilation of Extracts from the Edgar Cayce Readings*. Virginia Beach, Va.: Edgar Cayce Foundation, 2006.

Clark, Robert Thomas Rundle. *Myth and Symbol in Ancient Egypt*. London: Thames and Hudson, 1991.

Clark, Tom. *The Great Naropa Poetry Wars*. San Francisco: Cadmus Editions, 1980.

Claussen, Geoffrey. "Angels, Humans, and the Struggle for Moral Excellence in the Writings of Meir Simhah of Dvinsk and Simhah Zissel of Kelm" in *Jewish Religious and Philosophical Ethics*, Oliver Leaman, Curtis Hutt, Halla Kim, and Berel Dov Lerner, eds., New York: Routledge, 2018.

Coomaraswamy, Ananda. "Angel and Titan: An Essay in Vedic Ontology." *Journal of the American Oriental Society* 55, 1935.

Cooper, Rabbi David A. *God Is a Verb: Kabbalah and the Practice of Mystical Judaism*. New York: Riverhead Books, 1997.

———. *Invoking Angels for Blessings, Protection, and Healing*. Boulder, Colo.: Sounds True, 2006.

Dallapiccola, Anna Libera. *Dictionary of Hindu Lore and Legend*. London: Thames and Hudson, 2002.

Damascene, John. *An Exact Exposition of the Orthodox Faith*. Edited by Paul A. Böer Sr. and translated by S. D. F. Salmond. Virginia Beach, Va.: Create Space Independent Publishing Platform, 2014.

Daniélou, Alain. *The Myths and Gods of India*. Rochester, Vt.: Inner Traditions, 1991.

Darke, Diana, and Robert Leutheuser. "Who, What, Why: Who Are the Yazidis?" *Magazine Monitor*. BBC News. August 8, 2014.

Darmesteter, James, trans. *The Zend-Avesta: The Vendîdâd*. Oxford: Clarendon Press, 1880.

Das, Bhagavan. *The Essential Unity of All Religions*. Wheaton, Ill.: Theosophical Publishing House, 1966.

Davidson, Gustav. *A Dictionary of Angels Including the Fallen Angels*. New York: Macmillan, 1967.

Dhalla, Maneckji Nusservandi. *History of Zoroastrianism*. London: Oxford University Press, 1938.

D'Monte, Victor. *Discerning of Spirits*. Chennai, India: Notion Press, 2019.

Doniger, Wendy. *The Hindus: An Alternative History*. New York: Penguin Classics, 2009.

Drower, Ethel Stefana. *Peacock Angel: Being Some Account of Votaries of a Secret Cult and Their Sanctuaries*. London: John Murray Publishers, 1941.

Emerson, Ralph Waldo. "XI: Immortality." In *The Complete Works of Ralph Waldo Emerson*. New York: Houghton, Mifflin and Company, 1904.

Enthoven, Reginald Edward, and A. M. T. Jackson. *Folklore of the Konkan*. Vol. 2. Oxford: Clarendon Press, 1923.

Fillmore, Charles. *Metaphysical Bible Dictionary*. New York: Dover, 2000.

Findhorn Community. *The Findhorn Garden: Pioneering a New Vision of Humanity and Nature in Cooperation*. New York: Harper and Row, 1975.

Finney, Dee. "The Peacock Angel and the Templars." Greatdreams.com (website). October 29, 2011.

Foltz, Richard. *Religions of Iran: From Prehistory to the Present*. London: Oneworld Publications, 2013.

———. *Religions of the Silk Road: Premodern Patterns of Globalization*. 2nd ed. New York: Plagrave Macmillian, 2010.

Fox, Matthew, ed. *Breakthrough: Meister Eckhart's Creation Spirituality in New Translation*. Garden City, N.Y.: Doubleday, 1980.

Fox, Matthew, and Rupert Sheldrake. *The Physics of Angels: Exploring the Realm Where Science and Spirit Meet*. Rhinebeck, N.Y.: Monkfish Publishing, 1996.

Frawley, David. *Inner Tantric Yoga: Working with the Universal Shakti—Secrets of the Mantras, Deities, and Meditation*. Twin Lakes, Wis.: Lotus Press, 2008.

Freeman, Eileen Elias. *Touched by Angels: True Cases of Close Encounters of the Celestial Kind*. New York: Warner Books, 1993.

Funk, W. P., ed. "Kephalaia." Iranica Online (website).

Ganguli, Kisari Mohan, trans. *Mahabharata*. Delhi: Motilal Banarsidass Publishers, 1883–1896.

Geisler, Norman. *Thomas Aquinas: An Evangelical Appraisal*. Eugene, Ore.: Wipf and Stock Publishers, 1991.

Gelberman, Joseph. *Physician of the Soul: A Modern Kabbalist's Approach to Health and Healing*. Sunset Beach, N.C.: Crossing Press, 2000.

Geler, Professor. "Azazel." Mythology.net (website).

Gemsforliving.net (website), "How Many Angels Can Dance on the Head of a Pin?" January 23, 2021.

George, K. M., ed. *Modern Indian Literature, an Anthology: Surveys and Poems*. New Delhi, India: Sahitya Akademi, 1992.

Gimian, Carolyn Rose, ed. The Mahasattva Avalokiteshvara in *The Collected Works of Chögyam Trungpa*. Vol. 1. Boston: Shambala Publications, 2004.

Ginsburg, Christian David. *The Kabbalah: Its Doctrines, Development and Literature*. London: Longmans, Green, Reader, and Dyer, 1865.

Ginzberg, Louis. *The Legends of the Jews*. 5 volumes. Philadelphia, Pa.: Jewish Publication Society of America, 1913.

"God and Tawuse Melek." Cultural Center of Caucasian Yazidis. 2019.

Godwin, Malcolm. *Angels: An Endangered Species*. New York: Simon and Schuster, 1990.

Goswami, Amit. *The Everything Answer Book: How Quantum Science Explains Love, Death, and the Meaning of Life*. Charlottesville, Va.: Hampton Roads Publishing, 2017.

Grant, Robert J. *Edgar Cayce on Angels, Archangels, and the Unseen Forces*. Virginia Beach, Va.: A.R.E. Press, 1994.

Guiley, Rosemary. *The Encyclopedia of Demons and Demonology*. New York: Facts on File, 2009.

Gunaratana, Henepola. *The Path of Serenity and Insight: An Explanation of the Buddhist Jhānas*. Delhi: Motilal Banarsidass Publishers, 2002.

Gurdjieff, G. I. *Meetings with Remarkable Men*. London: Routledge, 1963.

Hafiz, Yasmine. "Yazidi Religious Beliefs: History, Facts, and Traditions of Iraq's Persecuted Minority." *Huffington Post*. September 6, 2016.

Halevi, Z'ev ben Shimon. *A Kabbalistic Universe*. New York: Samuel Weiser, 1977.

Hall, Manly Palmer. *The Secret Teachings of All Ages*. San Francisco: H. S. Crocker Co., Inc., 1928.

Hamblin, William, and Daniel Peterson. "Who and What Are the Yezidis?" Courtesy of *The Deseret News*. June 26, 2015.

Hastings, James, ed. *Encyclopedia of Religion and Ethics*. 12 vols. Whitefish, Mont.: Kessinger Publishing, 2003.

Hillman, James. *Re-Visioning Psychology*. New York: HarperCollins, 1992.

———. *The Soul's Code*. New York: Ballantine Books, 2017.

Hopler, Whitney. "The Angels on the Kabbalah Tree of Life." Learn Religions (website). August 20, 2018.

———. "Can People Become Angels After They Die?" Learn Religions (website).

———. "The Sefer Raziel." Learn Religions (website).

———. "Who Was the Angel Who Wrestled with Jacob?" Learn Religions (website).

Hua, Hsuan. *The Shurangama Sutra: Sutra Text and Supplements with Commentary*. Burlingame, Calif.: Buddhist Text Translation Society, 2003.

Hudson, Sonya. "How Angels Are Viewed by Different Religions." January 8, 2018. Lifebodysoul.com (website).

Johnson, K. Paul. *Initiates of Theosophical Masters*. Albany, N.Y.: State University of New York Press, 1995.

Joseph, Isya. *Devil Worship: Sacred Books and Traditions of the Yezidiz*. Boston: Richard G. Badger, 1919.

———. "Yezidi texts" in *The American Journal of Semitic Languages and Literatures* 25:2, January 1909.

Josephus, Flavius. *The New Complete Works of Josephus*. Rev ed. Translated by William Whiston. Grand Rapids, Mich.: Kregel Publications, 1999.

Kabbani, Shaykh Muhammad Hisham. *Angels Unveiled: A Sufi Perspective*. Fenton, Mich.: Institute for Spiritual and Cultural Advancement, 1995.

Kamenetz, Rodger. *The Jew in the Lotus: A Poet's Rediscovery of Jewish Identity in Buddhist India*. New York: Harper Collins, 1994.

The King of Glorious Sutras Called the Exalted, Sublime Golden Light Sutra: A Mahayana Sutra. Portland, Ore.: FPMT, Inc., 2001.

Klostermaier, Klaus. *A Survey of Hinduism*. 3rd ed. Albany, N.Y.: State University of New York Press, 2010.

Kohler, Kauffman, and Isaac Broydé, eds. "Eleazar ben Judah ben Kalonymus of Worms" in *Jewish Encyclopedia*. St. Petersburg, Fla.: Brockhaus and Efron, 1906.

Koltypin, Alexander. "Adityas, Daityas and Danavas." *Earth Before the Flood* (website). 2009.

Kreeft, Peter. *Angels (and Demons): What Do We Really Know About Them?* San Francisco: Ignatius Press, 1995.

Lachman, Gary. *Rudolf Steiner: An Introduction to His Life and Work.* New York: Jeremy P. Tarcher, 2007.

Laird, Thomas. *The Story of Tibet: Conversations with the Dalai Lama.* New York: Grove Press, 2006.

Lamsa, George M. *Holy Bible: From the Ancient Eastern Text.* New York: Harper & Row, 1985.

Larsen, Dr. Sarah. "Dr. Sarah Larsen, Angel Lobes, and EFT." Dr. Sarah Larsen (website).

Leadbeater, Charles W. *The Masters and the Path.* Adyar, India: Theosophical Publishing House, 1925.

Lewis, Franklin. *Rumi, Past and Present, East and West: The Life, Teachings, and Poetry of Jalal al-Din Rumi.* Oxford: OneWorld Publications, 2000.

Lilly, John Cunningham. *The Center of the Cyclone: An Autobiography of Inner Space.* New York: Bantam Books, 1973.

———. *The Deep Self: Consciousness Exploration in the Isolation Tank.* Nevada City, Calif.: Gateways Books and Tapes, 2007.

Lings, Martin. *Muhammad: His Life Based on the Earliest Sources.* Rochester, Vt.: Inner Traditions, 2006.

Lumpkin, Joseph. *The Books of Enoch: The Angels, the Watchers and the Nephilim.* 2nd ed. Blountsville, Ala.: Fifth Estate Publisher, 2011.

Marcus, Ivan G. *Sefer Hasidim and the Ashkenazic Book in Medieval Europe.* Philadelphia: University of Pennsylvania Press, 2018.

Mark, Joshua J., Violatti, Cristian, ed. "Zarathustra" in *World History Encyclopedia.* Ancient.eu (website). May 28, 2020.

Matt, Daniel Chanan, trans. *The Zohar: The Book of Enlightenment.* Pritzker edition, vol. 1. Stanford, Calif.: Stanford University Press, 2004.

Michael, Emory J. *The Alchemy of Sacred Living.* Prescott, Ariz.: Mountain Rose Publishing, 1998.

Midal, Fabrice. *Chögyam Trungpa: His Life and Vision.* Boulder, Colo.: Shambala Publications, 2012.

Mitchell, Stephen. *Genesis: A New Translation of the Classic Bible Stories.* New York: HarperCollins, 1996.

Moore, Thomas. *A Religion of One's Own: A Guide to Creating a Personal Spirituality in a Secular World*. New York: Gotham Books, 2014.

Moss, Robert. "The Book of Raziel." MossDreams (blog). October 14, 2016.

———. *Conscious Dreaming*, New York: Crown Trade Paperbacks, 1996.

Muir, Sir William. *The Life of Mohammad*. Edinburgh, Scotland: John Grant, 1923.

National Association of Spiritualist Churches. "Declaration of Principles." National Association of Spiritualist Churches (website). 2001.

Nasr, Seyyed Hossein. *Knowledge and the Sacred: Revisioning Academic Accountability*. Albany, N.Y.: State University of New York Press, 1989.

O'Brien, Barbara. "Eight Dharmapalas: The Protectors of Buddhism." Learn Religions (website). April 17, 2019.

———. *Rethinking Religion: Finding a Place for Religion in a Modern, Tolerant, Progressive, Peaceful and Science-Affirming World*. Charleston, S.C.: Ten Directions, 2014.

Oliver, Evelyn Dorothy, and James R. Lewis. *Angels A to Z*. Canton, Mich.: Visible Ink Press, 2008.

Packer, J. I. *131 Christians Everyone Should Know*. Nashville, Tenn.: Christianity Today, 2000.

Parrinder, Geoffrey, ed. *World Religions from Ancient History to the Present*. New York: Facts on File, 1971.

Patai, Raphael. *Encyclopedia of Jewish Folklore and Traditions*. London: Routledge, 2015.

Paz, Yakir. "Metatron is Not Enoch: Reevaluating the Evolution of an Archangel" in *Journal for the Study of Judaism* 50:1–49. Leiden, Netherlands: E. J. Brill Publishing, 2019.

Piankoff, Alexandre. *The Pyramid Text of Unas*. Bollingen Foundation, Princeton, N.J.: Princeton University Press, 1968.

Pickthall, M. M., trans. "The Meaning of The Glorious Koran; An Explanatory Translation." 1st ed. New York: Alfred A. Knopf, 1930.

Pinkham, Mark Amaru. *The Truth Behind the Christ Myth: The Redemption of the Peacock Angel*. Kempton, Ill.: Adventures Unlimited Press, 2002.

Podles, Leon J. "New Age Angels: Thrones, Dominions, and Mellow Fellows." *Crisis Magazine*. February 1995.

Pseudo-Dionysus the Aeropagite. *The Celestial Hierarchy*, Mahwah, N.J.: Paulist Press, 1987.

"Quantum Physics Explains How Your Thoughts Create Reality." The Healers Journal (website). January 9, 2014.

Rathod, Madhavi. "Into Buddhahood: The Story of Gautama Buddha." Yogapedia (website). May 17, 2019.

Rees, Valery. *From Gabriel to Lucifer: A Cultural History of Angels.* New York: I. B. Taurius, 2015.

Roberts, Reverend Alexander, and James Donaldson, eds. "Revelation of Moses." *Anti-Nicene Christian Library: Translations of the Writings of the Fathers,* 1870.

Rohr, Richard. "Christ, Cosmology, and Consciousness: A Reframing of How We See." Center for Action and Contemplation (website). October 27, 2016.

————. *Hope Against Darkness: The Transforming Vision of Saint Francis in an Age of Anxiety.* Cincinnati, Ohio: Saint Anthony Messenger Press, 2001.

Rose, Jenny. *Zoroastrianism: A Guide for the Perplexed.* New York: Continuum Publishing, 2011.

Roth, Cecil, et al. *Encyclopedia Judaica: Ja-Kas.* Vol 11. Jerusalem: Keter Publishing House, 1973.

Saldaña, Stephanie. "Reflections on Lalish, the Holy Valley of the Yezidis." Mosaic Stories (website). June 5, 2018.

Sangharakshita. *Transforming Self and World: Themes from the Sūtra of Golden Light.* Birmingham, UK: Windhorse Publications, 1996.

Saraydarian, Torkom. *The Symphony of the Zodiac.* Agoura, Calif.: Aquarian Educational Group, 1980.

"Scientists Discover Biophotons: Decode into Superhuman." Lifecoachcode (website). September 21, 2017.

Shah, Idries. *The Sufis.* London: ISF Publishing, 1964.

Shah, Vaishali Kamal. "Markandeya and Yama." HinduScriptures.com (website).

Singer, Isidore. "Eleazer ben Judah of Worms" in *The Jewish Encyclopedia.* New York: Funk and Wagnalls, 1903.

Skjærvø, Prods Oktor. *The Spirit of Zoroastrianism.* New Haven, Conn.: Yale University Press, 2011.

Slick, Matt. "The Origins and History of Kabbalah." Nampa, ID: Christian Apologetics and Research Ministry, 2018.

Smoley, Richard, ed. *The Kybalion.* New York: Penguin Random House, 2018.

Spät, Eszter. *Late Antique Motifs in Yezidi Oral Tradition.* Ph.D. dissertation. Budapest: Central European University, 2009.

————. "The Role of the Peacock Sanjak: Yezidi Religious Memory" in *Materializing Memory: Archaeological Material Culture and the Semantics of the Past.* Irene Barbiera, Alice M. Choyke, and Judith A. Rasson, eds. London: British Archaeological Reports, 2009.

———. "The Song of the Commoner: The Gnostic Call in Yezidi Oral Tradition" in *In Search of Truth: Augustine, Manichaeism and Other Gnosticism*; J. A. van den Berg and J. van Schaik, eds. Leiden: F. J. Brill, 2017.

———. *The Yezidis*. London: Saqi, 2005.

Steiner, Rudolf. *Angels: Selected Lectures*. East Sussex, U.K.: Rudolf Steiner Press, 1996.

Steinsaltz, Rabbi Adin Even-Israel, trans. *The Talmud: The Steinsaltz Edition*. New York: Random House, 1989.

Stevenson, Jay. *The Complete Idiot's Guide to Angels*. New York: Alpha Books, 1999.

Swedenborg, Emanuel, and John C. Ager, trans. *Heaven and Its Wonders and Hell: From Things Heard and Seen*. West Chester, Pa.: Swedenborg Foundation, 2009.

Temple Purohit. "The Untold Story of the Asuras: Hindu Mythology." June 1, 2015. Templepurohit.com (website).

Thompson, William Irwin. *The Time Falling Bodies Take to Light: Mythology, Sexuality and the Origins of Culture*. New York: St. Martin's Press, 1981.

Trussel, Dianne, and Anne Malatt. "The Double Slit Experiment and What It Means for All of Us." Unimed Living (website). 2014.

Van Auken, John. *Angels, Fairies, Demons, and the Elementals: With the Edgar Cayce Perspective on the Supernatural World*. Virginia Beach, Va.: A.R.E. Press, 2015.

Vanden Eynden, Rose. *Metatron: Invoking the Angel of God's Presence*. Woodbury, Minn.: Llewellyn Publications, 2008.

Watterson, Meggan. *Mary Magdalene Revealed: The First Apostle, Her Feminist Gospel and the Christianity We Haven't Tried Yet*. New York: Hay House, 2019.

West, John Anthony. *Serpent in the Sky: The High Wisdom of Ancient Egypt*. Wheaton, Ill.: Quest Books, 1979.

Williams, George. *Handbook of Hindu Mythology*. New York: Oxford University Press, 2003.

Wilson, H. H., trans. *The Rig Veda Sanhita*. Bangalore City: Bangalore Press, 1925.

Wilson, Peter Lamborn. *Sacred Drift: Essays on the Margins of Islam*. San Francisco: City Lights Books, 1993.

Winter, Miriam Therese. *Paradoxology: Spirituality in a Quantum Universe.* Maryknoll, N.Y.: Orbis Books, 2006.

Yezidi International (website). "About the Yezidi People." 2015.

———. "Lalish: The Yezidi Spiritual Heartland." 2015.

———. "Myths Buster." 2015.

———. "Reincarnation." 2015.

———. "Ser Sal or Charshma Sere Nissana." 2015.

———. "Tausi Melek." 2015.

YezidiTruth.org (website), "What is the Peacock Angel?" 2011.

———. "Yezidi Reformer: Sheikh Adi." March 20, 2008.

Yogananda, Sri Paramahansa. *God Talks with Arjuna: The Bhagavad Gita: Royal Science of God-Realization—The Immortal Dialogue between Soul and Spirit.* Los Angeles: Self-Realization Fellowship, 1995.

———. "Taittiritya Upanishad." Yogananda.com (website). 2017.

About the Author

Normandi Ellis, D.Div., has been known as a scholar, teacher, and leader of primarily Egyptological studies for three decades. The Reverend Olivia Durdin-Robertson of the Fellowship of Isis (Ireland) ordained her as a priestess of Isis in 2000, and in 2018 she was admitted into the Fellowship of Isis as an arch priestess. Having discovered a love of Egyptian hieroglyphs while attending a translation workshop required for her master's degree in English literature, with creative emphasis, from the University of Boulder, Normandi began in earnest to teach herself how to read and write hieroglyphs. Believing that curiosity is the best teacher, she immersed herself in the mythologies of ancient cultures as she examined Sumerian and Mandarin Chinese religious texts, as well as those of Mayan hieroglyphs, Linear A and B scripts of Crete, and Ogham and Pictish runes of the Scottish Highlands.

After studying the Egyptian hieroglyphs for eight years, she completed a poetic translation of the hieroglyphs that are found in *The Egyptian Book of the Dead: The Complete Papyrus of Ani*, which resulted in her highly acclaimed book, *Awakening Osiris*, published in 1988. *Awakening Osiris* has become a spiritual touchstone for those traveling in and studying ancient Egypt. It was followed by six other books: *Dreams of Isis* (1991), *Feasts of Light* (1995), *Invoking the Scribes of Ancient Egypt* (2011), *Imagining the World into Existence* (2012), *The Union of Isis and Thoth: Magic and Initiatory Practices of Ancient Egypt* (2015), and the more recent *Hieroglyphic Words of Power* (2020).

That same passionate searching for the inner mysteries led her to complete her doctor of divinity degree in comparative religions from All Faiths Seminary in New York in 2020. Her dissertation became the road map for her study of angels and this book.

Ordained as a reverend in the Spiritualist Church through the Indiana Association of Spiritualists in 2015, she has lived and worked in the Spiritualist community of Camp Chesterfield, Indiana, serving on the board of directors of the Indiana Association of Spiritualists, directing the metaphysical program, and teaching in the Spiritualist seminary. In addition to teaching a variety of metaphysical subjects, she teaches courses on angels, symbology, basic unity of religions, Spiritualist writings, the history of modern Spiritualism, and life after death.

Since 1990 she has led in-country sojourns through Egypt with Shamanic Journeys, Ltd.: Mysteries of Egypt, LLC; and in 2019 she established her own tour company, Two Ladies Travel Co. Normandi has also continued to publish her fiction and poetry in national literary journals, magazines, and in the following books: *Sorrowful Mysteries and Other Stories; Voice Forms; Fresh Fleshed Sisters; Going West;* and *Words on Water,* among other collections of award-winning fiction and poetry.

She has been a featured speaker at the Women of Wisdom Conference, the Hayden Dream Conference, the Great Lakes Retreat Center, the Academy of Oracle Arts, the National Association of Poetry Therapy, and the Association for the Study of Women and Mythology.

Index

Page numbers in *italics* refer to illustrations.